To Rajarshi and Suchita,

my pillars of growth

Praise for the Volume

A laudable contribution with penetrating insights on the theory and methodology of translation by one of the most active scholars of India. Every chapter of Translation as Growth is a nugget of information. Those interested in the theory of translation will find it stimulating and rewarding.

Braj B. Kachru
Professor of Linguistics and Juibilee Professor of Liberal Arts and Sciences
University of Illinois at Urbana-Champaign,USA

Translation as Growth presents many new views on the process of translation itself. For example, Singh discusses the question of what the difference really is between authoring and translating in a new light (given that translation is in a basic sense creative). He also relates Western theories of translation to Indian theories and relates translation to language development and to the, often socio-politically dependent, processes of contact and influence between languages (translation is a major force behind 'linguistic convergence'). The book, in short, makes a valuable contribution to the increasingly important academic field of translation studies.

Jens Allwood
Professor of Linguistics and Chair, Cognitive Science Program
The University of Gothenburg, Sweden

In *Translation as Growth*, Udaya Narayana Singh brings his insights as a poet, linguist and translator to bear upon his reconceptualization of the idea and the process of translation. He rethinks Western and non-Western approaches to translation in his attempt to refigure key concepts like text, language, ideology, culture, location, locution, othering, reading, *jouissance*, modernism and postmodernism. He semiotically links creativity with translativity, critically surveys the models of and metaphors for translation and closely examines the connections among language, translation, folklore and culture. The thematic range of the book is as admirable as the the freshness of its insights. This is no passive report on the scene; the author takes unambiguous positions on most of the issues and breaks many idols in the process.

K. Satchidanandan
Poet, critic and playwright, and former Secretary, Sahitya Akademi, India

This book establishes the centrality of translation in a globalizing linguistic scenario. Translation is not merely the shift of a given content from one language to another, but it is a cultural, emotional, interpersonal activity we engage in all the time. By thus expanding the connotations of translation, the author explores step by step the science of the translation process. At the end, we realize with amazement that translation is as creative as writing or doing something anew. This stupendous book adds a whole new dimension to the term 'translation'.

Martin Kãmpchen
Translation and Tagore expert, and former Visiting Fellow
Indian Institute of Advanced Study
and Rabindra Bhavana, Visva-Bharati University, India

TRANSLATION AS GROWTH

Towards a Theory of Language Development

Udaya Narayana Singh

PEARSON

Published by Dorling Kindersley (India) Pvt. Ltd., licensees of Pearson Education in South Asia.

Head Office: 7th Floor, Knowledge Boulevard, A-8(A), Sector-62, Noida 201309, India
Registered Office: 11 Community Centre, Panchsheel Park, New Delhi 110 017, India.

ISBN: 978-81-317-3086-7

First Impression, 2010

Typeset by Ebenezer Publishing Solutions, Delhi

Digitally Printed in India by Repro India Ltd. in the year of 2014.

Contents

ACKNOWLEDGEMENTS

I AM GRATEFUL to Suchita, who has been a source of inspiration, and for agreeing to be the first reader of most of my texts in original as well as in translation. To my son, Rajarshi—first, because so much of his time had to be denied to him as I was engaged in creating some of these pages—and later, when he grew up to be a fine litterateur, for having critiqued some of my more recent texts. For their patience, when the work was under preparation. For their impatience, too, when my pace of work was causing seemingly endless delay.

To all my doctoral students from whom I have had so much to learn. I love them all. Several of my M.Phil. and pre-doctoral students have been particularly helpful to me. It is difficult to name only a handful.

To the supporting staff at Hyderabad as well as at Mysore—particularly, Murthy, Apparao, Avinash, Bharathi, Swarnali and Manikantan.

To the editorial team at Pearson, particularly to Urmila Dasgupta and Praveen Dev in getting the project through and to Shinjini Chatterjee for editorial and academic input.

Among colleagues and fellow linguists, Professors Sisir Kumar Das, Rajendra Singh, Suresh Kumar, R.N. Srivastava, Suresh Joshi, D.D. Mahulkar, K. Satchidanandan, Nirmal Bhattacharya, Harish Trivedi, B. Mallikarjun, Rajesh Sachdeva, Sam Mohanlal, Anju Saxena, Debes Ray, Mahasweta Sengupta, Subha Chakraborty Dasgupta, Meenakshi Mukherjee, P. P. Giridhar, Swapan Majumdar and Probal Dasgupta have been very helpful in discussing different aspects of the thesis proposed in the chapters here. I am thankful to them.

Finally, to my readers of translations, for reacting to the texts I have articulated. The question as to whether I authored them or they authored me is still open.

I am grateful to the texts, too, for having prompted and provoked me to act and react in the manner I have.

Udaya Narayana Singh

Introduction

Languages develop or are developed. When languages develop on their own, the time it takes for historical events to unfold in a particular manner is impossible to specify.

Viewed in one way, like many other histories, the history of language is nothing but a catalogue of a series of accidents—some planned, some others spontaneous, and some that are chain reactions. In another reading, the history of a language would appear as a mirror of an age—a whole generation, a century or a millennium depicting the life of an entire nation or language. In the second sense, this history is the documentation of a series of ongoing and ever-evolving events that are all products of time.

Whichever view of history we may entertain, when languages develop as a consequence of a set of historical processes, they take a little longer time than those that develop because of planned interventions. Languages that develop on their own can be said to have undergone *primary standardization*.

Languages that are developed undergo *secondary standardization*. More often than not, in cases of the latter type, it is very difficult to differentiate between the periods of standardization and modernization. These processes go hand in hand with respect to these languages because of the time constraints within which these latecomers bloom. It is more than a convention that when a language undergoes primary standardization, the processes of modernization follow it soon after, in course of time.

Gone are the days when languages could develop on their own. One difference between the advent of modernism during the last two centuries and the postmodern situation prevailing today, is that all languages in today's world advance and develop because of various internal and external pressures, and because of the ensuing tensions. As against this, there was a time when a language could develop as a consequence of either natural historical forces or chance emergence of a towering literary personality. Such primarily standardized languages, however, had no model before them to emulate. In comparison, languages of today have a number of models of primary development before them, and they have an option to follow any one of these models (with suitable modifications, wherever necessary) or chart a completely new course by scrupulously avoiding the known courses of action. For today's languages to develop, therefore, there have to be policies that have already worked elsewhere, which need to be re-implemented. Alternatively, there must be models which can be translated if the elites that influence decision-making processes of the state want them to be so. The options here are between being innovative and being *translative*.

It would not take one long to realize that between these two options, translativity is a better, surer and faster way to develop. Innovation (howsoever ideal it may be theoretically), like any act of creativity, runs the risk of being counter-productive and a failure. If nothing, it is surely more time-consuming than any translative strategy. It is not surprising that many underdeveloped and developing languages today start from a point where they attempt at translating metaphors, myths, proverbs, terms, sciences, cultures, and language structures. Many, of course, end up translating attitudes and fashions first, which relegate the twin task of textual transference and language development to the background. Where this does not happen, and when a number of texts are actually transferred over a considerable period of time, the source and target languages show a tendency of 'coming together' or *converging*. I would not hesitate to imagine that much of what we call *linguistic convergence* emerges from translative actions which members of converging speech communities use as 'gap-filling devices', as techniques that erase distances. They also try recreating certain language functions, something that allows either linguistic dominance or improvement of status of one language over the others in the same speech community. That is the reason why many languages of the Third World—be it Hindi in India or Hausa in Nigeria—very quickly learn the art of dominating over other indigenous languages and varieties, at least in formal speech functions.

Since it is increasingly becoming evident that the translativity model is the fastest way of growing, it places a tremendous responsibility on the shoulders of the translators and language planners of the underdeveloped language communities. Persons engaged in such work of translating (voluntarily or willy nilly, because of pressure on them) have to be ready to listen to a lot of criticism and unkind remarks. But in all fairness, one has to give them and their products or attempts a certain amount of time (to see if they gain acceptance). For instance, in spite of the best efforts of a term planner or a translator, the terms created by her and planted in a user-environment may take time to gain acceptability, even when the domain is limited. Any critic of a glossary of technical terms would easily lay the blame on the translator without realizing how the Sapir-Whorf hypothesis (cf. Kay and Kempton 1984) on linguistic relativity also works in acceptance or rejection of such proposals for linguistic reform.

Almost all modern Indian languages have a number of grammatical devices including some syntactic operations, which did not exist in their early stages or in their initial prose literature. Such imprints existed, not only in known and visible aspects of grammar such as punctuation and lexis, they permeated into syntax, too. The tradition of translating the ancient Indian texts into modern Indian languages always existed but translation from non-Western, non-Indian sources began only in 1801 in Urdu (from Persian *Araish-e-Mahfil*) and in 1805 in Bengali (*Totaa itihaas* from Persian *Tutinaameh*; also *Paarasya itihaas* from Arabic, available in 1834). Beginning from 1803, one finds a regular flow of translations from English into modern Indian languages, starting with *The Oriental Fabulist* into Hindi, Urdu and Bengali (and later into Marathi in 1806).

These trends not only influenced the grammatical structure of modern Indian languages, they also started interlingual rendering of texts among the modern languages, such as the Bengali *Krttibaasa RaamaayaNa* into the Manipuri *Langoi Shagd Thaba* in 1802. Or, consider the Marathi *Raajaa Prataapaadityaace Carita* (1816), which was a translation from a Bengali book published in 1801 (cf. Das 1991:75–77). Notice that this is only a revival of the tradition of what I had called *horizontal translation* (cf. Singh 1989a, 1990) in India, whereas *vertical translation* from a Western classic or from ancient to a modern Indian language was a more accepted activity. But even in ancient times, translations between Indian languages and other Asian languages were a common phenomena. Whether one talks about

AshvaghoSa's *Buddhacarita* or the Thai *RaamaayaNa*, or the Tibetan translation of the Bengali *Caryaapada*, or the Japanese temple inscriptions of Pali sayings, there are a number of philological studies on this aspect.

As one is bound by one's language and by one's culture, both of which bind each other, one is also bound by the science and technology one inherits naturally. It is only normal for a critic to view any other type of categorization of knowledge and belief with a kind of scepticism. In fact, what is expressed as a dissatisfaction against a term is often actually a refusal to appreciate another kind of system. When one translates economics, politics, science or culture of another community, the terms and expressions one opts for have this primary aim of being a match for what they name. It is not fair to blame the translator for introducing something 'foreign', because the ultimate goal of the translator is to use his discretion in coining a term as an instrument of growth. The sooner the translations are naturalized, the faster will the language grow. The present text is planned as a rough script based on which such models of growth could be built. It is meant to be a contribution to both translation theory enterprise as well as to language planning and development.

Chapter 1 questions the common belief that authors are solitary geniuses for whom social contexts do not matter much. At the other extreme is the belief that authors are positioned by their society and language to act as social agents, and they are prompted to write 'social texts' that either reproduce or reiterate the existing social order or initiate a chaos that characterizes their time and space. The texts then act much like the deictic categories of syntax. Assuming that we take the latter position, we may then have to say that all 'texts' are constrained both by *language* and *social forces* that together 'domesticate' writing. As the demarcation between the text and the world collapses, reading and re-reading remain the only real authors. This pushes us to a position where one could claim that like all social products, texts too begin to author writers, constraining authorial sensibility and subjectivity—and introducing a socially acceptable formulation of society. Thus, when texts assume and appropriate the authors' 'self', the authors are pushed into the background as the 'others'. Once we bring translators into the scene to construct a social theory of the text that will make it multi-dimensional, this 'second' turn to a text, or this 'twice-removed' translation, if we may call it so, helps evolve a sociologic of writing. This would also prompt one to claim that as much as 'reading writes', it also destroys texts, because the responsibility of interpreting what is 'undecidable' rests on reading. In fact, with a few exceptions of texts that get recycled and eventually become metatexts of a given speech community, all other texts seem to live a definite life and have a fatalistic self-destructing tendency. There is only one tool that could act as a real hope for discourses of ideology, and save the text from destruction, and that is 'translation'.

The chapter opens up on a personal note to situate the present author in his social context and elaborate the social roles and obligations with lines of demarcation between the innate grammarian who sets up categories, and those who would avoid the company of a grammarian, if given a chance. The utility of grammar and linguistics as vocations notwithstanding, categories such as deixis, antecedents and terminations are shown as relevant even today for a theory of translation-interpretation. It is shown here that it is still relevant to talk about 'location' and 'locution', because one's empowerment or disempowerment of speech would depend on one's location. Although it is true that fashionable theories like the Western concept of 'postmodernism' appear as a cascade that moved from fracturing of ideals to heterogenization of signs (resulting in disintegration of social forces), giving rise to explanations that are 'partial' and 'relative' rather than being holistic, they have finally taken up a position where spatiality and temporality have lost all relevance. And yet, the fact that we are still talking in terms of 'location' and deixis are important, because they are invaluable concepts in understanding the value of 'othering' in translation and interpretation. It has been argued here that acts like writing, translating, interpreting and analysing that we perform on language are deictically tied up with the categories of person, number and gender. On the other hand, the dichotomy of 'location' and 'locution' show that there is dislocation and disposition all around. But much of these in today's critical discourse would often depend on what I would call anaphora and antecedent marking. Thus, as translators, we often have to work with false equivalents—with words that try, without much success—to bridge the cultural distance. It only shows that we must position ourselves in any debate or deliberation on 'self' vs the 'other' for the interlocutors to appreciate our position. The chapter argues that almost all cultural spaces carve out special locations for themselves, and try and relate themselves to three kinds of 'others': (i) other cultures, or the cultural 'other', (ii) the textual 'other', and (iii) the analytical 'other'. A translator negotiates with the textual other while deciding on his or her illocutionary strategies. This brings me back to my original statement on how authors often try to hide their own selves behind others.

Chapter 2 titled 'Creativity and Translativity: A Case for Double Articulation?' begins with an aggressive claim that there are interesting parallels between writing and translating, so much so that *all original literary work is translation and all translation, original creation*. Both are destined to deploy human language, which, by its very nature, is prone to change and decay. We recall here the words of Octavio Paz (1971: 9):

> Every text is unique and, at the same time, it is the translation of another text. No text is entirely original because language itself, in its essence, is already a translation: firstly, of the non-verbal world and secondly, since every sign and every phrase is the translation of another sign and another phrase.

This follows from the fact that human language has the inherent characteristic of double articulation, and that all original writing in a given language is nothing but a recreation—a translation twice-removed. In a monolingual situation, this may sound bizarre. To argue further on these lines, one needs to postulate an open-ended arena inside all potential and actual author's mind—which would be the logical space—where several texts are moulded in continuous semiosis and from where all the written texts evolve as products. There is a difference in an author's (or any creative person's) understanding and conceptualization of the outside world and the common man's universe, which gets reflected in the creative output of an author. This is where the concept of 'creative internal text' (CIT) emerges as a methodological field of happening where a continuous flux of signs revolves in an interrelated fashion (Singh and Pandey 1996). The point being made is that the author is the subject here—the main determinant. But at the same time, she also acts as a predicate—an agent of products that, in turn, determine the nature of signs.

The unfolding of CIT, thus, continues in an open-ended fashion where the author is often an unconscious participant, and is yet involved in a process of growth of consciousness. The creative impulses of an author transcend into the reader's space, which I call the *physical space,* that lies in the form of texts. It appears as if, an author, like a native speaker, is articulating twice. What comes out as a text is a *re*-creation, because what is aimed at—creation—lies in CIT, and it is more likely that there will be a mismatch between the two—the logical and the physical space—much in the same way as a translation is often not an exact match of the original. This is the reason that the source text and the translation do not fit into the same mould. In fact, it is this mismatch which makes literary activity most challenging. The mismatch happens even when the author of the original text herself happens to be her own translator. This is also why creative writing has been described here as a translation twice removed. The first order signification involves the creative person's creation of CIT, and the second order signification lies in the text she produces.

Creativity, in a way then, could be and should be defined as a rearrangement of existing signs. Creativity is a point of view to look at the world which is already in existence, and yet defining it in new permutations and combinations. The key to invention, therefore, is in the rearrangement of existing signs, and the unravelling of new routes of derivation that rules can take. It is emphasized here that this position does not emerge from the Barthean rejection of 'author-god', nor does it assume reader's supremacy. Not surprisingly, Umberto Eco and others have already questioned this kind of extreme bias towards readers' space and suggested an interactive domain instead. The premises proposed here tally with these ideas and build a bridge between 'creativity' and 'translativity'.

It then follows from the above that the author, like the translator, chooses sounds, smells, colours, words, symbols and icons, from the environs around her, and portrays a certain interpreted reality. The mask she wears or wants to wear are worn by the characters in her creation. The environs created around each interpreted character are linked in lineage to the cluster of many characters that live within the author's mind. Notice that it is comparable to the translator's use of the icons in the target text. The iconic use of certain noises, visuals, syntactic constructions or even idioms bears it out. Here the faithfulness, like the translation of bilingual situations, cannot be denied as CIT is the total repertoire—the *superset*—and its creations are all subsets to the superset. There are clearly two model worlds here, two worlds having different sets of icons, sets of rules, different signifiers and signifieds. These possible worlds do not have a transitive relation to each other. They have partial transitivity through somebody, like the translator, who can transit between two worlds. It does not mean that these two worlds of signifiers and signifieds, of creativity and translativity merge into one another, but they can be transcended by the subject concerned.

In Chapter 3 on 'Thoughts on Theories of Texts and Translation', we continue to relate the text and the world. It is not unknown that some writers write as social agents, usually considering the demand and supply relationship in the market, whereas there are some others who claim to represent the oppressed, and then there are some others who write with certain convictions or dogma. In all such cases, writers live a dual life—one which the readers are lured to discover in the text, and another often completely antonymic, in real life. At the turn of a new century, therefore, when there is a genuine possibility of closure of the universe of socio-political discourse, and when language, too, loses its ability to reason, criticize, and stand apart in a non-partisan manner, the activist concept of literary agency becomes important.

Having begun in this way, the chapter dwells on the twin-question in the world of critical theories today, namely, whether we want texts to change the world, or the world to change the texts, or both. When an author begins to write and thus expresses her intentions, she is still in the mould where authors write books. But soon enough, it is as if books begin constraining authorial sensibility and subjectivity, as if it is the books that write authors. Since it has already been said that texts are actually constrained both by *language* as well as by *social forces* that domesticate writing, it needs to be explored if the translators enter the scene as liberators or as a new set of agents who would create a social theory of the text that will remove its one-dimensionality (cf. Marcuse 1964).

The chapter deals with more questions such as these: Is narrativity a dangerous weapon with which to write a history that proceeds from the dilemma of setting a stage to reach a revolutionary anticlimax? Do the events which would otherwise have unfolded as unknown seem to fall into a pattern as we historicize them? There is this wide range of positions, where postmodernists such as Derrida and Foucault would argue that narrativity is indeed a potentially dangerous weapon, and that, therefore, narrativity be demystified. The relationship between textual activities and the culture industry that dominates them is also explored. The games that an author's or a translator's language play on people and reading, and the game that throws up possible alternative narratives, are also discussed here. We also discuss whether and how readers of different kinds 'suffer' as they read a text. Of particular interest in this context are those 'readers' who own various information technologies that run the popular cultural universe today. They try and take the maximum advantage of this situation so that their domination over the modes of speech in different media continue, and they celebrate the freedom they have suddenly discovered vis-à-vis literary texts. They try replacing the Bible or the Quran just as they attempt to dislodge known philosophical and political positions, and tell us (or dictate?) how to translate these texts into what they want them to mean.

These discussions throw up more questions such as the following: (i) What is the response of the author or that of 'reading' towards this cultural capitalistic onslaught? (ii) Is there a textual theory of writing, which tries to understand the contemporary nature of ideology at a time when one can easily transcend between *text* (which holds the world as a reflection) and the *world* (which holds the text as yet another product)? (iii) Do we need a social theory of the text to relate it with ideology or with the possibilities and limits of the critique of ideology? (iv) Can ideologies be criticized, their mythologies demystified and illusions pierced, in order to stimulate social change? (v) Is it at all necessary to retain a critical distance between the author and the translator, between the text and the reader, or between the reading and the world to comprehend an object without being influenced by it? Lastly, (vi) is it desirable to be so objective as to not be influenced by such proximations or breakdown of dyadic relationships? It is argued here that one must attempt to answer these questions, if one is to construct a sociology of translation. In order to do so, many negotiations are to be made between Marxian thought and modern/postmodern theories, between reading and deconstruction à la Derrida, between French structuralism and post-structuralism, and the American reception of such thoughts. These positions are explored further inasmuch as they could demystify the present discursive practices in writing and translating, which we could collapse and call 'authoring'. It is suggested here, not necessarily for the first time though (see Agger 1989b), that we need a new theoretical mapping that locates Marxism, postmodernism, feminism, environmentalism and anti-colonialism on the same cognitive map. It is also clear that we need both global and local explanations of various theoretical positions vis-à-vis writing and translating.

In Chapter 4, 'Translation: Try Thy Metaphor', we look into the various metaphors that dominate the scene of translation theory-building activities today. It is argued that the theoretical enterprise has taken a course where the old metaphors are being constantly replaced with new metaphors. The focus is on the metaphors of governance as to which text will rule in the target language (TL) culture, or on the metaphor of disease when they talk about 'uncontaminated' versus 'contaminated' texts. The war as a metaphor, as well as the legal metaphors of inheritance or even that of a contract, raises interesting issues for the practitioners of translation. The struggle of the literary translator to decide, or even create, a language that lies beyond all officialese has received focus here.

It then takes a position that all translation is essentially communication—not merely a motive force of culture, but also a method of fostering and preserving a culture. In the context of such cultural survivals, when both extremes (total isolation and autarchy versus the extreme degree of merger) are avoided, one realizes that isolationism leads us nowhere and it should be exactly the opposite, namely, that all postmodern societies today should be more receptive to translation because reception of translated literature has in all ages been an index to the broadening of literary taste. From here, we move on to the complex question of definitions of translation. One soon realizes that it is difficult to restrict the act of translation within any all-encompassing definition. This is because the complexity lies in the vast differences in the materials translated, in the purposes of translation and the existence of different types of prospective audience.

The interesting part of the game of definition comes from the consideration of the names or nominal words used for the activity of 'translating' and interpreting in Indian languages. In fact, when we talk of translation (especially 'literary translation'), we may not always refer to the act of translating between 'languages'. Such textual transference may also happen between dialects, registers and styles, or may even be inter-semiotic. The chapter takes this broad position that translation is primarily an act of transforming messages from one form of human expression to another, distanced by time or space, and this act interfaces variegated factors, each one capable of influencing the other. It is argued here that in the final count, all translation is, at best, an effort at mediation or negotiation (Belitt 1978: 38)—*mediation* between two people, their culture and their civilization separated by time or space.

The chapter finally addresses a few wh-questions with respect to the act of translating, namely, the 'why' question (such as why does one translate literary works at all?); and the 'how' question, that is, how does one study and interpret literary language, particularly when it shows remarkable differences from the common man's language? These two are followed by a consideration of what I have called the 'what' question, in terms of 'form' versus 'content' of translation. It is shown why this debate between the form versus content becomes very sharp in translating poems and, in particular, the great metrical poetry. It is shown why the real challenge for the translator is to maintain a balance between these two, because no rule, not of any science, can be applied to measure the sentiments, ideas, pleasure and pain or the feeling that poetry imparts to its reader. From here, we go on to discussing translators who act as 'intercultural mediators' today, as well as to other theoretical issues, and weave another set of questions around them: (i) Can a translation theory merely aim at a description of what goes on when a text travels across language boundaries? (ii) Could it be a validation of lexical and grammatical manipulations meant to attain the semantic equivalents? (iii) If so, can the wider question of discourse be neglected by concentrating merely on grammar and lexicon? (iv) Are the subjective and objective content of the linguistic sign as consistent as they are usually thought to be? And (v) what is the social implication of the Saussurian dichotomy of 'signification' and 'valeur' in the context of translation?

The most important point discussed in this chapter has to do with the two models of translation, namely, vertical versus horizontal translation, and various hierarchies that exist in the field of writing and translation. In particular, the typical colonial context in which a 'translating' culture would only vertically engage itself in 'borrowing' or translating a text from another culture (the 'donor' culture?) is discussed here with special reference to the growth of the indigene or the BhaaSaa literatures in India.

Chapter 5 on 'Translation, Transluscence and Transcendence' begins with a discussion on the joy of reading of a literary text or the lack of it when we read a translated text, either because of under-translation or due to over-translation. It suggests that a translator must 'appreciate', 'evaluate' or 'analyse' a literary text, and wear two hats at the same time—of a critic and of a creator. And as serious literary appreciation depends crucially on 'reading', it turns out that reading is the real thing. At the same time, one cannot deny that the moment we begin to read literary translations, particularly if we also happen to know the original work, the deviations stand out before us very clearly. But we must also appreciate that a translator may have to perform unavoidable operations on the body of target texts that are rooted in a very different cultural tradition. Such changes are also a part of strategies to circumvent virtually untranslatable portions, the knowledge of which may not be easy.

The chapter points out that the moot question is not whether translators have any right to deviate by deliberately under-translating texts or by bringing in suppletions or substitutions, but, rather, whether such deviations can also lead to literary innovations in their own right and, if so, whether they must involve rewriting. This is related to the cases where a translator voluntarily accepts a 'subordinate' role in allowing the transposition of an original author in her language. As Dryden (1711[1808]: 81) notes:

> A translator that would write with any force or spirit of the original must never dwell on the words of his author. He ought to possess himself entirely, and perfectly comprehend the genius and sense of his author, the nature of the subject, and the terms of the art or subject treated of; and then he will express himself as justly, and

> with as much life, as if he wrote an original; whereas he who copies word for word loses all the spirit in the tedious translation.

In fact, this chapter also reminds us that translated literatures have been responsible for major literary movements in all ages. It is in this context that we must understand why some structuralists interpret reading of a literary text as a productive and creative activity. Rather than viewing the reader of a text at the end of the line, waiting to 'receive' a text or a work and 'receive from' it pleasure, pain, fun, directions, advice or even responses to questions that she always wanted to ask but dared not ask, the reader is viewed as reading to produce 'interpretations', to create histories, ideas, mores, sciences and systems that are as valuable as the text itself. It is argued that a reader always rewrites the texts, and she comes back to do so again and again, because every time she revisits it and re-writes, the text appears ever more 'writable'. In comparison, works are shown as extremely 'readable' objects which are not written again and again. They are only to be read, enjoyed, and to be consumed, as it were. Words in these works move from a definite point to another definite or 'appointed' end, and hence they captivate the readers. The point of conclusion is that all literary works of certain standard or value are extremely 'lisible', but rarely 'scriptible'. Interestingly, the Indian literary tradition offers a similar distinction between *kaavya* (texts) and *saahitya* (works). It is shown here that another important point of difference between the text and the work is that the latter fades more rapidly than the former. The text lives through different ages and generations and gets manifested through works of different authors, merged with different philosophies and outlooks and, at times, even written in different languages. The text of the RaamaayaNa perhaps provides one of the best examples of this point.

It is shown with numerous examples here that there is bound to be a semantic loss, gap or mismatch in translated texts as compared with the original, even if we take the best translations. One answer to that could be multiple translations of the same text. But as practical examples show, even multiple texts show different kinds of losses. A translator often finds it difficult to decide whether he should (i) transcribe, (ii) translate, (iii) substitute with something similar from TL, (iv) naturalize, by making minor modifications (be they grammatical or phonological), (v) by loan translating, or (vi) by paraphrasing. If source language (SL) and TL differ lexically, grammatically and phonologically at both langue and parole levels there is bound to be a loss, especially of the lexical kind. Again, individual uses of language of the author and the translator may not coincide. Idiosyncrasies and private meanings may also cause losses. Further, the author and the translator may have different theories of meaning. The biggest problem emanates from the tension between 'over' and 'undertranslation' that all translators suffer.

The next segment of the chapter discusses the arguments that show translation as capable of positively contributing to literary appreciation and criticism, sometimes more than the work of monolingual, conventional critics. Notice that the typical critical analysts believe in a set of moral and formal values of the texts and works to be interpreted—whereas the translator, in trying to go through the twin processes of 'comprehension' and 'formulation', first tries to find out answers to questions about the origin, function, and future of a text. In particular, one would like to know who wrote the text and under what socio-political conditions; who were and are its readers and what were their social compositions; and at which point of time the text emerged. Second, although critics may restrict themselves to only a few apparently legible interpretations self-evident from several cues that the author may have provided, the literary translators are not bound by any of these guileless and simplistic interpretations. Third, since different translators are likely to give different translations, based on many differing interpretations, this appreciation of ambiguity is ingrained in the approach of a literary translator. Finally, it is pointed out that there is an interesting anomaly which is at work here: While 'to translate' in our world may be semantically void, there is, at the same time, a huge repository of actual translations existing in our languages. Further, what we do here has an interesting consequence for the building of a universal grammar (UG), because what would seem an impossible, illogical and ungrammatical structure in one language becomes a perfectly possible structure in another.

Chapter 6 focuses on the concept of *uttar-aadhunikataa* and elaborates on the debates from the BhaaSaa literary scene. It begins with the politics of theory-building in the area of translation and different assumptions such theoreticians make. Then it goes on to discuss the question whether the norms of [expression are] set in every speech community by native speakers (Mufwene 1998: 111), especially in the light of Saussure's claim on language, namely, that no individual can ever create or modify a language system by herself. The literary histories of our languages have shown that the greater the prowess and power of the individual, the better are the chances of these innovations surviving. Man as the centre of universe in the positions on *uttar-aadhunikataa* in the Indian theoretical scene, or the multiple embeddedness that Pramod Talgeri (1988a) talks about in a paper titled 'Intercultural Hermeneutics and Literary Translation' are taken as instances that have a parallel in creativity. The way sentences are embedded into other sentences which are themselves further embedded could be compared with the 'embeddedness' of a literary text in a cultural context. Thus, readers of the source text get an opportunity to find newer and as yet undiscovered layers of meaning through the translations of a text.

The chapter also discusses the issue of 'language purity' and 'linguistic corruption', with which students of sociolinguistics as well as of translation studies are familiar. The popular belief is that the ancient or early formation of speech is pure and it gets corrupted and 'vulgar' as the days go by. This has a parallel in the field of translation: the original text is pure, and it tends to become corrupted as it travels from one language to an other, and then to another, etc. At a given point of time in South Asia as well as in Europe, it was commonly and tacitly agreed upon that the purity of the 'original' must be maintained at any cost, and if necessary, by artificially inducing a certain degree of prescriptive planning or by opting for grand plans in the form of 'Sanskritization', which we can roughly equate with 'purification'. The modernists responsible for the spread of this particular theory believed that this was a highly desirable activity, and was actually possible. Thus, while everybody agreed that 'Prakritization' (often read as 'degeneration') of languages and texts was inevitable, it was to be arrested to create a platform of discourse that is widely acceptable, easily teachable and learnable so that it defies aging. On the other hand, it is argued in the *uttar-aadhunikataa* tradition that it is this force of 'Prakritization' that takes all creative endeavours in our languages to greater heights.

In fact, the high modern language is a higher value speech in comparison to all those which, for some reason or the other, did not get the chance of undergoing appropriate changes to qualify for this epithet. Now, this clearly creates a 'caste' distinction in speech. Some are declared as 'twice-born'—not only 'standard' but 'modern' as well—whereas a large number of BhaaSaas (often called the *vernaculars*) are expected to remain even below the first level. The chapter questions what is generally taken for granted, namely, that there are a large number of speech which do not get the desired push to end up as an acceptable form of literary expression, and that their development goals become ever elusive. The focus of the whole chapter is the claim by some critics in the modernist tradition that human language is being constantly 'devalued'. It is argued that if modernity is a product of civilization, *uttar-aadhunikataa* allows us to realize—in the words of Jean-Pierre Mileur (1985)—our 'post-enlightment dilemma' and that makes it possible to appreciate that 'the burden of our modernity involves the apparent necessity of a choice between the best interests of the past and those of the present and the future'. Postmodern philosophers too claim, to cite Berel Lang (1986), that there is a sharp divide between the past and present, a disanalogy. *Uttar-aadhunikataa* is rich in presenting the debate between the English and Sanskritic models of creativity and the writing that emerged from the BhaaSaa tradition as they were in the earlier centuries.

The chapter also clarifies the relationship that obtains between *uttar-aadhunikataa* and the postmodern approaches. In particular, the issues of canonization and universalization of literary canons are also discussed in detail. It is shown why the typical European modernity enterprise which was built upon the loss of cultural cohesion and which was largely elliptical and denying all previous content, mattered very little to the contemporary Bengali litterateur. The beginning of a postmodern attempt to divorce 'modernity' from time and space, as Tagore had done, and to which the post-Tagore era writers—the modernists in Bengal in the 1930s—did not subscribe, is detailed here. It is shown that the attempt to establish an equation between *aadhunikataa* and European modernity or Westernization was nothing but a derivative and initiative exercise in discovering one's routes of transplantation (as against the search for 'roots' among the 'eternally modern'). Although it is agreed that the emergence of 'new poetry' in different Indian Bhaasaas came at a different time, and as a result of their engagement with Euro-centric modernity, the real giant leap happened only when one took recourse to Prakritization. The decay of modernism as it happened in Bengal is also touched upon in detail, taking it up to the mid-1970s when the *uttar-aadhunik* criticism was first raised by a group of poets, writers and painters. It is shown that the first and foremost characteristic of decadent modernism of the 1980s even in the mainstream writing in Indian languages was this rejection of language—the search for an 'otherness' that is ever elusive. Quite related to this was the writers' anti-scholasticism. The chapter then discusses a few decadent modernist poets of the 1990s in Bengali and shows how their writings 'leak' in so many ways. Finally, the whole debate on the BhaaSaa literary scene is related to the enterprise of building of a non-Western theory of translation by drawing parallels between theories of language and translation. It is argued that speech has a chaotic existence, and chaos like speech has a unique pattern occupying a three-dimensional space, which requires different kinds of semantics to understand it, as discussed in detail in Chapter 9.

The chapter ends with a possible *uttar-aadhunik* position on translation theory, where many interpretations compete for space, functions, readings and influence over very large numbers of readers. The 'native' qualities of a text would come to the forefront only when society and politics resolve the ensuing problem of brokering interpretive power 'equitably' between source and target versions, as also among the various sincere interpretations of the same in either of the versions.

Chapter 7 shows that most people have misgivings about translation. Some identify it only as a classroom exercise. Some others find it merely a tool used to introduce popular literature or a rare knowledge-text of an alien language into one's own language. Some of course take it as a means to convert certain legal and governmental documents into other languages in a more or less routine manner. Very few consider it a serious activity. Translation is not considered to be an ideal discipline at par with other linguistic and literary studies. This is so because a translator and a translating culture have always been placed at the lower end of a line of vertical relationship of texts (cf. Singh 1989a: 5).

The Italian epigram *Traduttore, traditore!* ('the translator is a betrayer') and Robert Frost's comments, 'what is left out in poetry is translation', are examples of such misgivings about translation as a serious discipline. It is yet to be realized by many that translation is no longer a hit-or-miss pursuit, that it is an equally creative and dynamic activity in every respect, and that it gives us an entirely new perspective in creating a theory and aesthetics of interpretation.

It is argued here that writing takes us far away from what we hope to write about. All images are instances of double articulation (cf. Chapter 2), and in each lies a part that is born out of the 'manipulation' of reality. The author does not stop at such manipulation; she also tries giving it a name and a context. She is easily excused for such excursions from truth and text. However, we are not so kind with the translators who deviate from the original and try to 'transcreate'. We should, rather, try to find out under what circumstances one does opt for the strategy of 'transcreation', or what kind of changes could be (or, should be) brought about when one transcreates. To start with, one has to admit that neither the author nor the translator can assume a distinct identity vis-à-vis the text, and this fact has been noticed by many already. Some would, of course, describe their products as pieces of fiction or fictition. As against this position, there is a school of thought, though, that states that poets and authors owe their 'imagination' primarily to their surroundings, and therefore their writing must grapple with all such problems that life presents—political, social, religious, scientific, social or even personal.

This chapter also discusses how a comparison between literary creativity and magic is brought about, where both the poet and the magician see links and connections between things not easily perceived by a common person. It also mentions scholars like Humphrey Jennings (1987) who take the position that while poetic vision and imagination are a part of life and their importance cannot be belittled, one must make a distinction between the means of production and the means of vision. He laments that the function of the poet has been historically limited by a division of labour, so that poetry becomes more and more specialized, until at last it is left with no subject but itself.

From the above, the chapter moves on to another difficult question, namely, whether culture is anti-technology, anti-modern, or even anti-popular. Some may take the position that culture and civilization are in a kind of antonymic relationship, and that civilization has on its agenda an undeclared writ to subvert culture. This reminds one of the relationship that obtains between *sangskrti* and *prakrti* on the one hand, in the realm of culture, and between Sanskrit and Prakrit, in the field of language. The distancing that, say, poetic language will naturally achieve without even consciously attempting it will not necessarily be appreciated by all. The point is that whenever we read a literary text, we derive a pleasure that is neither nameable nor measurable. This unquantifiable reaction touches a chord where one feels a rare kinship with its progenitor, because this pleasure, in greater or lesser form, must have been hers, too. The author who herself tries to recreate her own text in another tongue, feels constrained: she finds her hands seemingly tied by a lack of equivalent idioms, collocations and metaphors. The frustration lies in not being able to relive the same pleasure. Where an original author fails, a sensitive and a seasoned translator may succeed. But this success cannot be ascribed merely to her having been able to find the correct correspondences, nor to her achievements in capturing the meaning intended by the original author but to her ability to do what Abhinavagupta would probably call *anukiirtana* in Sanskrit—something that allows one to churn, munch, taste, sing and understand the *kiirtana*, the text. All poetry is *anukiirtana*, according to Bharata. This supports what has already been argued in Chapter 2, namely, that all writing is double articulation. That means that the language of literature is bound to become a little different from the rest of its application. A reader can understand and appreciate a text, provided she reads and re-reads not only the lines in the text, but also between the lines. The chapter then proceeds to outline the coordinates and conditions in any act of critical 'reading' when one approaches a work of art.

In today's context, packaging of the text for the consumers, including its presentation for the audience of translations, is the most important thing. As nobody has time to read, there is no question of re-reading. So if a text or a point of view has to be emphasized, one has to talk about what was once called *anuvaada* in *Kaadambarii,* where the word stands for repetition or *punarukti*. Literally, *punarukti* means 'saying it again'. Even in the famous medieval Bengali text, *Caitanya-caritaamrta* by Vrndaavanadaasa, translation or *anuvaada* has been described only as *anukiirtana* (literally, 'singing after'), or *anukSaNa kathana* (or 'repeating all the time'). Here, translation is grouped into three different types: (i) *anukathana*, or imitation, where the original text is followed quite closely, and is rendered into the target word-for-word: (ii) *punarkathana*, or 'paraphrasing', where the meaning is accepted as an invariant and, accordingly, a text is transferred into another language by 'meaning' transference; and (iii) *adhikathana*, or complete rendition of the source text, where adherence to the syntactics of the original, or its structure, is not essential.

The chapter ends with a discussion of Tirumalesh's (1990) approach where he views translated texts as another kind of original writing. It is shown that two texts, one original and the other its translation or transcreation, may both achieve such a literary height in their respective cultures for entirely different reasons. It is suggested that this phenomenon calls for our serious attention, because from these instances there is something to learn for prospective translators. On the contrary, when we see that the early translation scholars have been concerned with the 'literariness' of a given text or with 'primary' and 'secondary' sources of translation, we become aware of the assumptions they make even before they actually begin to 'appreciate' or 'analyse' a literary text in translation. In reading and understanding a literary text in translation as under the present scheme, we cannot afford to repeat their mistake. Although deviation is an inevitability, translations can also lead to literary innovations in their own right, as it has been already proposed here that all translations are instances of 'rewriting of an original text'.

Finally, it discusses the conjecture that while translating, the most important thing that happens could be described as 'replacements', and that there are three levels at which replacements can happen: the lexical, grammatical, and semantico-pragmatic levels. One is not always creative in finding the three kinds of equivalents as one tries to translate. An ideal translator will not only worry about proper expressions in TL, she will also have to see that the way she has created/drafted/written the target language text (TLT) makes its meaning coherent. For achieving this goal, the translator will have to take a number of crucial steps, which are enlisted here:

(a) identification and clarification of the original theme,
(b) selection of an appropriate language structure and language use according to the context,

(c) precision in utilizing the non-linguistic factors such as socio-cultural background and pragmatic values, and
(d) intelligible reproduction of the fullest possible *signifié* or sense structure in TL.

Since translation deals with the formal replacements of structures from SL to TL, the replacement does not only mean physical replacement of graphic form (by transliteration to various other strategies including various types of borrowings) but also of some supra-graphic features, i.e. the social, economical, cultural and political information either demonstrably loaded in or clearly implied through the text. In this respect, too, translation becomes a multi-dimensional art. The discussion ends with different imagery associated with the characterization of 'translation' as a social action.

Chapter 8, 'Saying it Again: On Building Models of Literary Translation', is a modest contribution to mutual illuminations—where a theory of literary translation draws from an otherwise unutilized repository of knowledge that goes by the name of common sense. It aims at understanding the nature of *intra-lingual translation* of texts. As a literary critic and teacher of literature, one is used to doing 'paraphrasing', but there is hardly any literature available on its methods, conditions, constraints, and its place in the politics of creating literary and linguistically standardized styles. At the same time, it is a well-known fact that all practising translators derive help from basic conversational strategies such as 'paraphrasing', used by both monolinguals and bilinguals. Here, particular emphasis is put on paraphrasing as a strategy of literary translation, where both inter-lingual paraphrasing among bilinguals and paraphrasing between two or more styles and speech varieties in a monolingual situation are discussed.

Translation as paraphrasing is very different from translation as a plain inter-lingual transfer in many ways. While inter-lingual rendering is a product of history, and is constrained by the politics of a given period, paraphrasing is a response to one's requirement at a particular point of time. At a given moment, when an interlocutor (or the person one is engaged in conversation with) is unable to follow the speaker or is unable to get the full import of their statement, the speaker cannot but try to say the same thing 'in other words'. This position has been elaborated with a few texts of both types to instantiate two kinds of activity—paraphrasing and translation on the one hand, and inter- and intra-lingual paraphrasing, on the other.

There are many assumptions that form the basis of discussion here. For instance, one such assumption is that translation is an extension of speech activity. The basis here is the stand taken by Pegacheva (1959: 138) who defines translation as a 'peculiar instance of speech activity in course of which a number of psychological difficulties have to be overcome'. Most of us learn to get over such difficulties based on our common sense and experiences and not on the basis of any formal training. Zimnyaya (1993: 88–89) too contends that 'Translation is essentially [an] activity. My aim is to show that translation is a complex, specific, secondary type of speech activity. This statement holds good for all forms of translation....' Obviously, viewing translation as a kind of speech activity has many interesting consequences. This common sense approach to translation lets us take it for granted that every native speaker of a language has an intrinsic competence in translating just as they are claimed to have linguistic competence as a speaker-listener of their language. In that case, the only question that arises at this point is the following: Is translation comparable to secondary speech activities or is it like a primary speech activity? I would claim that all native speakers constantly paraphrase themselves or redraft their statements (potentially all statements, but practically at least some) and, therefore, everybody takes recourse to intra-lingual translation or paraphrasing. When someone is a born bilingual or when one acquires a language other than one's mother-tongue, one is expected to know how to express the same feelings in different languages. There are exceptional bilinguals, however, who know how to use another tongue only in limited domains, or who use two (or more) languages mostly in mutually complementary contexts.

As against this, one could also take a position that translation is a secondary speech activity, such as preparing summaries or precis-writing and paragraph writing. It is argued here that it can be both primary and secondary activity. Yet another consequence is that a large number of speakers in each community is born to speak a particular speech variety, which in their later life may be used mostly in the familial domains, whereas in other contexts the standard speech variety is used.

It is to elaborate on these points that several types of translations have been discussed in the chapter. In this context, Crystal's views (1987: 344) on 'translation' as a 'natural term used for all tasks where the meaning of expressions in one language (the "source" language) is turned into the meaning of another (the "target" language)', become important. The chapter then also discusses the concept of 'total translation', which Catford (1965: 21) describes as misleading. This is because it involves a total replacement of SL grammar and lexis. Consequently, one may even have to replace SL phonemes/graphemes by non-equivalent or not necessarily fully equivalent (or say, 'comparable') TL phonemes/graphemes. This position is then compared with 'partial translation', where some parts of the SL text are left untranslated: they are simply transferred and incorporated into the TL text. In the latter case, even if an equivalent emerges at all or is found or created, it is either based on chance similarities or on the phenomenon of convergence. It is argued that an inter-lingual paraphrasing will be closer to partial translation, whereas an intra-lingual paraphrasing has some in-built advantage of the same script and is generally similar with respect to phonological devices, and at least comparable at the word level; therefore, it will be closer to total translation.

Similar comparisons are made with respect to other kinds of distinction, namely, between rank-bound translation and unbounded translation (Catford 1965), or between communicative and semantic translation (Newmark 1981, 1988). Finally, the chapter discusses certain texts that exemplify the above positions as well as the consequences of these positions.

Chapter 9, 'Translating Alien Cultures: Search for the Native', begins where the sixth chapter ends, namely, in the claim that speech has a chaotic existence, and that chaos, like speech, has a unique pattern occupying a three-dimensional space and three different kinds of semantics—the semantic of confusion, the semantic of amorphism and the semantic of the void. I begin drawing the parallel in a reverse order. First, when a speaker is born with an inborn urgency to overcome functional hurdles and is yet dependent on these very hurdles to build a theory of behaviour, when she has the capacity to use her tool with which she may initially fumble or fiddle but not err for long, she appears in an intermediary space, formless and unspoilt by grammar. The speaker who is still more a 'potential' than a 'real' communicator, provides the much needed hiatus between one man and another or between an individual and the society. Second, when we as speakers step into this world, our faculty or ability will have a rare flexibility, which will allow us to bend our senses in whichever way our immediate and not-so-immediate environments may require. It is this flexibility that enables us to prevaricate, prognosticate and interpret through speech and writing. Thus, although our 'interpretive competence' had not assumed any shape by then, and was, therefore, not governed by any rule or pattern, it was still not outside the realm of reason and rationality. Third, there is no doubt that much of speech is chaotic to the uninitiated but not to native speakers. All these go on to point out that it makes sense to talk about all semiotic constructs, including human language, as having a chaotic existence. If speech has both pattern and chaos inherent in it, let us see how theorists try to represent them in their characterization. The reactions of linguists who try to understand this duality are twofold: *vertical* and *horizontal*. For a long time, the expression 'duality of patterning' as a description of human speech has dominated the theoretical scene. However, it has been accepted only in one sense which is basically a vertical interpretation of the concept of duality. In this sense, it is commonly understood that language is basically a layered construct which is organized in some sort of a hierarchy.

The chapter argues that one should not be surprised if psychological as well as sociological theories show that layered compartments exist in that part of their brain, which are responsible for speech production and comprehension. There is, however, yet another way in which the expression 'duality of patterning' could be understood as elaborated by Annamalai in his 'Nativity of Language':

> Language has double existence. One is grammatical existence and the other is social. Both are not a priori existence, but they come to exist by human construction. The grammarian constructs the grammar of language, which is a manifestation of its grammatical existence. His construction of the grammar is founded on his theory of grammar. This makes the grammar a theoretical construction... (1998: 148).

He then goes on to elaborate the other pattern of language:

> The social existence of a language comes about through its social construction by the community of speakers. The social construct may be about the boundary of the language ... It may be about the norm of the language ... It may be about the propriety over language ... It may be about what the language stands for; that is, about its cultural and political symbolization (ibid.: 149).

It is pointed out here that both the grammatical and social existence of language show such patterning as are beyond individuals and idiosyncrasies, and that language is as much general as it is specific. Although Annamalai requires that speakers' mental grammars and the grammarians' theoretical grammars should ideally match, this matching is problematic as there are many versions of these constructs.

Chapter 9 thus shows that the equation between grammatical and social constructs of language is not one to one. Second, we are often told about 'language purity' and 'linguistic corruption', and sociolinguists working on linguistic attitudes of speakers are quite familiar with such ideas, just as students of translation studies are. The parallel in the field of translation, namely that the original text is pure, and translation makes it impure, or the vertical relationship between 'Sanskritization' and 'Prakritization' (or even between the 'deep' and 'surface structure') already discussed in Chapter 6 are brought here once again.

Chapter 10 on 'Lamentations and Celebrations' treats folklore studies as an extension of translation studies, and begins with the question on 'purity' of lore and the absence of a *pure folklore studies*, on the lines of similar-sounding disciplines such as *pure mathematics*. It is argued that as a discipline, folklore suffered at the hands of literary critics as well as linguists. Anthropologists are to be blamed equally. This explains the lack of an autonomous discipline of folklore. If, however, one looks at the enterprise from a different angle, the study of folklore should be viewed in a twofold manner: first, as an interdisciplinary endeavour where each participating discipline sheds its apparently pristine requirement of purity, and second, at the same time, as a discipline in its own right. I take a position here that language and purity do not go together, particularly because 'prevarication' happens to be the most essential quality of both language and its principal product, literature (and consequently, also of translation). And since the essential ingredient of folklore happens to be language, this applies to folklore as well. From here, I pursue a line of argument that goes like this: If prevarication must be an ingrained characteristic of our folk-knowledge and folk-expression systems, all our *real* productions and reproductions vis-à-vis language are instances of 'double articulation', twice removed from what could have been *ideal*. In fact, for any lore or myth, it is this apparent removal from reality that adds colour to what one says or does with language, even when a given text is not so pretentious as to be scoring a point or sending a message. Our folk-narratives, folk-drama, or folk-poetry cannot be a mere mirror of reality. And yet, they draw heavily from our context, our environs and our vision of space and time.

It is shown here that when we talk about apparently more respectable modes of text-generation in different genres, the imprint of a folklore on them is often undeniable. Whether in the journalistic writing or programmes in the mass media, the same creative uncertainty (= the same prevarication?) gets reflected. No wonder then that what we are expected to do scientifically under oath of honesty and truthfulness is not what we actually do whether we stand as witnesses or when we sit in judgement on others, because there is this general uncertainty in all instances of speech. It is from this uncertainty, the removal from reality, and this double-articulation that both modern folklore and translation activity flow and enrich our existence.

The chapter ends with an emphatic claim that both folklore and linguistics share one major concern, namely, the primacy of speech over writing. Following Saussure, I argue that writing is a parasitic form, the representation of a representation. This apparently innocent move of Saussure was probably a part of the politics of theory-building that he had engaged in. Recall that he had warned us that linguists could 'fall into the trap' of attending to written forms which could eventually 'usurp the role' of speech. If writing was set aside as dependent and derivative, accounts of language could take as the norm the experience of hearing oneself speak, where form and meaning seemed to have been given simultaneously. In fact, the privileging of speech is not only a weighty matter, it is also very nearly inescapable. It is so because whether in linguistic analysis or in folklorist studies, and by extension, in semiotic analysis of any kind, everything depends upon the possibility of identifying signs, for which it is necessary to grasp or identify signifieds. It is, therefore, neither an accident nor an error that semiotic theory should find itself implicated in phonocentrism and logocentrism.

It is argued that these new binary oppositions, such as outside/inside or transcendental/empirical, depend on a point of differentiation. The claim is that the moment of speech, where signifier and signified seem given together, where inner and outer or physical and mental are for an instant perfectly fused, serves as the point of reference in relation to which all these distinctions are posited. In an interview on his positions in 'Semiologie et grammatologie', Derrida identified his double science or double reading not with a mode of discourse that would lie outside or beyond semiotics but with a special practice within semiotics (Derrida 1972: 49–50). Although Derrida's deconstruction reveals 'irrationalities' in our systems and theories, it is not a kind of 'new irrationalism', as is often suggested. It only reveals contradictions and paradoxes, which neither semiotics nor translation studies can escape.

The chapter also raises certain interesting questions that have remained hidden. First, are oral texts—which is what folklore is—subject to 'double articulation'? In what way are they different from the written act of creativity? These are not easy questions and they don't have easy answers either.

I have claimed here as well as elsewhere (cf. Singh 1990) that horizontal translation must be the base on which one can build a new translation theory. This kind of a translation theory is sure to be different from the one based mainly on vertical translation—from the languages of power to those that lack it. Here, translation provides us with a model of growth of underdeveloped languages. Any theory of translation based on the political equations such as SL = dominant and TL = dominated (because 'the dominated' is often colonized and oppressed) is bound to carry a bias that will ultimately affect the use of translation as a tool of development. This is because it is now clear from the work of Trivers (1985) and Layton (1989) that there is no objective basis for speaking in terms of higher or lower forms of entities either in physiological evolution or in the evolution of social behaviour. If so, there is no reason why we should let the ills of vertical vision colour our theory of translation or development.

Let us make it clear that while evolution knows no verticality, development (whether natural or planned) may give rise to an unequal relationship close to the notion of verticality. We are only trying to raise the question that challenges the validity of using the experiences of the 'developed' as the basis of building a theory of language development for the 'undeveloped', as has been done by almost all Western scholars initially, including Joshua Fishman, Charles Ferguson, Jonathan Pool and others, although some of them changed their positions later. We take the stance that much of the monistic theoretical arguments on language development came from the sociolinguistic background and bias of Western scholars who grew up in a very different kind of social condition than the one experienced by the world waiting to be developed (cf. Singh 1992a). However, I would not subscribe to a conspiracy theory here as theirs was not necessarily an organized effort to drown the voice from the East. This was probably because it is otherwise difficult to explain how so many scholars with different disciplinary backgrounds could agree upon a common characterization of development, namely, that it was a 'homogenizing' process (cf. Huntington's [1976] ninefold characterization of modernization).

At this point, some readers of this piece may find a contradiction in the position we have taken here, because we reject homogenization as a characteristic of modernization (and development), and rate translativity as a better way of growing than innovation, and at the same time argue in favour of a horizontal translation process as ideal for the developing world. One might say that translation from the developed to the underdeveloped would in effect promote 'homogeneity', and defeat all our talks of 'pluralism'.

However, I do not see any contradiction in this because translation, in the first place, can never be like an act of duplication or photography. Translation is a creative activity—as much as original writing is. The demands that are usually made on translation in terms of fidelity and exactitude seem ill-advised as they can only be approximations, the closeness or distance between two texts depending on a number of factors. Translation is thus always (+ or –) SL text. And it is this indeterminacy that is interesting about translation, because it makes translation parallel to creativity of other kinds. This is what makes translation an extension of literature.

It also explains how translation is a way of growing—growing to be different. In the present volume, we bring different perspectives on translation with reference to the ideas floated by some of the best researchers on translation, and related areas, but we do not engage ourselves in an exhaustive discussion of the theoretical positions of all schools. The chapters in this volume not only dwell on various issues of the act of translating, but also tackle the question of defining our time and space or other creative activities in which we are engaged as a part of the social semiotic. The chapters explore and use rich instances of actual translation of texts between Indian languages and English, and among Indian languages, often to make a theoretical point. What is generated from this move has the potential of becoming an important academic discipline with tremendous potential for applications.

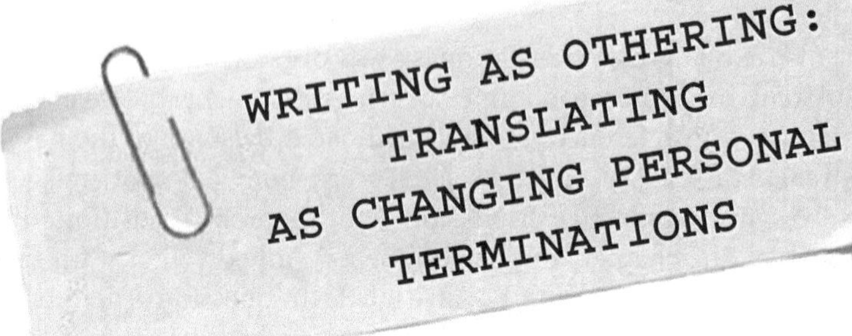

1

OPENING UP

WHENEVER I SPEAK, someone in the audience is bound to demand a clarification: Who's speaking, please! I wouldn't blame the interrogator.

In fact, when you enact several roles, it may be necessary to draw some line of demarcation. Before I proceed further, let me admit that when confronted with abstract categories, the innate grammarian within me often props up in setting up categories, and I am aware that I am probably speaking to people who would avoid the company of a grammarian, if given a chance. On a personal note, I would often have this verbal duel with my grandpa on what was right and what was wrong, or how to do good things with words. At the end, exasperated, he would only grumble, 'Never cross your path with a grammarian!' If I asked, 'Why?' he would elaborate with an age-old proverbial statement in chaste Maithili which, in translation, would read like this:

> Befriend a grammarian and all your letters will return red-faced with errors spotted all over; pick up a fight and you are bound to lose on 'moods'; try making a case to argue, and you would forget all 'articles'; kill a grammarian and the ghost will fumble with the weak verbs; bury the devil, and there will grow a tree on it with

tautologos. You can't put him down. So, should you meet a grammarian and a snake, kill the grammarian first. Kill him anyway!

No matter what may be said about grammar and linguistics as vocations, there is no doubt that categorical notions such as deixis, antecedents and terminations (referring to person-number-gender) are relevant even today for a translator-interpreter. It is still relevant to talk about 'location' and 'locution' (Bhabha 1994), because one's empowerment or disempowerment of speech would depend on one's location. Fashionable theories like those of 'postmodernism' appear as a cascade that moved from the fracturing of ideals to the heterogenization of signs (resulting in disintegration of social forces) and gave rise to explanations that are 'partial' and 'relative' rather than being holistic, taking us to a position where spatiality and temporality have lost all relevance. But the fact that we are still talking in terms of verbs of 'movement' and post-positions of 'from' and 'to' tells us that 'location' and deixis are important in what I would call the category of 'person'. But that does not undermine my concerns for 'gender' or 'number', because they are invaluable concepts in understanding the value of 'othering' in translation and interpretation.

It is a different matter that some literary theorists may feel that many of the foundational terms (such as 'gender') are fast losing relevance now. While elaborating on the dichotomy of 'location' and 'locution', Claudia de Lima Costa (2000: 728) makes an interesting observation:

> ...in light of multiple fractures within the condition of woman, followed by her continual decenterings in poststructuralist times, it has become increasingly difficult to theorize in feminism. Feminism's once foundational concepts—such as gender, woman, and experience—are rapidly yielding their explanatory power and being forced into invisibility in the critical vocabulary of the 'post'. I can foresee a time when we can read about them in bedtime story books: 'Once upon a time, there was gender....'

Even if we do not share her concern, there is no doubt that there is dislocation and disposition all around. But much of these in today's critical discourse would often depend on what I would call anaphora and antecedent-marking—to use some more grammatical terms. To take an example, although we love to talk in terms of African or Latin American literature, we are often dealing with cultural spaces that do not share antecedents with respect to cultural tendencies (in myth, history, rituals, progress, market, for instance) as pointed out by Nelly Richards (1993). This only goes on to show that we must position ourselves in any debate or deliberation on 'self' versus the 'other' for the interlocutors to appreciate our position.

LOCATION

Therefore, beware, ye readers! Here I come. This is how I would like to locate my 'self'. I play three principal roles:

(a) One as a *writer* of insignificance, penning poems to essays.
(b) The second is that of a *translator* (of dubious distinction, I would say—I don't know what others would) travelling from and into several languages, but mostly into English, Maithili, Bangla, and Hindi—in this order.
(c) The third is that of a *linguist* who specializes in both structural and social aspects of language. These are notwithstanding the role played by a reader or a teacher or by a planner of languages.

As a *writer*, my primary purpose seems to be hiding my identity. When I write in any one of the languages of operation, I try and erase all cues that would link with my discipline or my plural presence—even my age or marks that might otherwise bear my generational affiliations. (It is a different matter if some cues are still visible or discernible.) It is not surprising, therefore, that I would choose a pseudonym[2] in Maithili. I have seen and known writers pretending to be someone or something else, and I am sure each one of us has some story to tell about authors whose game it is to 'other' the self. The strategies are numerous; some lean on prevarication in defining their locus; some choose to fabricate in depiction of the frames (in which a text is to be grounded); some try and hide the pair of eyes (of the protagonist or the proverbial 'I' of the narrative or poem) through which the readers are asked to see the unfolding of events; others make public statements rejecting peers or predecessors as junk authors; or even rubbish all critics and academics who dare look at them. I take it all as the game we all play. Some make the game all too obvious, while some others hide it in so many ways. As a writer, my initial response to myself was to push my *self* to the background, and to foreground instead the social commentary on feelings, fellows, and their frictions. In other words, this is like changing one's personal terminations from the first to third person singular.

As a *translator*, I would always try to foreground myself, and try and occupy the front seat, as it were. Although the textbook style of operation of translation would teach us to make our presence a subdued one, letting the author of the original be underscored through the operations we perform, my attitude as a practitioner of this trade has been of that of an equal, taking liberties if liberties are to be taken, and sewing or mending corners where needed, or tucking pieces underneath a carefully chosen garb where I could not avoid doing so. Those in the trade, and very knowledgeable ones, have always warned me that I was only a recipient of a text, at best, an interlocutor for the author of the text. The author, with an explicit or carefully skimmed effort in playing down her voice, I was told, should always be allowed to show a 'grand presence' of her first person writ large over each word a character from her text speaks, or each turn a text takes. It is true that the author interlocutes with the reader through the text, thus forming a first-person–second-person dyadic relationship of some kind. But I was told I had no authority to question the author or her intention, because I was a mere reader. But unfortunately, even as a reader, many of us were uncomfortable with each decision taken by an author, or even fretting and fuming over the fate of a character who had almost become our own by the time we reached somewhere deep inside the text. It was not surprising, therefore, if the readers began to question the author's sense of space and time, reading, background or even scholarship, to have taken that stand in the text. At certain moments of creativity, when the reader decides to switch his passive role and assumes the task of providing a creative response to the text as a translator-cum-interpreter, I see a distinct scope in more cases than are actually reported, a chance that the translator has shed the inhibition of remaining a passive sounding board. This, I think, could be called a silent revolution—happening with many great works of translation, as more and more time passes by. It was this that I would like to view as a transition from second person to assume the role of a first person.

As a *linguist*, I have worked on linguistic situations I did not know much about, before I began to investigate (Ladakhi or Adi or even Telugu), but most of my time has been spent on languages I knew best, and on projects where my intuitions of a native speaker would play a major role in deciding which of the available solutions would be the best. Whenever I worked on Bangla, Maithili and Hindi, the three languages I had acquired naturally,[3] the greatest challenge according to the classical school of linguistics was to first forget that I knew these languages. The greatest challenge was thus to eliminate one's personal bias and look at one's own languages 'objectively' and reasonably 'impatiently', we were all told. This othering as a linguist was perhaps thought necessary to come up with expressions after expressions that would be perfectly nonsensical apparently, but turn out to be 'possible' expressions given certain contexts. Further, even when I dabbled in the social aspects of languages, this othering was a necessary condition. When a sociolinguist goes out to a field, to discover the patterns of interaction among people, he acts like an outsider, or at least, he should act like that. However, since I was mainly a syntactician and a phonologist in my initial incarnations, with the advent in theory-building thanks to Noam Chomsky and his school, there emerged a reaction to this strategy of othering. In the new methodology, intuition and looking inward were to play key roles in unearthing a lot of hidden logic behind expressions that often elude our everyday perception. Until the still newer paradigms of universals and typological studies emerged, the generative grammar approach reigned supreme and came to be accepted almost universally, where a descriptivist of linguistic patterns probed into the deep structure by adopting an intuitive approach. It was thought that the ideal strategy is to open the vistas of mind and churn out those expressions that matter in the context of a given structural construct. I think here one is turning oneself from the third person to a first person.

Thus, I think in whatever role I assume, I seem to be changing my personal terminations through some kind of transformation.

LOCUTION

The great moments are defined deictically. Halfway through the KurukSetra battle, Arjuna had doubts again about the morality of the war in which he was engaged. Halfway through the battle, when his chariot wheels had been immobilized, KarNa wondered where he went wrong. Sitting under the tree where he would die a few moments later, halfway through his life, KrSNa began pondering over the meaning of all that he did or said, or that he did not. These dilemmas and doubts arise out of a particular position one is placed in or as a result of clustering of certain deictic moments.

As I have already argued, acts like writing, translating, interpreting and analysing that we perform on language are deictically tied up with person, number and gender. And each one of these three is important in one way or another. Those who might have by now got sufficiently tired of the onslaught of grammatical concepts could pick up any critical discourse coming up from numerous corners of the world to see how these categories have invaded the critical psyche. In fact, our concerns for foregrounding or interest in centring as well as de-centring a thought, or a section or a belief would emanate from our concern for the grammar of the text.

It is a different matter that our act of translation often perpetuates a violence on the original text and language so much so that each such act appears to be a revolt against the 'grammar', and yet, each such resultant text is also a product of another set of grammatical rules. Eric Cheyfitz in *The Poetics of Imperialism* (1997) argues that as a rule, translation is a violent operation on the text being transformed because such attempts restate the idea embedded in the original text through a significant which is not really equivalent. Thus, when one culture translates another, it perverts the original. If this is true, then any cultural translation is a violation of the other culture's identity, and, like all violent acts, it generates first an awareness of what is happening and then a resistance against the translation (Averbach 2000). This is how Cheyfitz elaborates the point: If we define the cultural institution known as *weroance* in Algonquian, as king or emperor in English, we would perpetuate a gross violation of the original as well as be unjust to the target readers as the Algonquian term *weroance* is understandable only in a kinship economy of the tribe, while the words king and emperor are related to capitalism and rules of inheritance. Thus, as translators, we often have to work with false equivalents—with words that try, without much success—to bridge the cultural distance.

What we notice at the outset is that almost all cultural spaces carve out special locations for themselves, and try and relate themselves to three kinds of 'others': (i) other cultures, or the cultural 'other', (ii) the textual 'other', and (iii) the analytical 'other'. Let me give an example of the third kind first. In an essay, Guo Jian (1999) comments on China as the 'other's other', and describes the post-1989 period in the following words:

> The year 1989 marked a turning point in China's cultural history… the aftermath of cultural revolution came to a tragic end with the government's suppression of the democracy movement in June of that year…. A small group of Beijing-based academics appropriated contemporary Western critical theory and set going a 'postist' trend. Grafting postmodern/postcolonial discourse on the Chinese soil, they coined the term 'Post-New Era' for the Chinese 1990s … in which China was finally free from the spell of a Western myth called 'modernity'.
>
> For Chinese postists, 1989 … left behind that stage of Chinese history dominated by a hegemonic power called the 'Western Knowledge of China'. This power, they argue, had posited the modernity discourse of European Enlightenment as a frame of reference, and assigned China a humiliating position as the West's 'backward' and 'exotic' Other, and effectively rewritten China's cultural identity for the Chinese. Under the influence of this power, Chinese intellectuals accepted the Western ideas of reason, justice, democracy, and individual rights as universals and led China in the course of modernization in the past 150 years, designed to catch up with the West. But according to postists, such a process was simply 'self-otherisation', conforming to the 'China image' in the 'Western cultural imagery'. The project finally reached its breaking point and went bankrupt in 1989. In the 1990s, the postists argue, China was pregnant with a new consciousness: the awakening of the self synonymous with the dawning awareness of China's colonial identity as an 'Other' of the West. (pp. 213–14)

In this example, we can see how postist China tries to negotiate with the analytical twin others—modernity as well as postmodernity. Somewhat similar is the case of the Latin American space. Let us now consider a recent observation on 'de-centring' in this cultural space, where one is trying to relate one's own culture with another cultural space—an instance of the first of the three types I mentioned above. The following reading of Latin American space is relevant both in terms of its thematic as well as rhetoric:

> The fractured syntax of postmodernity allowed the center to be the first to mediate about its crisis of centrality and about recovering the transversal proliferation of its margins. The periphery, one of the margins now re-integrated into the rhetorical complex of the disintegrated, sees itself today forced to re-diagram its axis of polemical confrontation due to this perverse inflection of this center, which aims at appropriating the periphery's alterity and its anti-hegemonic protagonism. Part of the challenge revolves around the conversion of the postmodern theme to a Latin American key.... Latin American marginality and the post-modern defense of the margins, the crisis of authority and the metanarrative of the crisis, the theory of de-centering and the center-function of this theory as a symbol of cultural prestige, and the rhetoric of difference and the politics of difference (Richards 1993: 157–58).

The polemical terminations or 'inflections' here merge with personal terminations that I had referred to earlier. I find an echo of Nelly Richard's ideas in the context of Latin America in one of my own essays titled 'Another India: Voices from the Periphery', presented at Saarbrücken in 2001:

> Which India shall I talk about? The space that is presented in the words woven by our writers who write or re-write in English may appear to be a conundrum—a universe plotted as a pastiche on a canvas which looks remote and diverse at the same time—to the reading public in other parts of the world.... But for those of us who think and write in—let me use the much-maligned word, 'vernacular languages'—those that stand on the other side of the lamp that is sustained on an English wicker, it is evident that rather than illuminate the concept or the space we would like to call India, Indian English writing allows a large part of India to perpetually remain outside the focus. What is in focus suddenly becomes the centre, even if it is a dormant Kanthapura, or a sleepy town in Kerala. But what is outside this written world remains in the periphery for the Anglophone Indian, no matter how interesting Labtolia or Purnea may be in Bibhutibhushan Bandopadhyay or

> Renu's unforgettable stories. There is yet another India, often not understood by the readership of mainstream Indian literatures. I am talking about the stories of Chandayana in Rajasthan or Raja Salhes in Mithila, or the Manteswami episode of the Tulus in Karnataka, which typically lie outside our known worlds. It is often seen that what is happening in Kurmali, Bodo, Adi-Galong or Bhojpuri is not a concern of the mainstream Indian readership. These cultures become newsworthy only when a caste war occurs, or when they throw up a tainted political figure. They are the perpetual 'Other' within India—and yet far removed from us (Singh 2001).

Let me now give an instance of what a translator does to negotiate with the textual other while deciding on her illocutionary strategies. Jerome Rothenberg makes the following 'confession' on translation and appropriation, and we can see a recollection of it even in his *Writing Through: Translations and Variations* (2004a: xvii–xviii).

> All of that remains central to me—the translations, I mean, and those other suppositions and legitimate acts of 'othering' that underlie my total project. In *The Lorca Variations*, a series of poems from the early 1990s, I took a step beyond translation by writing with Lorca (or my translation of Lorca's book-length poem series called 'The Suites') as my source—isolating his nouns and other words (which were by then my own in English) and systematically recasting them into new compositions. In another series of poems, *Gematria*, I used a traditional Jewish form of connecting words by numerological methods and a word list of numerically arranged words and phrases from the Hebrew Bible, to make a poetry—as with the *Lorca Variations*—that I thought was both personal to me and was created by means that shared in what Blake saw as 'the most sublime act [:]... to set another before you.' And in recent work, while continuing to make translations from Picasso and from the great Czech modernist Vitezslav Nezval, I have interspersed appropriations from their work with my own—composing three series of a hundred numbered verses each that I have called *Autobiography*. Still more recently—in *A Book of Witness*—I have used the first person voice, the pronoun 'I,' to explore whatever it is that we can say for ourselves—not only my *personal* self but that of all others—and by that process can even and meaningfully put identity into question.

I needn't over-emphasize the fact that many translators are engaged in what translation theorists often call 'manipulation'. The instances of appropriation Rothenberg describes could have been my own when I translated the entire children's literature of Tagore into Maithili (Singh 1997) or when I was negotiating face-to-face with a number of living poets of Maithili to bring their poems into Bangla (Singh 1998) in the manner that makes it possible to 'read' them as Bangla poems. More importantly, the statement on the strategy used to play with the grammatical category of 'number' proves the point I was making on the relevance of PNG (person-number-gender) as grammatical space that allows manipulation, appropriation and othering. This brings me back to my original statement on how authors often try to hide their own selves behind others. While talking about a fiction-writer, Janet Frame, Tara Hawes (1995: 40) says the following about the strategies employed by Frame, where we see once again how 'personal terminations' become important:

> Frame's literature contains many examples of othering the self/selfing the other, such as 'Jan Godfrey' (one of her earliest short stories), where the narrator takes an identity, then deconstructs it in the process of the story. The exercise of writing an autobiography is essentially one of othering the self, Frame describing it as an exercise of legitimacy, or 'making [herself] a first person.

WAITING FOR FOUCAULT

A lot of what I said about 'reading' and 'writing' (which includes 'translating' of course) must be diluted now to read from a parody of Samuel Beckett's *Waiting for Godot*, 'prepared' by Matthew Maslin (1996) where he creates an interesting 'other' for Beckett so true in all discussions and deliberations on translation and creative writing. In the place of Vladimir and Estragon, we find Mikhail Bakhtin and Jacques Derrida appearing as old friends in this text. They are shown as engaged in an imaginary conversation, as they *wait* endlessly *for Foucault*. I use this as there is a lot to learn from the way we as authors and translators can laugh at ourselves as we begin a serious discussion on 'translation and othering'. Let us look at the play of 'words' and the play with 'roles' here, and how an ever-elusive 'third person' becomes a topic in an illocutionary act.

As the play opens, we see Derrida writing. He is obviously frustrated, crumpling up paper and cursing to himself. He is soon joined by Bakhtin:

Derrida: Oh, I can't write a thing.
Bakhtin: Of course you can't. Neither can I.
Der: How can I write if I don't know if I'm a writer? What if I'm an author?
Bak: What if you're an author and I'm a writer?
Der: And what if you're a writer and I'm an author?
Bak: Right.
Der: Write? But how?
Bak (*angrily*): I said right as in correct, not write.
Der: We've been here for hours.
Bak: Days.
Der: Years. (*sighs*) Let's go.
Bak: We can't.
Der: Why not?
Bak: We're waiting for Foucault.
Der: Why are we waiting for him?
Bak: Because he can tell us what an author is.
Der: He knows?
Bak: He might. He did ask the question. When he defines the author-function, he should know what an author is, and then ... well, then we'll know.
Der (*confused*): I don't understand you
Bak: That's good!!
Der: Why?
Bak: Because if you understood me, we wouldn't be talking.
Der: I don't understand.
Bak: That's good!
Der: Why?
Bak: Because if you understood me, we wouldn't be talking.

Thoroughly bored, they continue in the following manner to 'keep the conversation going. That way we can pass the time'. The topics seem limited as they can't 'talk about a novel yet', 'because it isn't done yet', and nor about the concerns such as 'Do you think we're writers?', because if they were not, and were 'authors' instead, they were dead 'because of what Barthes said'. If so, Derrida suggests:

Der: Let's hang ourselves immediately!
Bak: But what if we're already dead?

Der: Then it won't matter!
Bak: But what if we don't have to be dead?
Der: Oh. But how will we know?
Bak: We'll wait for Foucault. He can tell us.

In the segment on 'Writing', Derrida falls asleep and Bakhtin kicks him to warn that he 'must stay awake', for which 'we have to talk about something' such as:

Bak: I was thinking: suppose we're writers.
Der: What else would we be?
Bak: We could be authors.
Der: What's the *differance*?
Bak: The what?
Der: Never mind...

The play continues in the same multiply nested mode, which made a virtue out of boredom, as Bakhtin is depicted raising a fundamental philosophical debate on writing, morality and Plato:

Bak: Even if we're writers, do you think we should even bother being alive?
Der: Why?
Bak: Didn't Plato say that writing was bad?
Der: No, you fool. We don't even know what Plato meant. Some words mean opposite things.
Bak: So?
Der: So Plato could have meant anything. What he really meant is that writing is good.

That is when enters Roland Barthes. They decide to 'write him a letter' as Derrida is reported to have said somewhere that 'writing is better than speech'. But before the two can write anything, Barthes approaches them and speaks to them:

Barthes: Good day, gentlemen.
Bak and Der: Hello.
Brth: What are you doing here?
Bak: Waiting.
Brth: For?
Der: Foucault.
Brth: Why?

Bak: He knows the author-function.
Brth: Why do you need to know that?
Der: Because you told us we were dead!!
Brth (laughing): No, I told you that the author was dead.
Bak: What are we?
Brth: Writers!! Writers, you fools!!
Der: I always thought we were authors.
Brth: Well, it depends on whether you perform a function or an activity. Which is it?
Bak and Der answer simultaneously: A function!! An activity!!
Brth (*laughing*): Ha!! Just keep waiting for Foucault.
Bak: But are you an author or a writer?!
Brth: Never mind, boys, never mind. I'm a critic.
Der: But...

Exit Barthes.

CONCLUDING REMARKS

By way of concluding remarks, I would like to add that authors are often inaccurately portrayed as solitary geniuses, and what more, many strongly believe in this depiction. But they tend to forget that they, as social agents, are positioned, by language and society, to write 'social texts' that reproduce the existing social order or the chaos that characterizes their time and space—once again, deictic categories. Let us not forget that 'texts' are actually constrained both by language (Wittgenstein 1976, 1986) as well as by social forces that 'domesticate' writing. Since the boundary between the text and the world blurs to the point of collapse, *reading* and *re-reading* remain the only real authors. Very soon, as Ben Agger (1990) would like us to believe, books begin to author writers, constraining authorial sensibility and subjectivity, and introducing a socially acceptable formulation of society. It is at this point that texts assume and appropriate the authors' 'self', and the authors are pushed into the background as the 'Others'. But, I would urge that we must bring translators into the scene to construct a social theory of the text that will remove its one-dimensionality. It is this 'second' turn to a text that helps evolve a sociology of writing and help frame a theory and critique of ideology (see Jameson 1991). Although the French postmodernists like Derrida and Foucault would claim that 'reading writes', it is also the case that 'readings' destroy texts. The responsibility of interpreting what is 'undecidable' rests on reading. With the exception of those texts that get reincarnated and enter into the circuit of meta-texts of a given community or cultural space, all other texts seem to live a definite life and have a fatalistic self-destructing tendency. In such cases, translation seems to be the only real hope for discourses of ideology.

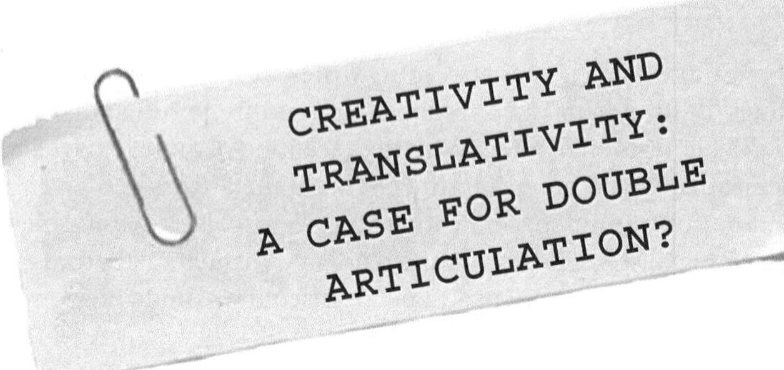

2

THE PARALLEL

LET ME MAKE a claim at the outset that, broadly speaking, all original literary work is translation and all translation, an original creation. Both are destined to deploy human language which has it in its nature to change and decay. Don't we hear an echo of these words in what Octavio Paz had to say?

> Every text is unique and, at the same time, it is the translation of another text. No text is entirely original because language itself, in its essence, is already a translation: firstly, of the non-verbal world and secondly, since every sign and every phrase is the translation of another sign and another phrase (quoted in Basnett-McGuire 1980: 38).

Thus, one is tempted to take this position further because of the fact that human language has the inherent characteristic of double articulation. However, the same argument can be turned around without sacrificing its validity: all texts are original because ideally every literary translation is an invention and is, as such, a unique text.

I think it needs to be mentioned that some of us have already taken a theoretical position that all original writing in a given language is nothing but a recreation, a translation twice-removed (cf. Singh and Bhattacharjee 1999). In a monolingual situation, this may sound bizarre. But the claim needs more clarification. To argue further on these lines, one needs to envisage an open-ended arena inside all potential and actual authors' minds—which I would like to describe as the *logical space*—where several texts are moulded in continuous semiosis and from where all the written texts evolve as products. In the absence of a better term, let us call it a creative internal text, with an acronym, CIT (cf. Singh and Pandey 1996).

The persistent interaction between the world at large and the living being confined to bondage that goes by various names—culture, society, family or even marriage—is a life-long phenomenon. An author is no exception to this scenario; albeit, there is a difference in the author's (or any creative person's) understanding and conceptualization of the outside world and the common man's, which gets reflected in the creative output of an author. The concept of CIT emerges from here. It can be defined as a methodological field of happening where a continuous flux of signs revolves in an interrelated fashion. The author is the subject here, being the main determinant but at the same time, she also acts as a predicate—an agent of products that, in turn, determine the nature of signs.

The unfolding of CIT, thus, continues in an open-ended fashion where the author is often an unconscious participant, and yet involved in a process of growth of consciousness. The creative impulses of an author transcend into the reader's space, which I would like to designate as a *physical space*, in the form of texts. It appears as if an author, like a native speaker, is articulating twice. What comes out as a text is a *re*-creation, because what is aimed at—creation—lies in CIT, and it is more likely that there will be a mismatch between the two, much in the same way as a translation is often not an exact match of the original. It is often the case that the source text and the translation do not fit into the same mould. In fact, it is this mismatch that makes literary productivity one of the most challenging activities. The mismatch happens even when the author of the original text herself happens to be her own translator. This is why creative writing has been described here as a translation twice removed. The first-order signification involves the creative person's creation of CIT, and the second-order signification lies in the text she produces.

Creativity, in a way, then, can be and should be defined as a rearrangement of existing signs. Creativity is a point of view to look at the world which is already in existence, and yet defining it in new permutations and combinations. Thus, the approach, though not completely original, draws support from Shannon and Weaver's (1948) mathematical model of information as to how much can be 'new' and how much 'given' in any text. If one naively goes through the annals of the history of inventions, it will be evident that no scientific invention or literary piece is original. Each one is built on top of another or on several 'others'. The key to an invention, therefore, is in the rearrangement of existing signs, and unravelling the new routes of derivation that rules can take.

Notice that this position does not emerge from the Barthean rejection of 'author-god', nor does it assume the reader's supremacy. Not surprisingly, Umberto Eco and others have already questioned this kind of extreme bias towards readers' space and suggested an interactive domain instead. The premises proposed here tally with these ideas as well as modify their theoretical position.

Today's writers are very particular about who their readers are. As Barbara Godard (1995: 75) points out in 'A Translator's Diary', it matters to authors like Nicole Brossard 'that it is a woman (re)reading the fiction' of this woman writer. Brossard is herself interested in the positive potential of lapses in translation because 'it is in the aura of words that feminist consciousness and lesbian emotion can be found, that which we like to express does not enter into the spirit of "official" languages that we speak' (Brossard 1992: 25). Sherry Simon (1996: 35) points out that code switching can be 'a way of inscribing multiplicity in a text governed by universalizing modes of representation'. In her diary *Journal intime* (1984), Brossard does exactly that between French and English, and plays with fonts and styles to make it a textured diary.

Let us, therefore, take a concrete example of an author such as Nicole Brossard from Quebec, who has been writing since 1965 and has already published close to 30 volumes of poetry, novel, journals, literary essays and so on. Brossard (ibid.: 23) thinks that the question posed in translation is one of choice. Which signifier should she choose that will stir up the multiple meanings that act invisibly and efficiently on the consciousness? The process of translation fascinates

Brossard 'as an act of passage from one language to another, but also, for me as passing from reality to fiction, or from fiction to reality' and as a process that engages a woman as both a reader and a writer, negotiating meaning in an open space of ontological enquiry.

According to Siemerling (1994) and Siemerling and Huggan (2000: 96), Brossard (1984: 22–23) has been 'an explorer in language'. This is because she finds translation interrogates the links between language and identity:

> To be translated is to be questioned not only in what you believe exists but also in the very way we think in a language, as well as how. This is to ask oneself, how would I be if I thought in English, in Italian, or in some totally different language.

Because Brossard's *Journal intime* is a lesbian diary, the most important problem for Bev Curran and Mitoko Hirabayashi in translating it into Japanese was how to make the translation explicitly gendered and women-centred in Japanese. Curran says in *Translation in Three Dimensions: Nicole Brossard in Japanese* (2000), that this is because 'the writer's purposefully political misuse of grammar and linguistic structures forces new meanings from the symbolic systems that pre-program our thoughts and words'. Her feminist writing thus demands feminist translation strategies such as the supplementing and commentary. The text misleads sense, that is, the text is 'a trickster' or it 'seduces' by an engaging appearance of reality. The more a text tricks the sense of what we have learned by heart in our lives, the more it seduces, captivates, the more it brings us closer to writing' (Brossard 1988: 151).

It then follows from the above that the author, like the translator, chooses sounds, smells, colours, words, symbols and icons, from out of the environs around her, and portrays certain interpreted reality. The mask she wears or wants to wear are worn by the characters in her creation. The environs created around each interpreted character are linked in lineage to the cluster of many characters that live within the author's mind. This is comparable to the translator's use of icons in the target text. The iconic use of certain noises, visuals, syntactic constructions or even idioms bears it out. Here the faithfulness, like the translation of bilingual situations, cannot be denied as CIT is the total repertoire, the *superset*, and creations are all *subsets* to the superset.

There are clearly two model worlds here—two worlds having different sets of icons, sets of rules, different signifiers and signifieds. These possible worlds do not have transitive relation to each other. They have partial transitivity through somebody, like the translator, who can transit between two worlds. It does not mean that these two worlds of signifiers and signifieds, of creativity and translativity merge into one another, but they can be transcended by the subject concerned.

If the translator or the author wants to pass on some message or her/his understanding of reality from a source language to a target language, as the worlds are different, the translator has to deconstruct the total reality of the first world (or a text) in order to understand and analyse the icons and sets of rules. She has also to reconstruct the total understanding she hit upon and transfer them onto the TL world using the TL axioms and sets of rules. The same deconstruction and reconstruction processes go on in a cycle.

WHY TRANSLATE?

Why do we require new translations? Belitt (1978: 114) is very clear about the reasons: 'Each age must find Virgil and Horace and Sappho and Homer and all the others for itself.' That makes translations inevitable. The reasons for translation are manifold. They are inherent in the nature of language, intrinsic to the art of language, and imbued in the nature of creativity. Then there are external reasons as to why translation occupies an important place today, and these have to be found in politics, economy and culture. The original remains permanently wrapped in a language—bound by both time and space, and which grows obsolescent very soon—calling for new words and newer sentences. This only proves that literary translation is a 'time-art' (Rose 1981: 4). Translations decay, just as styles do, says Belitt (1978: 33), but the message—the content, the core—is always constant. The message lies dormant within the obscure language and needs to be reinterpreted in contemporary tongue. Therefore, one should always translate inside the wide-open premise that re-translation is an ongoing process.

There is another argument for translation. The existing translation of any text, as Savory (1957: 29) rightly observes, is quickly antiquated. It becomes obsolete and as an art (which is timeless), translation can also reappear to appease the stimuli felt by every new generation. The translator, as a mediator, recreates the 'mediating vehicle' in renewed shape.

Third, like the plays or performing texts that are in constant state of change, all literary works are also in a state of flux, the main actor in this drama being language. Be that as it may, it is also language that decays soon and needs renovating. Frederic Will (1993), therefore, stresses on not the work but the energy or 'thrust' of a work that is important for translating. To quote Will (ibid.: 155):

> Translation is par excellence the process, by which the thrust behind the verbal works of man ... can be directly transferred, carried on, allowed to continue.... Works of literature are highly organized instances of such thrust ... these blocks force themselves on, through time, from culture to culture.

The dynamic process of reinterpretation is accelerated by an inward power of language and art. To turn outside this cycle, why one translates a particular work and how one does it depends on political, economic and cultural forces at work.

Culture is by far the most important force that pushes one to surge ahead and bring in a river into the plains, as it were, something that reminds one of Bhagirath bringing in the Ganges in the Hindu mythology. By bringing in the holy river from the virgin mountains down to the plains, it was not merely canalizing a force of nature, it was a bringing about of a whole new attitude, new means of life and livelihood, a novel cultural landscape. It is such cultural needs that force texts to be 'situated'. At the same time, cultural isolation of a text is regarded as a 'dangerous matter' (Raffel 1971: 157). So translators need to relate the creative work they handle with the people for whom the original work was created. Whether we look at the re-creations of the RaamaayaNa story in Tulasidaasa's Awadhi text or Kamban's Tamil versions, re-translations can happen both inter-culturally and intra-culturally. Kaliprasanna Sinha's rewriting of the RaamaayaNa in Bengali in mid-nineteenth century—something that his predecessor poet Krttibaasa had already done in eighteenth-century Bengal and Ishwarchandra Vidyasagar would do soon in *Siitaar Banabaas*—shows that translations can also happen intra-lingually, just as they do inter-lingually. Each one of them has its own pleasure, for they make it possible to know our own selves and others and make it possible for others to know us.

THE CONTEMPORARY AUTHOR AND LINGUISTIC MANIPULATIONS

As for original writing, I strongly believe that no creative writer can meditate in a realm that precedes language. This is because language is the primary modelling system, literature and art being the secondary modelling systems. I also believe that one's aesthetics of translation will derive from one's background. From what we have discussed so far, it is clear that like translators, the original authors too are engaged in constant linguistic manipulations, which swing between grammatical violence to semantic compromises. Be that as it may, let us use the metaphor of grammar to understand this situation better. We shall discuss the question of linguistic manipulation in terms of a few visible approaches, and begin with a 'nominal' approach.

Like duality of patterning that characterizes human language, 'images' used in a literary text are also subjected to another kind of duality which has been called the dynamics of 'reverberation' as against the energetics of 'causality' (cf. Minkowski cited in Bachelard 1958[1964]: xii). A textual image has the quality of 'trans-subjectivity', even when it shows variations as against the other concepts that are constitutive and that are, therefore, open to causal relationship. An author creates his own language, and even when he 'does not confer the past of his image upon ... [us], yet his image immediately takes root in ... [us]' (ibid). At the level of 'reverberations' then, a text possesses us entirely. Knowing that the image in the text has been given by another person, the image that we as readers derive makes us feel so involved with the text that we begin to feel that we could have created it ourselves. The twists and the turns that we, enlivening such texts, give in speaking, retelling or enacting this oral acquisition derive precisely from this confidence that the text has become 'really our own'.

In the vernacular of imagery then, literary texts can be viewed (Barthes 1978) as a field of *pomme frite* (French fried) on a frying pan where 'on any object, a good language-system function, attacks, surrounds, sizzles, hardens, and browns' (Barthes 1986: 355). I would like to call these imageries 'pronominal' because 'language' here stands only as an object which is not the real thing but without which nothing real or substantial can be stated.

There may arise a question here as to what the author does with language in order to actuate such images or such qualities in writing. I believe that the author distorts the world of words, corrupts vocabularies, cripples the canonical syntactic norms, and introduces unprecedented grammatical violence. She bends and mends language to accommodate his images. And the task of the translator is to transfer this violence into another community, into another language. To the extent that this is true, we can see how the dominant 'nominality' works in the area of critical appreciation. The literary interpreter as well as the translator as the 'subjects' of the given texts begin to qualify and quantify their 'dual objects'—the direct (text) as well as the indirect (SL or TL reader).

Let us now move on to yet another kind of imagery, prevalent in the literary texts of our time. In order to contextualize our translator/ interpreter, or to take an 'adverbial' approach, one must appreciate that the source and target texts are quite often referring to completely or substantially different space and time or that the encoder is 'manipulating' the message form to achieve a certain kind of unreadability/ incomprehensibility. In such cases, it becomes crucial for us to know the 'when', 'where' and 'how' of a given text. Particularly, we must know whether the manipulation was done because the author wanted to write in a 'private' look for a wholistic meaning in a text, that is, look for 'the' meaning, not caring to appreciate that language (and consequently, literature too) is essentially ambiguous.

Second, although critics may consider the search for alternative or supplementary meanings futile, or they may, at the most, restrict themselves to only a few apparently legible interpretations evident from the cues provided by the authors, the literary translators are not bound by any of these guileless and simplistic interpretations. This is because they are not only interpreting the original text, they are reading it to re-read and re-create. They are finding meanings in a text in relation to the world of meaning of the target language semantics as well as in terms of its possible readings (which each one of them thinks is possible) in the source culture and community.

Third, since ten different translators are likely to give ten different translations, based on many differing interpretations, this appreciation of ambiguity is ingrained in the approach of a literary translator. In fact, it is now increasingly realized that one can only interpret a literary text if one dares attempting to render it inter-lingually, inter-semiotically or even intra-lingually, although the third approach is usually uninstantiated. Notice that some of the best critiques of a literary text have come from their cinematic renderings (hence the inter-semioticity).

In fact, one can extend this position further and say that 'our aesthetics will derive from the canon of our worldview', which in turn is 'determined by our own languages' (Singh 1990). If we argue that our languages and cultures (stated in plural because more often than not an Oriental person is split between at least two cultures and almost surely two languages) constrain our perception and are constrained by it, building a 'standard' critical theory can only be viewed sceptically as a new way of establishing hegemony.

In fact, if we are to believe that 'there is no magic land of meaning outside human consciousness', following semanticists like E. D. Hirsch (1967), it will follow from there that all attempts at building a monolithic critical discourse are to be viewed as attempts to level up this magic land of meaning by obfuscating all uneven terra and by precluding any future corruption of space. Cognitive psychologists like Edmund Husserl would even go one step further and state that 'meaning' may be conceived as a self-identical schema whose boundaries are determined by an originating speech event, while significance may be conceived as a relationship drawn between that self-identical meaning 'and something, anything else' (Husserl 1939[1973]. Compare this position with Barthian idea of signification which argues that ideas cleave and cohere to the body of text like a leech does and that 'criticism' is a system of demystification or de-leeching language. Also consider Rosenblatt's (1984: 123–28) position where poetry is defined as an event of reading poems (i.e. poetry 'happens' only when one 'reads' poems). The claim is that literature is that thing which a reader discovers in a text.

THE DIFFICULTIES OF BUILDING A THEORY

As for the impossibility of translation, a translator may have an aim which she may not be able to fulfil. The reasons for such failure could be many. She may not be able to decode the text fully. This difficult-to-decode text need not be a difficult literary text alone. It can be a difficult scientific or legal text too. But obviously, this is more likely to happen in case of literary translation. This may happen even if she knows the language well.

The other possibilities are that her competence in the target language (TL) may not be the same as her knowledge of the source language (SL). Alternatively, the structure of SL and TL may be so different that even the best translators cannot do justice. And then there is this danger that she may read more meaning into a text than was intended by the original author. Further, the act of translating will produce different results depending upon the translators' linguistic backgrounds. Of particular importance are answers to these questions: Is the translator a native speaker of the source language (SL) in question? Or, is she translating an SL text into a given target language (TL) that happens to be her mother tongue? Or, is the translator a grass-roots bilingual in both languages?

It does not rule out the possibility that some translators may achieve their desired end, whatever their goals may be. The goals, as we know, may vary. Some may aim at being true to the original, whereas others may try to provide us only a commentary of the original text. Some may even think of removing all frills from translated texts but others may like to leave the unevenness there on purpose, particularly to remind the TL reader that what they are reading is a translation. There may be several factors that may contribute towards what either readers of TL texts or their translators may consider to be successes—perceived or real. The most important of these is the knowledge of both SL and TL that a translator operates with. More often than not, in such cases, the translator is a mother-tongue speaker of the TL or a grass-roots bilingual with both languages available at home. There may be other reasons too. The translator may share the concern, philosophy and other aspects, excluding the professional expertise, of the text writer or the author of the text. Yet another reason for success could be that the SL and TL were genealogically and typologically close to each other.

SOURCE LANGUAGE: BHOJPURI

Once again, there was a Panchayat meeting in the village today. Autar Baba was seated on the highest seat. The seat was nothing but a pendulant cot with bamboo straps tied below and woven with ropes made out of seasoned grass. As Autar Baba settled down on it, the ropes of the cot bent down unusually. Baba was wearing a half of five yards cloth below, and tied the rest across his legs behind his back from where it was swinging in the air, back and forth. The Panchayat there would also swing along. Dangling his dhoti like this, only God knows how many cases were handled by Autar Baba. One has lost count of them. There was no quarrel in the village, which could be resolved without his intervention. The people in his family would call Autar Baba a 'recluse'. You must have seen the bulls—let loose—which could not be tied to any stand. The Lord of Bulls could still be grounded, but the Taurus must graze as it wished! Let anybody say what pleases him! But these critical words had no effect on Autar Baba. What harm could anyone do to him? Wherever he went, he was sure to get a square meal! He won't mind sleeping off on the tilling land of a follower or even in his stable! When it was dinner time, the grandchildren would come and invite him, 'Grandpa! Call for dinner, please!' And he would rebuke them, 'Go away! Am I dying in hunger? I have had my belly-full. The Panchayat is due to meet in a few moments, and you want me to go home to eat?' The children would go back.

Gojar Chowdhry would then appear mixing khaini and chuna on his palm and would instantly begin shooting his cryptic comments, 'What's the matter Pundit Baba? The members of the Panchayat haven't come yet?' In a few moments, they would arrive anyway. Autar Baba would until then lie baring his back and legs. He would now rise and sit up straight. As he did that, that piece of cloth tied around his back and legs would begin dangling once again. Spitting his betel water in a corner, he would thus begin by looking up at Gojar Chowdhry, 'Yes, tell me Gojar-bhai! Why are we assembled here?'—Taking cue from this question, the accused would begin almost immediately, 'Sircar, My Lord! Listen to me! Just imagine the courage of Khadarua's wife! She is stealing at this nascent age? Let her skull be smashed!'

> Birju Pundit thought it his birthright to intrude. If it was a woman's cause, and particularly if she was young, he could not be silent. He shouted at the fellow, 'Did you catch her in the field?' Even Khadarua couldn't control himself. He made his already small eyes even smaller and commented, 'Why don't you keep your mouth shut, Grandpa?' At this, the judges, the common people, and the accused—all burst into laughter. The proceedings of the Panchayat got submerged under that (Singh 2000a: 51–59).

In this text, a non-initiated Western reader would probably require footnotes on what a 'Panchayat' is, or what a 'square meal' means any way. The ones not familiar with a folded 'dhoti' often worn by village elders or grown-up males would not understand the details of descriptions such as 'a half of five yards cloth below, and tied the rest across his legs behind his back from where it was swinging in the air, back and forth' or what kind of seat would be a *khatiyaa* which is 'a pendulant cot with bamboo straps tied below and woven with ropes made out of seasoned grass' in this text. Interestingly, the original Bhojpuri text had these details and not merely single words or compounded expressions. Lord Shiva referred to as 'the Lord of Bulls' here, or 'mixing *khaini* and *chuna*', are common expressions for an Indian. Although urban Indians living in the four metropolises may not have come across *khaini*, there would hardly be anyone who would not know what 'betel water' is.

Let us now look at another prose-text, this time from a classic short story in Maithili published in the post-Independence period by Laliteshwar Jha writing under the pseudonym 'Lalit'.

SOURCE LANGUAGE: MAITHILI

> Her name was Kanchan, but they call her Kanchaniya. She was poor and untouchable, which was why everybody would call her Kanchaniya, and not Kanchan. She has been a silent witness of fourteen springs. Her father Harjanma was a farm labourer of Bauku Choudhury. Last year, during the summer, he fell down from a rose-apple tree and died. He left behind, like other labourers, the only property he had—two earning hands of his daughter and the legacy of a loan in her lame mother. The only way of livelihood for the family was Kanchan's ability to slog.

> Dibble and drill in the paddy fields during the rains and reap, glean and gather before the winter sets in. Her mother was crippled all right. But she too was able to earn as much as she could. She used to make cowdung cakes for Balo babu and got half of what she made.
>
> Her hut was away from Babhan-toli. It wasn't really a hut. It was only a shanty shed which had somehow been made livable after a door was fixed. The lamey had been having fever for over a month now. And besides, she had a large spleen in her stomach. 'Where will she get money from to buy the medicines she needs? Now once again the fever has got better of her. She gets into a delirium in the morning ... and remains subdued in fever the whole day.' With a wolf in the stomach, Kanchaniya sat motionless in a corner of their courtyard the whole day, placing her head on her knees.
>
> ...
>
> Where are you?' she heard the feeble voice of her mother from inside the room. But even this fervent call of the sick woman could not break her inertia.... 'Where did you disappear, girl?' The lamey cried out in a hoarse voice, 'Doubt if there's something at home. Is there anything?' the lamey asked, licking her own dark lips, without even looking at Kanchan.
>
> Nothing! How can there be anything?... Nobody has given even a grain today.... It is Sukrati today, that's why! (Singh 1996).

Here, let us take up only one of these, namely the first text, for further discussion and analysis. One should not view this particular translated text independently of the strategies used by the translator in rendering Sukumar Ray's nonsensical stories and rhymes.

SOURCE LANGUAGE: BENGALI

> He really was a most extraordinary creature.
>
> 'Who are you?' I asked him. 'What's your name?'
>
> He thought for a while and said, 'My name's Higgle-Piggle-Dee. I'm called Higgle-Piggle-Dee, my brother's called Higgle-Piggle-Dee, my uncle called Higgle-Piggle-Dee....'

I cut him short. 'Why don't you simply say the whole family's called Higgle-Piggle-Dee?'

He pondered the matter again. 'Oh no', he said at last, 'I'm really called Tokai, my uncle's called Tokai, my nephew's called Tokai, my cousin's called Tokai, my father-in-law's called Tokai....'

'Are you sure?' I asked sternly. 'Or are you making all this up?'

He grew confused and stammered, 'Well, actually my father-in-law's called Biscuit' (Chaudhury 1987: 36–39).

The translator very intelligently used expressions such as 'higgle-piggle-dee'. The probability was that the translator was doing what is called 'saving (or improving upon) the text'. Let us consider the source language text:

jantuTaar rakam-sakam dekhe aamaar bhaari adbhut laaglo. aami jijnaasaa karlaam, 'tumi ke? tomaar naam ki?' se khaanikkSaN bhebe balla, 'aamaar naam hijibijibij. aamaar maamaar naam hijibijibij, aamaar baabaar naam hijibijibij, aamaar pisher naam hijibijibij....' aami ballaam, 'taar ceye sojaa ballei hay tomaar guSTi-shuddha sabaai hijibijibij'.

se aabaar khaanik bhebe balla, 'taa to nay, aamaar naam takaai. aamaar maamaar naam takaai, aamaar khuRor naam takaai, aamaar meshor naam takaai, aamaar shvashurer naam takaai...

aami dhamak diye ballaam, 'satyi balcho? naa baaniye?' jantuTaa keman thatomato kheye balla, 'naa naa, aamaar shvashurer naam biskuT'... (Ray 1921[1986]: 132–33).

The same tract, when reproduced in the source language, reflects the broad *changes more clearly*. There was no paragraph division in the Bengali text as in the English one (between the first two paragraphs in the English version). The last two paragraphs in the English text (including one more paragraph which is not quoted here, comprise just one unit in Sukumar Ray's Bengali original). This kind of division—except perhaps in poetry—may be allowed, particularly because they are usually in conformity with the target language way of organizing things in a fiction or such other prose texts.

Also worth noting is the fact that referential words and names, which act as proper names as well as words defining one's characteristics, were not possible to handle properly in the translation. The blooperous rendering was of course in the paragraph which starts the 'Tokai' narration. There is a logic in what Higgle-Piggle-Dee says, just as there is a logic in the concept: *Ha-ja-ba-ra-la*. He does not and cannot say that his name was takaai. As we see in the excerpt, he says that his maternal uncle and various other relatives are called takaai, which he says to counter the allegation of the listener (= the self), namely, that the whole clan (*guSTi-shuddha*) is called Higgle-Piggle-Dee. Therefore, the sentence spoken after the creature pondered for a while cannot start with 'I'm really called Tokai'. This probably was not a chance error. Probably, the translator did it deliberately to forge a link between the two apparently senseless statements of Higgle-Piggle-Dee. But if one thinks about it seriously, now that we know a little more about the endlessly different and creative manner in which human languages show semantic and grammatical categorization of any concept, it is not entirely impossible to think of a culture where naming patterns have such rules as given by our *hijibijibij* here. It is perfectly possible for different kinds of people in your little world to have three sets of names: *hijibijibij*, *takaai* and *biskuT*.

Although most readers would point out that the expression *ha-ja-ba-ra-la* in Bengali has now become synonymous with *hijibiji* or *hijibijibij*, that is, in English—nonsense, fiddlesticks or poppycock—I think there is a deeper logic in the name. It is possible to appreciate this if one considers the apparently crazy (but actually very scientific) organization of the sound system or the arrangement of *varNas* in the great grammar of Panini written 2,500 years ago. Notice that Panini's 'shivasuukta' had fourteen 'words' (constructed out of possible sources and syllables), the last two being: *hayavaraT; laN*, which is what gives us '*ha ya va ra la*' (In Bengali, the Sanskritic *ya* becomes *ja*). One who does not know out critical tradition would miss the parallel intended by the author.

MORE PROBLEMS

Consider this brief piece of translation without the original (for a better appreciation of this point) from a Hindi poem by Suryakant Tripathy:

> I'm a Brahman's son
> And I love her.

She belongs to the Kahars
And at the first crack of light
She brings the water-jugs to my house,
And I'm dying for her.

She's black as a cuckoo, oh,
Her walk straight and steady
And not yet married. My heart
Bursts with wanting her.

She comes every day and wakes us all
But I'm the only one who understands her game.
She takes away the big water jug
And I bide my time.

If such texts are placed before a reader from the Western world (as David Rubin [1976] did), one cannot expect that they will be fully appreciated, because this reader may not be able to understand the natural and social background of this piece. One will naturally fail to understand with what magic the tedium of the village belles bringing water-pitchers from a long distance is transformed into an aesthetically glorious visual that a male beholder longs to cerebrate and ruminate again and again, day after day. Besides, a culture or a society that does not have caste-based stratification will miss out some other aspects of the relationship between the two here—the hero, a Brahmin and the woman, a Kahar.

CONTEXTUALIZING THE TEXT

The next text is again deeply entrenched in the environs and society it belongs to. An Indian reader reading it in English will surely have a better chance of its fuller appreciation. The swear words used, or comparisons such as *Mallarme* > *Mallar-Meta* (in the pattern of *Narsingh-Me[h]ta*), the pun intended to be made out of *Kafka*> *Kofka*, or the *Sardar-ji* being referred to will be difficult, if not impossible, puns for an English-English or an American-English reader to appreciate. Obviously, the Indianism of expressions such as '*all wanting to leave*', etc., are intended by the translators here. Consider this following longish poem by Sitanshu Yasaschandra translated from Gujarati by Saleem Peeradina, Jayant Parkh, Raasik

Shah and Gulam Mohammed Sheikh (again, only the English version is given to make the point):

SOURCE LANGUAGE : GUJARATI

1
It all started with stubborn Magan saying
I want to live.
The Gujarati literati were dumbfounded:
You dolt, is that ever possible?
The young clamoured on one side—what about
our experimental periodicals?
On the other the elders rebuked—this
way centuries may pass idly.
All agreed upon this—if you choose to live
then quit the sanctum of literature.

Done, said Magan.

The moment he stepped across the threshold
a miracle occurred.
From the niche appeared the Goddess Saraswati

and informed the king
that where Magan went she would follow.
And behind her—Goddess Experiment,
Miss Realism, Mr Rythem—all wanting
to leave, all adamant.
So they decided, all right, you trouble-maker,
stay and rot in that corner.

2
But the fellow whose name was Magan,
a few days later says I want love.
All right, you nut.

So we took him to Apollo Street.
In the picturesque square, an
impressive building. In the building
a secret chamber under lock and key.

Took Magan to the State Bank's safe-deposit vault—
as stated in the scriptures, brought a priest
along to recite mantras

—handed one key to Magan and kept the other.
Then with chant of glory to
Ramachandra, Sita's spouse, opened the locker.

Here, take love.
But the son of a bitch Magan says—this is not love.
If this is not love then what is it, you
bastard?

All the bigwigs—prize-winners, medalists—have
taken love for their stories, poems and plays
from this very source.

And you, fancy idiot, claim that this is not love.
What is it? If this is not love what is it?
What is the purpose of keeping it in the
safe-deposit vault then?

So you can use it when necessary and return.
It never goes out of style.
All those veteran professors use it year after
year and some of them have used it for
twenty-five years—yet it stays brand new.

But
this prick Magan, he says—
I want to live and I want love.

3
Well then..
Crazy Magan was locked up in the House of Letters.
The place has western-style latrines.
In the morning everybody used paper.
Need a lot of paper: but that Sardarji
from the Times of India distributed huge rolls
of paper which were left hanging there.
Then all the literary big-shots
—old and new—
put their signatures at the bottom of the
paper after use.

And the contents would be published in
periodicals or read over Akashvani.
In the case of an upset after bad food.
an entire novel could be serialized.

On anniversaries and festive occasions, special
numbers and anthologies would be brought out
from this stock only.
This swine of a Magan did his work
really well.

Early every morning, he would do the job—
and forget to sign.

But those literature-loving editors would
always be lurking around.

They would grab a new poem (even it it had been discarded)
and print it under the name of Magan,
poet extraordinary.

Only rarely would they put their own signatures.
(Generally speaking, there is some ethics in
our Gujarati literature. No one would pinch
another's poem.)
And within a year, Magan got the State prize
and five or six gold medals.
And then there were celebrations and
felicitations: Every paper announced that on
a certain date and day, a felicitation programme
for Magan, the poet emeritus, would take
place with the following speakers and
who the chairman would be, plus a long list
of well-wishers.

Each one of them spoke. What oratory!
Someone mentioned *Kofka*, another spoke of
Mallarmeta and still another of *Narsinhmeta.*
Someone spoke of the love between a camel
and a cow.

And each one had an anecdote to relate.
Auspicious and inauspicious—all was revealed.

Finally someone happened to remember:
Let that swine Magan say a few words.

The chairman was all set to press the bell
saying one, two, three, speak—
And Magan, the dolt, the poor idiot (one
pities him) says (the same, what else?), he
says (and this after receiving the prize for poetry),
says I want to live. I want to love.
I want to write a poem.
(Peeradina et al. 1991: 221–24)

As one would notice, any English-English or American-English grammar checker would simply go crazy in trying to identify the 'errors' that have been committed here: *Stubborn Magan* in the very first line attracts our attention. Those who know about the *Little Magazine* movement in the context of our BhaaSaa literature would know what is meant by experimental periodicals. The overt employment of both conditional trappings—'if … then'; faultily preceding adverbial clause—'where Magan went she will follow'; the juxtaposition of '*informed* … that where …'; or even names of possible characters—*Goddess Experiment, Miss Realism,* or *Mr Rythem* (let us not mind the spelling) are all evidence that point towards this localized backbone of the English version. This gets to a point where Indianism begins to get clearly exposed, but this seems to be a deliberate act. Where the experimentation of the translators reaches a height in needless elongation, multiple nestings or even almost impossible collocations and combinations is in the following expression:

…Every paper announced that on
a certain date and day, a felicitation programme
for Magan, the poet emeritus, would take
place with the following speakers and
who the chairman would be, plus a long list
of well-wishers.

As it must be obvious from this discussion, stylistic deviation has been used as a tool by the translators consciously. In addition, the Western reader may discover a number of other problems here.

CULTURAL DIFFERENCES

As mentioned already, the problem of genetic unrelatedness or structural distance becomes more difficult to deal with where cultural differences exist in addition to linguistic differences. An understanding of structural complexity and typological distance along with its socio-cultural context among the languages is indeed useful in determining the equivalence of translation. Further, it will be of more help to translators to orient their actions and develop theories on an empirical foundation. For instance, English represents the SVO (subject, verb, object) pattern and Tamil the SOV (subject, object, verb) pattern of languages. The shift from one to another is possible and permissible in the process of translation but as a student of translation studies, one must find out whether in doing so there are a set of constraints that hinder smooth tranference or translation. It should not be surprising to find A. K. Ramanujan not translating the title of U. R. Ananthamurthy's *Samskaara*, even though he does translate the word differently in the text. Similarly, Radhakrishnan's retention of the word *dharma* in his translation of the Giitaa in certain contexts in his English text is justified on the same grounds.

Let us take up the example of Jaishankar Prasad's *Kaamaayanii* and its well-known structuration into the following 15 canto:

> cintaa; aashaa; shraddhaa; kaama; vaasanaa; lajjaa; karma; iirSyaa; iRaa; svapna; sangharSa; nirveda; darshana; rahasya; aananda

Anybody familiar with the Indian philosophical thoughts will realize that many of these words are difficult to translate in that they will have many renderings each in any Western language. In one of the several translations of this classical text, Jaikishandas Sadani (1975) opts for the following:

> anxiety; hope; faith; desire; passion; bashfulness; action; envy; intelligence; dream; struggle; renunciation; revelation; mysticism; bliss

While there will be general agreement on some of these renderings as the one for *svapna, sangharSa,* etc., for many others, one doubts if the choice is acceptable if one considers the full connotation of such words. Take for instance the following naming words, each one of which has so many interpretations in English:

shraddhaa: reverence; respect; faith; trust; confidence; regard; esteem; admiration

karma: action; deed; work; function; occupation; fate; rite; ceremony; affair

If these options with reasonably different meanings or different semantic shades exist in the source language, it seems difficult to choose any one item in the TL. To further re-emphasize the problems that typically emerge out of language pairs that are unrelated, let us look at the last stanza of *Kaamaayanii*, and compare a few published translations, and this argument will find further support. Consider the following lines from the original Hindi text:

samaras the jaR yaa cetan
sundar saakaar banaa thaa;
cetanataa ek vilasatii
aanand akhaND ghanaa thaa.
(Prasad 1936[2003]: 1)

Let us now look into the different renderings that are available:

1. Matter and spirit were harmonious
Exquisite was the form of beauty
Consciousness alone was blossoming
Transcendental infinite Bliss.
(Sadani 1975: 251)

2. All objects conscious or unconscious were
Pervaded by the saviour of one life,
And beauty was incarnate everythere,
And Bliss intense and undivided reigned.
(B. L. Sahney, quoted in Lal 1975: viii)

3. Spirit and matter both seemed one,
Assuming beauties fresh and new;
One consciousness pervaded all
And joy from heaven dropped like dew.
(D. C. Dutta, quoted in Lal 1975: vii)

4. Spirit and matter joined,
Beauty took form,

One consciousness sported round,
It was intense unbroken bliss.
(Rameshwar Gupta, quoted in Lal 1975: vii)

While the fourth translation seems unduly concise, the second option is the opposite: In P. Lal's words (1975: vii) this one seems to be 'an amplified interpretation more than a translation'. The third one suffers from the defect of introducing new elements merely for the metrical reasons: 'dew', for instance; or even 'heaven'. These do not find mention in the original cited above. The options given here for the Hindi words *jaR* and *cetan* again reveal similar problems as discussed earlier. In the first, third and fourth translations, the choice is unanimous: spirit and matter for *cetan* and *jaR*, respectively, while the second uses conscious (*jaR*) and unconscious (*cetan*).

CONCLUSION

The main purpose of this chapter has been to make one aware of the fact that it is a comaparable set of things that happens when one *creates* new literary texts vis-à-vis when one *translates* such texts. The chapter also discussed the need to identify the problem areas in translation, and underscored the differences between the text and the work to relate them to translation. The translator was viewed as an interpreter here, and was shown as someone who would suffer from the tension between over- and under-translation, choice of styles, cultural differences as well as genetic and structural relationship (or the lack of it) between the source and target languages.

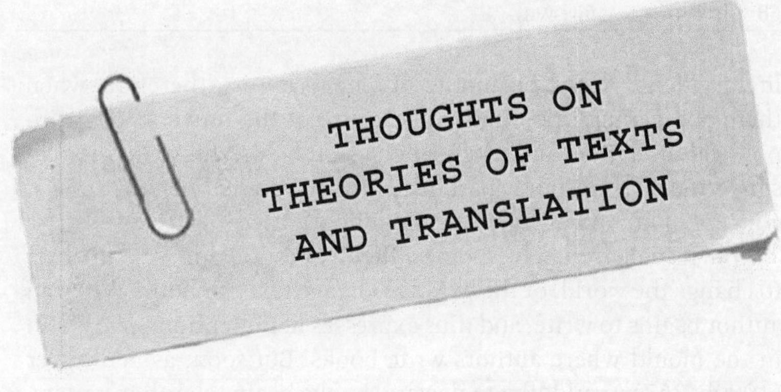

3

THE TEXT AND THE WORLD

ANYONE WHO HAS been through Noam Chomsky's work will remember the once-famous but now-forgotten example of 'Colorless green ideas sleep furiously' (Chomsky 1957: 2). Let us replace *ideas* with *authors* and then the action of *sleeping* with *writing*, and what do we get? We have a sect of social agents called writers, who often do not want to commit themselves politically, and who write furiously, composing all sorts of texts. Not surprisingly, these agents, like any other entrepreneurs, write their way into vast fortunes and usually possess a keen sense of the market. Some, who claim to represent the oppressed, write their way out of oppression and the ones with certain convictions know how to write beyond their dogma. False heroism abounds as false ideologies in the texts that get churned out of this mill, while the writers live a dual life—one which the readers are lured to discover in the text, and one, often completely antonymic, in real life.

It has already been contested that authors are often portrayed inaccurately as solitary geniuses, and what is more, they themselves forget their role as well as responsibility. In fact, today very few people have time or patience to read challenging political polemics, and many tend to create their own—often expressed in jokes, snide remarks, or party talk—which they derive from their reading of literary texts. At the beginning of a new century, therefore, when there is a genuine possibility of closure of the universe of socio-political discourse, and when language, too, loses its ability to reason, criticize, and stand apart in a non-partisan manner, the activist concept of literary agency becomes important.

But let us ask ourselves some difficult questions: do we want texts to change the world, or the world to change texts, or both? When an author begins to write, and thus expresses her intentions, she is still in the mould where authors write books. But soon, as Ben Agger (1989b: 367) would like to declare, books begin to author writers, constraining authorial sensibility and subjectivity, and introducing a 'socially acceptable' (and, may be, politically agreeable) formulation of society. Texts are actually constrained both by language (Wittgenstein 1976, 1986) as well as by social forces that domesticate writing. Since the boundary between text and world blurs to the point of collapse, reading and re-reading remain the only real authors (as Derrida implies). That is the point at which translators enter the scene to construct a social theory of the text that will remove its one-dimensionality (according to Marcuse 1964). It is this turn that helps evolve a sociology of writing and help frame a theory and critique of ideology (see Jameson 1991).

More questions: is narrativity a dangerous weapon with which to write a history that proceeds from the dilemma of setting a stage to reach a revolutionary anticlimax? Do the events which otherwise would have unfolded as unknown seem to fall into a pattern as we historicize them? Postmodernists such as Derrida (1976, 1978) and Foucault (1972, 1977) believe that narrativity is indeed a potentially dangerous weapon and hence they recommend that narrativity be demystified. We are told that a text is an undecidable marsh that hides in it polyvocal semantics that get exhibited only through a series of small pictures (cf. Lyotard 1984). Also, that textual activities as dominated by the culture industry (Adorno 1973a; Horkheimer 1937; Marcuse 1964) turn thoughts into commodities and rob critique of its sharp edge.

Although French postmodernists like Derrida and Foucault claim that reading writes, it is also the case that reading destroys a text. Since the responsibility of interpreting what is 'undividable' rests on reading, and since each text seems to live a definite life (except for those that get reincarnated and enter into the circuit of metatexts of a given community) and has a fatalistic self-destructing tendency, translation to my mind seems to be the only real hope for discourses of ideology.

In a possible sociology of writing and translating, if the author is viewed as a pawn with a keen sense of the game—the game that her language plays on people and reading, as well as the game played by the more crucial elements on the board, the rook, etc.—she must be buying things to sell as 'her own words'. What do they buy as raw materials? And who sells them? Supposing we say the system always has a set of official stories to sell, one that is blared out on radio and tele-networks, and the other which circulates through riddles and rumours common people have to offer as possible alternative narratives. The agencies at work in that society, whether they are group-internal, or external interest-groups, would like to create their own little deviations or versions. Those that resist change have their own myths, and the advocates of change spread their own beliefs. But does the author depend on any one of these? Or, must she do so? It often appears that the literary political economies within which the authors have to function frustrate their rationale and critique. But if we believe that it is the readers who actually write, then they are free to dispel a belief, discard an approach and dislodge a theory so as to write new versions not only of texts but also of the social relations.

Given the above scenario, who is likely to suffer? Who else but those interested in academization of critical theory. Whenever an attempt is made to doctrinate the ways in which one should react to literary texts, or to any social event for that matter, there is a further decline in the public discourse (Agger 1990). People who read also suffer because they translate a lot of these texts into their own lives, thoughts, dreams and fantasies—just as some of them render them into other forms to replicate them, be it another genre (films, the theatre, music, painting, sculpture or photographs) or another language—they do not wait for such doctrines. But, nevertheless, some do get influenced by such set modes of reading, and try re-reading texts to categorize them in some other set ways (cf. Jacoby 1976, 1987). On the other hand, those who own the various information technologies that run the popular cultural universe today take the maximum advantage of this situation. These are the people who 'dominate' the modes of speech such as radio, television, advertising, newspapers, magazines, or even textbooks, and they celebrate the freedom they have suddenly discovered vis-à-vis literary texts. They try replacing the Bible or the Quran just as they attempt to dislodge known philosophical and political positions, and tell us (or dictate to us?) how to translate these texts into what they want them to mean. Today's 'lives are depicted here as utopian, narrowing the distance between what is and what ought to be through images of plentiful consumerism, adventurous leisure, revivifying travel' (Agger 1990). With the emergence and dispersion of 'virtual' reality, there seems to have arisen a nearly frictionless coordination of production and consumption—a frictionless capitalism (cf. Agger forthcoming) which brings in new forms of exploitation and domination. Here we find a domination of one language over many and of certain kinds of culture industry over a vast potential of multiplicity of unexplored cultural conclaves and cultural expressions. Here this ideology seems to be trying to dominate the circuitries of information and consumption of all texts, and choke the arteries with only those images and entertainments which they have manufactured.

All these discussions throw up more questions than one could possibly answer at present. They include the following:

1. What is the response of the author or that of reading towards this cultural capitalistic onslaught?
2. Is there a textual theory of writing, which tries to understand the contemporary nature of ideology at a time when it can easily transcend between *text* (which holds the world as a reflection) and the *world* (which holds the text as yet another product)?
3. Do we need a social theory of the text to relate it with ideology or with the possibilities and limits of the critique of ideology?
4. Can ideologies be criticized, its mythologies demystified and illusions pierced, in order to stimulate social change 'which seizes on the openness of history to reauthor it' (Agger 1989b: 366)?
5. Is it at all necessary to retain a critical distance between the author and the translator, between the text and the reader, or between the reading and the world to comprehend that object without being influenced by it?

6. Is it desirable to be so objective as not to be influenced by such proximations or breakdown of dyadic relationships?

As the first step to construct a sociology of translation, let us draw upon the metaphors of grammar.

SOCIOLOGY OF TRANSLATION

For purposes of representation, while all sentences are divisible into categories—call them categories of words, phrases, phrase structures, clauses, X-bars, or nodes of trees—each one offers yet another kind of classification. These are classifications in terms of what the sentence does in a locution or what the constituent categories do, both within the construction and outside it, in the world of logic. Which is why we get notions such as 'subject' and 'object'. A social theorist of the text may start with a conviction that subject and object, the writer and the world, are linked inextricably, grounded in each other. But a social theorist of the text would also know that there are different kinds of objects—the direct (the world), the indirect (the image or the text), and the oblique (institutions and practices). She understands, for instance, that there are 33-odd kinds of subjects, as logicians like Keenan would like us to believe.

In a sociology of writing, these different subjects—the logical subjects (reading) and the surface subjects (interpretations)—are often prone to socio-political passivization (the authors), the chômeur (or the displaced), subjects (the people), and so on. They are as important in social grammar as different types of objects. In course of all this construction activity (just as in the case of sentence-generation), there are a number of fuzzy areas that remain as unresolved mysteries of social grammar. Writers occupy worlds that they author, and worlds invade literary sensibility and the social and economic organizations of literary production, making it difficult to decide theoretically the issue of literary agency. Many questions remain unanswered here:

1. Are we to write and translate 'secretly' so that we are not overlooked by the forces that commodify texts?
2. Or, has writing become a public space where copy-writers, web-content developers, screenplay authors, news-breakers

> (including journalists ready to intrude into bedrooms and bathtubs), book or film-reviewers, literature-teachers, communication-experts, positivist social scientists, and even critical theorists vie with authors and translators of literary texts?

It also appears that texts that once 'directed' our social behaviour have been banished today ideologically. These grand texts have been dispersed into the impressible environment, and these books that command millions of lives are not understood by the common reading public now. They all require translators, and it is here that the politics begins. Who qualifies to 'construe' an ideology? Do authors have rights to 'distort' what are conventionally interpreted as 'celestial' verses? The plea to conform and consume are encoded in the unmediated environments of the quotidian. As Foucault (1977) would have us believe, one does one's job in the various spheres of everyday life—the workplace, family, various political formations (unions, political parties or pressure groups), voluntary organizations, places of worship (temples, mosques, or churches, etc.) and in religious associations—unmediated by canonical texts of discipline. But there is still a 'discipline' in doing all these or any one of these, which is written into our micro-environments in a subtle and unalterable manner, so much so that they are sealed off from critical examination. This was precisely the Frankfurt School's point about the inescapability of domination. Instead of being purely a doctrine, domination becomes a discipline, perpetuated and reinforced by discourse. These cultural discourses and the ways in which they are read/heard/viewed/understood are eclipsed by the culture industries that replace thought with slogan, dictated by their compulsions of marketing.

THE POSTMODERN: PROBLEM WITH PREFIXATION

In a recent work titled *Postponing the Postmodern* (2002), Ben Agger tries to wriggle out of numerous definitions of the term *postmodernity* by suggesting that the decision on which one of these was nearer truth be postponed. His own conviction was that postmodernism was to be viewed as a goal to be achieved, and in this sense, was an extension or a version of Marxism. It was neither to be defined as a period that comes after or before another -*ism* (as in Harvey 1989) nor was a *cause célèbre* (Lyotard 1984).

For many in the yet to be developed world, postmodernity reflected the victory of the spoken word over the written. It was like a narrative to outline a possible utopian future not as a definite and predictable outcome of what could be called *social laws* but rather as one conceivable discursive achievement among many. Shorn of 'necessity', postmodernism builds bridges between the global and the local, linking up the system and action. Although the postmodernist does not usually make a political claim at the current social moment, she does not suggest either that socialism is, or should be, dropped as a political aim. It assumes socialism to be an 'imaginary' vision, model, or blueprint which has lost a great deal of its currency at a time when the communist experiment in social construction seems to have failed. Simply because socialism has been tainted by Cold War experience does not mean that it is unworthy as a utopian goal of critical social theory. On the contrary, we seem to be in greater need of socialism now that both American and Soviet destinies have been found wanting.

To say this in other words, one could well contend that postmodern theory grants the left a new imaginary with which to revive Marxism at a time when 'class struggle' has been severely criticized from all sides, including by the champions of plurality—the multiculturalists, the feminists, the subalterns as well as the coloured. The requirement of the postmodern movement would of course be that one can refashion Marxist categories in the light of historical transformations unforeseen by Marx. In that sense, these functions of postmodernism are crucial for critical thinkers and actors who refuse to concede that Marxism has been bypassed by the so-called postmodern (Agger 2002).

The irony is that some critical postmodernists (Jameson, Aronowitz and Harvey, for example) use postmodernism as a way of defending the significance of Marx's world-historical ideology as against Baudrillard and others who would like to celebrate postmodernity's break with modernity. While one group would like us to believe that postmodernity fulfils Marx's dream of a disalienated society, the other offers the same postmodernity as proof that Marx was wrong all along to posit a disalienated society articulated in terms of classlessness.

This postmodernist discourse engages the question of what the Frankfurt School called late capitalism, lateness being an issue of historicity resolved differently by theorists who variously defend and abandon Marxism. The issue of lateness, as argued by Agger, acknowledges that capitalism needs to be theorized today not only in ways one would trade on capital but also in ways it addresses the questions of culture, gender, race, colonialism and the environment—something that was attempted by Habermas under his new social movements theory.

What endures about Marxism is both Marx's understanding of the contradictory logic of capital and his vision of a disalienated society. In his *Capital*, Marx showed understanding that the so-called fetishism of commodities reified human relationships, producing their representation as relationships among things in nature. One could even claim that what Marx called commodity fetishism was the first postmodern interpretation of capitalism, in the sense that it recognized that alienation (here, the economic exploitation of labour power) requires a certain discursive formulation for it to be reproduced in everyday life. The workers reproduce capital by failing to understand the *historicity* of their lives, the fact that they are themselves oppressed by capital, which has emerged historically and thus can be challenged. Instead, they experience everyday life as unchangeable or immutable. The everydayness of their alienated lives is neatly packed and hidden in the supposed laws of the bourgeois market economy, which discursively produce the illusion of a fair deal in the form of labour contract. Both law and economic theory produce and thus protect the contradictions that go with postmodernism.

MARX AS POSTMODERN

One could describe Marx as a postmodern to the extent that he understood how, as texts, economic theories come alive, secretly creating those lives. He questioned the increasingly porous barrier between textuality and materiality by arguing that the logic of capital is objective in the sense that workers have only their labour power to sell, and they thus stand on the brink of destitution. But it is subjective and intersubjective at the same time in that culture must produce the representation of alienated experience and practice as nature-like, hence reproducing a nature-like society. Thus, the objective, subjective and intersubjective comprise a complex totality that cannot be dissected into base and superstructure or into economics and culture. Marx was pre-postmodern because he recommended unmasking via the critique of ideology, revealing the falsehood of certain nature-like representations of capital. The Frankfurt School in proposing its critical theory no longer took for granted Marx's optimism about how representation could unmask representation on the battleground of competing truth claims (Jay 1984). Marcuse (1964) argued with copious examples that radical discourse is increasingly coopted by an affirmative culture in which dissent becomes lifestyle, hence robbing language of its demystifying and galvanizing power. Empirically, Marcuse was correct: the New Left and counterculture failed to resist their own commodification as the 'sixties' became a growth industry capitalizing on pure nostalgia.

The postmodern theory of the West then focuses on the crisis of representation as, in effect, the crisis of late capitalism. No longer should we assume that representation can be demystified through discourse which is not fraught with *undecidability* (Derrida 1994). Representation is no longer possible, because the text and the world have become enmeshed today to an extent that they are practically indistinguishable. Though this merger of concept and thing is never total (Adorno 1973a), there remains an *indissoluble something* which eludes representation and thus makes truth possible.

In these ways, postmodernity of the European kind can be viewed as a fulfilment of Marx's idea of disalienation, which he characterized as the end of prehistory (modernity). This could be confusing because French theorists like Lyotard have positioned Marx as modernist, as they had the challenge of establishing their own 'postmodern' position as *post-Marxist*. Marx, of course, worked within the social moment of modernity, and did not use the term postmodernity. However, both Berman (1982) and Agger (1992) have shown beyond doubt why we should treat him as a postmodern, and I have only re-stated them here. Marx's attempt to transcend modernity was evident in his position that was qualitatively different from those of others.

Marx's original notion of false consciousness inverts the real and the ideal, arguing that freedom lies beyond the realm of 'necessity', which is subject to 'known' social laws that only vouchsafe that capitalism continues eternally. Capitalism's internal contradictions of being bound by a dichotomy of capital and labour notwithstanding, Marx obviously could not have foreseen the extent to which state intervention, cultural sedation and globalization of information technologies would protect capitalism against the final expropriation. Thus, a social theory of the text today has a difficult task to perform. It is expected to be a theory of ideology that retains Marx's promise of truth and liberation. But it is also expected to address the newfound diffusion of textuality into signs and simulations that are difficult to read as texts.

This is not a transcendence of the ideologizing powers of writing to reproduce a given order of social things. This is rather a concealment of the authoriality of writing and thus allowing room for one or more other versions of a text in original or in translation. The contemporary critique of ideology must address the fact that ideologizing texts are no longer old-fashioned books that are removed from reality and are a distortion of it. There have been some distortions though. For instance, it is often argued that with Habermas, there has been a linguistic turn in critical theory. But he restricted his focus to speech and did not further expand it to cover writing, probably because of his commitment to the general principles of the descriptive linguistics enterprise where speech was more important than writing. Thus, in *The Theory of Communicative Action* (1984, 1987b), Habermas ignored writing and culture for the most part; it is difficult to make an empirical use of his concept of the ideal speech situation, characterized by uncontrolled dialogue between thoughtful interlocutors in constructing a theory of texts.

THE TWO 'D'S: DERRIDA AND DECONSTRUCTION

It must be mentioned that for a long time books used to be the trusted and reasoned tracts that made best use of their distance from reality in order to criticize it. Today, it is more difficult for writing to stay aloof and offer commentaries on socio-historical events. Today's authors are standing both within and outside the world, and are constrained by the inadequacies of language to express the truth. Speech and Writing—both having become undecidable (as Derrida would suggest)—one has no other option but to defer final solutions of quandaries and instead live with their opacity, vagueness and circularity. Language is inadequate also because the distance of writing from the world has been shortened so much so that language has difficulty in transcending ordinary meanings in helping us view the present data as frozen bits of history that, through bracing ideas, can be changed. In fact, the decline of public discourse came with structural and cultural shifts since World War II. The main problem with academics has been their preference for obscurantism, which seems to have become an unavoidable occupational hazard. To the extent this has happened, the reading base of academic criticism has further shrunk. The decline of discourse is also linked to a failure of authorial nerve, as today's authors are worried about the vagaries of freelance writing. Also, the culture industry has reduced them to being providers of 'products'—manuscripts for a readers' or viewers' market. It suggests an alienation so complete that it is useless to retain images of literary heroism, even as authors such as Derrida or Adorno write and resist. But for every rare Adorno, there are dozens of academic underworkers who build their careers by publishing essays of little interest on topics addressed a thousand times on. Gone are those days when a Gramsci would write his notebooks in prison.

Derrida says many of the same things, although he does not offer any historicizing. What Derrida and French theory add to the Frankfurt School is an approach to what is often known as 'cultural studies' (Agger 1992). Ideology is a version, a positivist version, as Horkheimer and Adorno recognized; it has been authored by many—scriptwriters, social scientists, marketing specialists, producers of Hollywood blockbusters, textbook authors. Ideology is not simply imposed, as the Frankfurt theorists sometimes imply. It is a 'lived practice', as Althusser (1970) called it: the notion that ideology is a version that emerged out of an author's 'subject position' and is haunted by the undecidability, so typical of all writing. It also goes beyond Marx's understanding of texts as clear-cut representations that could be challenged by scientific readings. In fact, all ideologies can be challenged, but only by rhetorical versions that acknowledge their grounding in non-logocentric expression systems. Horkheimer and Adorno argued that civilizational texts were authorial artefacts. They deconstructed Homer's *Odysseus* as well as 'read' Hollywood films to understand ideology deeply. They similarly 'read' the emerging electronic culture, auguring latter-day cultural studies. But they did not consider these cultural works as authored oeuvres which could not be matched by new versions, achieved through emancipated authorship. The Frankfurt theorists, on the other hand, viewed the cultural universe as 'one-dimensional' (Marcuse 1964) and virtually closed to resistance. Thus, where Marx viewed ideology as a false representation of a dialectically moltened world, the Frankfurt theorists conceptualized ideology as domination, a cultural ether so impenetrable that only a handful of intellectuals who have mastered civilizational texts as well as the works of Marx can glimpse nonidentity amidst postured identity, harmony, and consensus. But, Derrida and Agger would view ideology as a version that can be rewritten by being read deconstructively, its inner chaos and contradictions having been brought to light.

In fact, deconstruction becomes a critique of ideology where it exhumes hidden authorship as a way of demonstrating that ideology is a text, a committed literary position, and not simply a representation of the frozen world. Our dilemma, then, is that in a bookless world, a world nearly depleted of accessible social criticism that distances itself from the reality in order to appraise it, ideology needs to be considered and countered as an authored text—a position piece for late capitalism. Although Adorno took his writing seriously as a craft, he did not theorize writing and reading in the way that postmodern theorists do. Foucault portrays domination as a technology that transpires not only over the heads of people but within their quotidian lives and even on the pages on which they imprint themselves. Texts were inscribed by the impulses of the surrounding society, driving to exhaust things with concepts that explain them completely, draining them of mystery and nonidentity—precisely to look for their identities to claim their liberating power. Ben Agger (1992) would, of course, argue that this secret writing can only be overcome by readings that write, that go public with alternative versions of the economy, polity, culture, family, sexuality, and nationality. Ideology must be met by counter-ideological versions that historicize a frozen present, depicting capitalism, racism, patriarchy, the domination of nature, nationalism, religion as moments of world history that can be overcome. A social theory of the text, then, must combine critical theory's and postmodernism's perspectives on culture, discourse and literary agency.

As one can see, domination deepens ideology past the point of no return. But when critical theory is able to resist the pull of domination that absorbs consciousness into the black hole of self-reproducing discipline, it must attend to its own discursive abilities to resist this pull. Adorno, entertaining the metaphor of post–World War II society as a concentration camp, did not let his own discursive powers offer resistance and thus failed to reground critical theory on a discursive, cultural and textual foundation. In this context, both Derrida and Foucault add a great deal to our understanding of the ways texts inhere in societies, portraying texts as nucleic societies of writers and readers. As such, the French theorists empower reading as a strong version that authors books, as much as it is authored by books. Reading is empowered because readers give sense, interpolate, resolve contradictions and glosses, and deal with authorial deferral. Of course, all versions are inadequate, occasioning a politics and discourse of humility. Reading necessarily writes because texts do not achieve closure, perfect representation, or transparent meaning. These versions, of course, are not public until they see the light of day as articles, books, pamphlets, editorials, posters or Internet postings. Literary agency, then, is a form of political agency, which is ever at risk in a disciplinary society that blends economic reproduction, entertainment, education and information. Yet texts require readings that, without too much friction, can convert into writings, which is what makes public discourse important.

Derrida attempted to subvert the hierarchy of writing over reading, explaining that writing unravels deconstructively when its apportioning of meaning, deferrals, and displacements are exposed. Deconstruction is viewed here less as an act performed upon texts than as texts' own unravelling. Rather than viewing it as a successful tool, one is looking at its failure to achieve pure representation. This is the opening, however opaque it may be from the perspective of traditional political theory. This is because readings, as strong versions in their own right, augur new worlds, much as Marx and Engels augured a world beyond capitalism in their *Manifesto*. A social theory of the text, then, stresses that texts, in their indeterminacy and undecidability, call forth other texts—readings—that both model and embody agency. The people for whom Marx intended *The Communist Manifesto* were readers as well as workers, and the inherent belief was that these workers would author their own lives, including theory, philosophy and culture.

THE FRENCH THEORISTS AND THE AMERICAN REACTION

The popularity of the French theorists such as Baudrillard in the United States has been almost ritualized as semio-celebration. Where Foucault and Derrida remained committed to a radical interrogation of modernist philosophical and theoretical assumptions, Baudrillard has gone ahead to make some important points about the semiotics of late capitalism in his *For a Critique of the Political Economy of the Sign* (1981) and even in *Simulations* (1983). Here he has dissolved 'reality' into the endless play of simulations and also dissolved material reality into 'simulations', thus replacing the political economy of labour power with the political economy of the sign. This was directly comparable with Horkheimer's work (1972) because his programmatic 1937 essay on 'Traditional and Critical Theory' links the material and ideal, and economics and culture. Notice that to marry postmodernism to Marxism, we need to historicize modernity in such a way that we recognize within it the possibilities of dialectical transcendence, of radical social change. In this sense, postmodernity will have to be viewed as a stage of modernity not yet fully developed. There is a strong temptation simply to equate the postmodern with the present.

The problem with this version of critical theory is that 'lateness' (supposedly also represented by the prefix 'post-') is seen to precede the dawn of a new world, a rhetoric used by Marx and many other utopians. But it is often forgotten that modernity is elastic, containing both the possibility of the Holocaust and of radical social change deserving the prefix. Marx was insufficiently dialectical in that he failed to see that postmodernity was in fact not a rupture with late modernity but a moment of modernity that exists as a dialectical possibility. Postmodernism is usefully ironic in that it stresses the undecidability of discourse and action while at the same time preserving the possibility of meaning conceived dialectically as an engagement with nothingness, meaninglessness, and alterity. In this sense, it is to be seen as an attempt to 'fulfill' modernity, establishing a regime of reason that the left today proceeds with no cosmic guarantees about the inevitability of radical social change.

The American reception of postmodernism has stressed this post-political quietism. But it has tended to ignore postmodernism's stress on the linkage between discourse and democracy, a linkage that I contend is precisely the opening of Derrida's critique of Western logocentrism to radical politics. Put differently, the American reaction suppresses the social and intellectual history of French postmodern theory, which emerged out of the 1968 May movement as a critique of Stalinist and orthodox Marxist authoritarianism. Far from turning away from politics, people like Derrida and Foucault viewed their own philosophical work as intensely and obviously political, contributing to the heterodox French Left project. The French theorists attempted to install deconstructive perpetual interrogation, especially the questioning of and debating to empower those who have historically occupied the subject positions of alterity and otherness, enabling them to enter a community and thus achieve political and social power. Deconstruction, as Derrida understood it, is the activity whereby dichotomies are revealed to be hierarchies (whether in terms of gender or other categories). Once deconstructively revealed, these hierarchies are to be displaced by the invention of new discourses/practices. Thus, deconstruction is at once a negative and positive activity, not only demystifying present discursive practices but also attempting to replace them with 'different' ones.

This leads us to the development of new discursive practices that do not depend on dichotomies alone, but rather underscores the importance of the trinity of race/class/gender, and reach a formulation that does our thinking for us, undermining the very difference deemed so important by multiculturalists. This further points out that a *good* multicultural community would vigilantly protect itself against the reification of its own hallowed concepts which, over time, harden into a code of political correctness. When Derrida says that there is nothing beyond the text, he appears to be telling us that there are no grounds of judgment outside of judging itself. This does not disqualify judgment but only situates judging in the undecidable discursive activity beyond which there are no aprioristic certainties.

That is, there is only historicity. Indeed, Derrida has done all sorts of political 'judging', on behalf of various French and international new social movements that he supports.

IN CONCLUSION: MAPPING POSTMODERNITY

The postmodern discourse theory of the West suggests that we must not any longer pose Marxism/postmodernism as disjunctive alternatives—a point that is very important for students of both original and translated texts. We need, rather, a new theoretical mapping that locates Marxism, postmodernism, feminism, environmentalism and anti-colonialism on the same cognitive map. To name this overarching cognitive map is somewhat like attempting to map the 'outside' of the universe, a fruitless exercise in meta-mapping. It is increasingly clear that we need both global and local explanations, especially where they are dialectically connected.

4

TRANSLATION: TRY THY METAPHOR

ALL THEORIES BEGIN and end with debates. But in the debates on translation one finds different kinds of metaphors being used. Many may seem out of place today. But then, they are being constantly replaced with new metaphors.

For instance, some use the metaphor of governance, where they discuss as to which text will rule in the TL culture—the source or the target text. Some others use the metaphor of *disease* when they talk about 'uncontaminated' vs. 'contaminated' texts. Do we not see the metaphor of *war* in 'wins' or 'gains' as against 'losses' of meaning in translation? There have also been cases where the legal metaphors such as one of inheritance have reigned, the focus being whether 'translated texts' are to be described as 'partly inherited' or 'partly made up'. Some claim that the target text has to be given a new garb, a novel locus, a virgin name and, thus, a new identity, as Pramod Talgeri (1988a) had argued. We are also told that the 'tacit *contract*' among the members of both source and target speech communities is not an easy thing to happen, because no community is pressureless and apolitical. In each, members often vie with each other to agree or disagree on all such contracts. Is one being *cannibalistic* when one claims the 'embeddedness' of a translated literary text in a cultural context? Many practitioners of translation demand an answer as to the agency relationship obtained by a text, namely, whether words of an original literary text are an inseparable 'agent' of cultural memory or if they are the 'patient' of social history?

The debate does not end there. Savory (1957: 57) would like us to believe that translation provides a key to an otherwise forbidden treasure-trove. Mufwene (1998) raises an important question and then tries answering it himself. To his question, namely, 'Are the norms [of expression] set in every speech community by native speakers?', he observes that native speakers' intuitions do not have the same privilege in all texts. Assuming that it is true of original writing, one can imagine how target language native speakers are likely to be treated. And this happens even when we know they have the ability to add on to the content, contributing to the collective memory of the culture. Having created and sustained this convention, the ordinary speakers cannot simply remain ignorant of what lies beyond their own space and time in their quest for knowledge about the 'others'.

The literary translator struggles to decide the nature of language that lies beyond all officialese (cf. Gorjan 1970[1987]). She wishes 'to interpret and to translate this language and thus preserve the supranational and superideological unity of all that is human'. In fact, this is the glorious task of writers and translators. There is a general agreement now that it is only the translators who, through their labour of love, have promoted what Goethe called 'world literature', and the universality of spirit of poetical work (Talgeri 1988b). For centuries they have managed to transmit human ideas and words from one people to another, and build a culture and literature, one on top of another, or one fashioned after the other.

For the literary historian working today, and looking back in time, then, it all appears like an 'onion syndrome'—the more they peel the outer layers, the greater is the revelation of the core inside. It is common knowledge that the Romans built on top of Greek culture, and that the Toledo School transmitted Arabic and Greek learning to Europe. The whole European culture until a few centuries ago was drawing on Latin and Greek translations. It is not surprising, therefore, that some scholars rightly describe translators as the heirs of all the cultures because it is they who make these traditions available to us (Congrat-Butlar 1979).

TRANSLATION AS COMMUNICATION

All translations are essentially communications. Toporov (1992) underscores the point that more than being a motive force of culture, translation is a method of fostering and preserving a culture. When a culture survives, it does so by avoiding two extremes—(*a*) total isolation and autarchy and (*b*) extreme degree of merger and fusion. That is, the choice seems to be between a situation of no-translation versus another situation of all-translation. In fact, isolationism leads us nowhere and it should be exactly the opposite to what is desired: all postmodern societies today should be more receptive to translation because reception of translated literature has in all ages been an index to the broadening of literary taste (Paniker 1994: 31). But here again, forcing translation on an unwilling and otherwise unprepared speech community will be considered as an act of violence against translation itself, as Victor Hugo observes.

The definitions of translation vary depending upon how its affiliation to certain disciplines is assumed. For example, for some scholars, translation is believed to be a linguistic activity (Catford 1965; Nida 1964), whereas it is a literary endeavour for others (Savory 1957). It has been alternatively viewed as a philosophical and cultural act (Steiner 1975; Toury 1998), and also as an integrated activity (Snell-Hornby 1988). So it is difficult to restrict the act of translation within an all-encompassing definition. The cause of this complexity lies in the vast differences in the materials translated, in the purpose of the work and the needs of the prospective audience (Nida 1964: 161), and consequently, in the different types of translation studies that have emerged so far.

The name *translation studies* has also been accepted as a study of the production and description of translation (Bassnett-McGuire 1980: 1), but as a young discipline it has undergone many changes. For some (Nida 1964: 58, for instance), the term translation stands both for process and result, whereas for de Beaugrande (1978: 7) the process is *translating* and the product *translation*. Translation has been categorized variously as an art (Savory 1957; Selver 1966), as science (Nida 1964; Wilss 1982) and even as a combination of science, art, craft and skill (Newmark 1981, 1988).

The common word used for this activity of translating and interpreting in Indian languages is *anuvaada*, etymologically, 'to speak after' defining it as a sequence. Other words that have been used, such as *bhaaSaantar* (literally 'linguistic transfer') in Hindi or '*paribhaaSaa*' in Malayalam (literally 'definition' in other languages) have not carried the ambiguity associated with the expression of translation, as much as *anuvaada* has.

Theoretically, when we talk of translation, we may not always refer to the act of translating between 'languages'. Such textual transference may also happen between dialects, registers and styles. But a line of demarcation should be drawn between this kind of situation and an actual, purposeful activity of translating inter-semiotically in which one is confined primarily to a written text with the purpose of recreating it in another form. Thus, translation is primarily an act of transforming messages from one form of human expression to another, distanced by time or space. The activity interfaces variegated factors, each one capable of influencing the other.

By citing a number of definitions, Nida (1964) shows that no single definition is complete and that the tension between formal and dynamic equivalence of text in any practical act of translation is always present. Further, a single definition cannot apply to both poetry and prose translation. From the literary point of view vis-à-vis translation, Nida quotes Pound's dictum of 'more sense and less syntax' (ibid.: 162–64). From the linguistic point of view, he quotes Garvin who says that 'the translation should make the resultant impression on the reader as the original does on its readers' (quoted in Nida 1964: 164). Finally, he summarizes that an adequate translation or its definition should meet these four requirements, namely, that of (i) making sense; (ii) conveying the spirit and the manner of the original; (iii) having a natural and easy form of expression; and (iv) producing a similar response. These together are called the 'Pidippidies condition' on translation, named after translators like Piddipidies in ancient Greece, who were supposed to travel a distance in order to convey the spirit and manner of the original words 'nobly' and 'gently', so that the response to them was predictable and as desired.

In Catford's (1965: 20) words, translation is the process of replacing the textual materials of a language with equivalent materials in another, and this stand explains the notion of equivalence, which he elaborates here. Newmark (1981: 7) believes that the theory of translation must draw upon the theory of language. He takes the position that translation is also a craft. As a consequence, he views it as 'a procedure which leads from a written SLT [source language text] to an optionally equivalent TLT [target language text] and requires the syntactic, semantic, stylistic and text-pragmatic comprehension by the translator of the original text' (ibid.: 112).

Thus, the term 'translation' is defined according to the convictions of the theorists. But the history of translation theory is full of a few polarized dichotomies and neutral terms such as 'decomposition' and 'recomposition' (Nida 1964: 68), 'deverbalizing' and 'reverbalizing' (Wilss 1982: 62), 'deterritorialization' and 'reterritorialization' (Venuti 1992: 53), 'deconstruction' and 'reconstruction' (Derridean maxim). But use of such terms as 'communicative intention or sense' is focused more, where the translator tries to maintain 'sense equivalence which includes denotative, connotative and extralinguistic knowledge presupposed by the author' (Kastovsky 1990: 45). Though equivalence is much acclaimed in different theoretical positions, what could be called a perfect equivalence is neither achievable nor should it be the aim of translating. As Halliday acknowledges, translation is only an approximation (Maddern 1977: 1).

In final count, all translation is, at best, an effort at mediation or negotiation (Belitt 1978: 38). It is not surprising, therefore, that Niranjana (1992) should hold the view that it voices certain authority and legitimacy, expresses some power, imposes certain politics and writes a particular history—of *mediation* between two people, their culture and their civilization separated by time or space.

LITERARY TRANSLATION

When we dwell on the issue of literary translation, we can divide our attention into several questions, the answers to which together will tell us about the nature of this specialized kind of activity.

THE 'WHY' QUESTION

First, we could ask ourselves why one translates literary works at all. The answer seems obvious if we consider the enormous contribution translations have made to every literature. Even if we set aside the traffic of texts that have been transferred from Greek and Latin into English, Arthur Waley, who gifted the Americans *Genji* and other Chinese poetry in moving English (Raffel 1971: 156), and Ezra Pound, who translated Li Po, have positively contributed to English poetic sensibilities. But for Fitzgerald, Omar Khayyam would have been an obscure poet in his own native Persia (Jermyn 1989: 243). I. A. Richards, Achilles Fang, Patrick White, Alexander Solzhenitsyn, and Samuel Beckett have been great writers as well as translators of equal eminence. Fictions of George Simon and Agatha Christie and voices from distant corners of the world—Milan Kundera from the Czech Republic, Pablo Neruda from Chile, and Octavio Paz from Mexico—are translated and read worldwide today.

Similarly, the world came to know of the Vedas, the UpaniSads and the Giitaa outside the charmed circle of the Brahmins in India only through translations. As Narasimhaiah and Srinath (1985: v) put it, the world would have had to live without Buddha's Dhammapada, Panini's grammar, Manu's Dharmashaastras, Bharat or Anandavardhana—to speak only a little of the great galaxy of Indian glory—but for translation. Stoberski (1972: 21) wonders how hard it would have been to imagine what our modern culture would be if one removed all works that had been made accessible in translation.

THE 'HOW' QUESTION

The next obvious question is a 'how' question: How does one study and interpret literary language, particularly when it shows remarkable differences from the common man's language?

In fact, translation studies suffered because of linguists' normative labelling, namely, that translation is highly 'deviant' and that it lacks 'objective explanation'. For a long time, therefore, it remained outside the realm of linguistics until critics like Uriel Weinrich (quoted in Snell-Hornby 1988: 51) argued that 'a semantic theory is of marginal interest if it is incapable of dealing with poetic uses of language'. Linguistically, literature is defined as the product of a special function of language. It cannot simply be dismissed as a 'deviant' language because as Coseriu (1988) observes, it represents the creative exploitation of the language potential, against which ordinary language represents a reduction. Man's urge to interpret and disseminate the literary heritage of civilization is undertaken by two groups of people—the critic and the translator. The critic mediates between the author and the audience, and the translator creates the original's equivalents in a different language (Lefèvre 1970: 76).

Literary translation is thus defined as 'the reflection of artistic reality of the original.... There can be no absolute reflection, it is always approximate' (Gachechiladze 1967: 89). In the early 1970s, Lefèvre (1971: 13) found literary translation still hopelessly cluttered by too many, too vague, and too impressionistic 'contributions'. Thus, it has hardly been two decades now when literary translation has begun to emerge as an independent activity and an area of common concern for creative persons with different backgrounds.

Literary works are classified into a four-point scale spectrum: lyrical poetry, the short story, the novel, and drama. Of them, poetry is the most personal and concentrated form 'where, as a unit, the word has greater importance' (Newmark 1988: 163). Just as literature is a special function of language, so is translation a special function of literature (Lefèvre 1975: 5). The immediate consequence of translation of poetry, like that of poetry itself, is pleasure first and then truth (Belitt 1978: 20). As Arrojo says:

> Poetic language organizes, tightens the resources of everyday language, and sometimes does even violence to them, in an effort to force us into awareness and attention.... Every work of art imposes an order, an organization, a unit on its materials in which it may be almost impossible to change a word or the position of a word without impairing its total effect' (1996: 209).

The theory of poetic art is inseparable from the theory of literary translation. The level of content and form are intricately woven and deny separation, and translating it into another language means to break them, separate them, to find another recombinatory unit which in practice functions differently. A conglomerate of 'heterogeneous elements' needs to be organized adequately so as to produce 'homogenous character' (Popovič 1988). Almost all problems and issues in literary translation have been centred on the translation of poetry. Translation is vital to poetry because there has been a claim that the nature of all verbal languages is woefully non-universal

(Belitt 1978: 156). This, however, does not mean that other kinds of literary translations are less exciting or less challenging.

THE 'WHAT' QUESTION

Debates in literary translation have concentrated on both form and content, but certainly more on the former than on the latter. The other dimension often discussed is the stand on absolute possibility to practical impossibility of translation. While describing the activity of translating poetry in particular, specialists have often used different epithets, ranging from 'difficult', 'most testing', 'almost impossible' to 'just impossible', nowhere is the debate of form versus content sharper than in translating poems. Among them, metrical poetry (verse in fixed forms) is regarded as the most formidable activity where even a single syllable cannot be added, nor can it be omitted. Even in free verse, 'the cadence and color of the word chosen and the word placed' (Babler 1970: 195) have their own harmony that are not to be tampered with. The tension between form and content in poetry poses a tremendous difficulty. Between them, the formal aspect attracts greater attention because the form primarily distinguishes poetry from prose and it also contributes to the rhythm, emotional intensity and flavour of the poetry.

The real challenge for the translator is to maintain a balance between form and content. The coherence of words, lines and sentences requires continuous compromise and readjustment (Newmark 1988: 162). In fact, no rule, not of any science, can be applied to measure the sentiments, ideas, pleasure and pain or the feeling that poetry imparts to its reader (the translator being the most important of them). The reader weighs them intuitively and objectively by using inner eyes and ears and words to make it possible for her inner voice to reproduce similar effects, usually auditorily and sensorily. Poetic translation, therefore, is 'an art, not a science, and much of the art is concerned with choosing—choosing what to put in, what to leave out, and what shape to give the work as a whole' (Raffel 1971: 22). The final test is that a translated poem must essentially be a poem first. Its difference from the original work lies mainly in the 'restriction of working upon matter that is already composed' (Wilss 1982: 139).

Since to translate a whole poem is to compose another, some argue that the translator should be allowed 'vatic authority' and full freedom 'to contemplate the universe of the given poem' in the same way as the original author is. This is because the translator's task is full of risk and uncertainty, risks that are at times greater than that of original authors, in the lonely game of signification where the translator is 'forever on the other side of [the] original' (Belitt 1978: 80).

The translator who devotes herself for purely humanitarian purposes stands at the crossroads of history as an 'intercultural mediator' today (Talgeri 1988b: 2). Translation has inculcated values such as knowledge, truth and beauty. The greatest contribution of translation is regarded as 'civilizing cosmopolitanism' (Wilss 1982: 18). Some translation theorists like Gentzler (1993: 9) think that translators must meet the challenge of globalization. As this world shrinks together like an aging orange and all peoples in all cultures move closer together (however reluctantly and suspiciously) it may be that the crucial sentence for our remaining years on earth may be very simply: 'Translate or Die' (Engle and Engle 1985: quoted in Gentzler 1993: 9).

THEORETICAL ISSUES

There was a time when even an enlightened reader would have been surprised to hear of a theory called 'translation theory'. Not any more, however. The fact that we can now think about constructing a translation theory is itself an important milestone.

All theories are woven around certain questions. The questions that one can legitimately ask here are the following: (i) Can a translation theory merely aim at the description of what goes on when a text travels across language boundaries? (ii) Could it be a validation of lexical and grammatical manipulations meant to attain the semantic equivalent? (iii) If so, can the wider question of discourse be neglected by concentrating merely on grammar and lexicon? (iv) Are the subjective and objective content of the linguistic sign as consistent as they are usually thought to be? (v) What is the social implication of the Saussurian dichotomy of 'signification' and 'valeur' (value)?

These and many other questions remain unanswered till today. But the activity of building a theory is not halted merely because there are no clear-cut solutions to these unresolved issues. Of course, some scholars talk about the 'adequacy' of a translated text. This I consider to be a potentially dangerous weapon to knock down any attempt to translate, because *adequacy* is an unstable and undefinable concept. Moreover, as a measure, 'adequacy' is a concept that lies at the mercy of individual interpretations. If that be so, that is, if all the approaches fail us, where do we go from here?

It is in this context that I would like to draw the attention of our colleagues in translation studies to the insightful paper that one of our leading poet-translators had given two decades ago. I am referring to Alokeranjan Dasgupta's 1988 lecture entitled 'Translating: Practice Creates Theory', given at a poet-translators' month-long workshop at Kolkata in which many of us writing in seven Indian languages were participants. True, Alokeranjan does refer to older debates at times when he raises the point made by Sri Aurobindo, who had argued that 'a translator is not necessarily bound to the exact word and letter of the original he chooses, he can make his own poem [read 'text' instead, if you like!] out of it if he likes, and that is what is often done' (quoted in Dasgupta 1991). But let us not understand what Dasgupta says in terms of the free versus literal, or the transcreation versus translation debate. What is important is that Alokeranjan makes us realize that cognateness and genetic relatedness does not necessarily make the task of a translator easy.

In fact, Alokeranjan highlights a genuine difficulty he once faced in trying to render Suuradaasa's BrajabhaaSaa poetry into Bengali. He says, and I quote: 'In one of the ambiguous *padas* I chanced upon the word "*saaranga*". On consulting the most reliable dictionary—*BrajabhaaSaa-SuurakoSa*—I found that 51 meanings are given there for this intriguing lexeme.' To mention a few here, they included: Siva, sun, swan, horse, lion, lotus, woman, ornament, hair, day, clouds, dove, breasts, collyrium, clothing, lighting, flower, melody, etc. (Tandon 1913: I. 1320). Alokeranjan then admits: 'To my utter dismay, none of these meanings was of any help till, judging the term by its context, I was convinced that it served the sound function of pararhyme.' In the rest of his lecture, he quotes many other mysteries that had remained unsolved in this particular translation.

VERTICAL AND HORIZONTAL MODELS OF TRANSLATION

The hostility and despair of the earlier era was because a translator was always considered an untouchable among creative writers and a translating culture was placed at the lower end of a line of vertical cline. This is because the writers in Republican Rome to those of today, from Terence (190 BC), the dramatist, to Jiri Levy in the 1960s, have a firm 'folk-belief' that translation is merely a branch of literature. Hence the paradigm of hierarchy: Those who fail to be a poet become literary critics and those who fail as a critic, turn into a translator.

Obviously, this cynical view had to be dropped eventually.

The typical colonial scenario entailed that a 'translating' culture would translate a text from another (shall we say, the 'donor' culture?) because the former did not have the text, nor did it have the means to 'create' it. This was not only true of India, it was true of many other colonized nations. What was, however, interesting about the literary scene in India in the early stages of the Western impact was the contradictory facts about our ('translating') languages having an inherent vitality and a rich tradition of literary as well as philosophical productivity (besides a history of 2,000 years of translation practice), and yet lacking in certain genres or areas of knowledge.

The situation after the mid-twentieth century has fortunately changed, so much so that (thanks to our continuing with this vitality even in the modern era) it is no more inevitable that our languages must only play the role of a recipient community. In other words, as I have stated elsewhere (Singh 1989a), the postcolonial reality is that we are slowly moving towards a *horizontal* translation traffic from a *vertical* unidirectional and unilinear model of translation.

TRANSLATION AS GROWTH

This discussion brings me to the other point which I have already made (Singh 1994a) in *Meta* (also evident from a discussion paper by Ikôme (1994a) in the same issue where he was elaborating on the stand taken by me in the earlier studies) that translation has now become an alternative way of growing in both theory and practice, but not growing alone. A translator who is instrumental in augmenting novelty to the ever-flowing stream of a language and culture, is also an interpreter who has to know the intricacies of the landscape of the source language 'works' on which he has to operate. This understanding depends heavily on the identification of the ideas and images depicted in a given text. The ideas cleave and cohere to the body of texts (which the translators would like their 'audience' in the target language to read with them) (cf. Barthes 1986: 352–53). In the process of what has been called the 'de-leeching' of texts, in order to be able to transcreate a work written in a contemporary mode of expression from one culture to another, they come to know about the crises of our time in literature, too.

When we discuss the problem of reading of literary texts, we come across many examples to show how novelty in lexical and synthetic construction creeps in, often from the structure of the target language.

Examples of this kind abound. Read the following piece transferred from Bengali into English where no attempts nor any pretensions have been made to hide the frills that are typically associated with translation, and where the translator does not make any effort to do away with Indianism in the syntax:

> I talk in verse and in no time, the lines turn into
> ornaments. Having put them on
> I spend my days and nights
> And drops of blood—all merely to make this pattern;
> You may wear it once and see
> Where it glimmers—does it shimmer your make-up
> Or glisten your heart? Look at its thousand edges—
> Do they touch your skin,
>   or prick your bones,
> somewhere along the bleeding route?
> Put them on and see.
>
> ('Ornament', Mitra 1990)

We will not discuss this particular text here because possible syntactic deviations as in Surabhi Banerjee's translation of the same text where the end-line is an un-English iteration, *'Wear, wear and see'*, are obvious here. But very often two such texts—one, a translation and the other, a transcreation, derived from the same source—may both achieve comparable success for entirely different reasons.

There are times when an original-language literary genius accepts, quite voluntarily, a 'subordinate' role in assuming the responsibilities of transposing and creatively presenting an original author from another culture in her own target language. We know about the Spanish ballads mainly through Byron's English versions. Further, when Wilhelm Meister was translated by Carlyle (1824), he is said to have 'freed' the resultant text from the mannerisms and tricks of the original. It is not that the classical and canonical German texts were not translated by others. Even before Carlyle, William Taylor had translated German texts like *'Iphigenia in Tauris'* by Goethe, 'Lenore' by Gottfried Burger, and *'Nathan der Weise'* by Gotthold Lessing. But it was Carlyle who, through his translations, underscored the point that Germany had produced works of the highest order. The consequences were noteworthy. The serious interest English nations were induced to take in German literature dated from the appearance of Carlyle's translation. Such could be the influence of a translation.

What the world knows as the *Iliad* and the *Odyssey* today was thanks to the excellent, but sometimes quite creatively deviant, efforts by Pope (in 1715–20 and 1725–26). The model was followed by Cowper, too, who rendered Homer in 1791. James Fitzmaurice-Kelly (1917), the Gilmour Professor of Spanish from Liverpool University in the early years of the last century, said the following about these translations:

> These neat translations nearly fail to convey any impression of Homer's epical grandeur and they set a mischievous fashion of artificial 'elegance' which has been too often adopted by their successors (i.e. by those who wanted to read or render Homer into their own languages); but both Pope and Cowper conform faithfully to the mistaken canon of their age, and both have fugitive moments of felicity.

Dryden's free translations of Juvenal and Virgil also try and preserve the meaning, but take considerable liberty and, therefore, these too belong to this class.

At times, a translator is also subjected to unkind remarks because of the deviations he is forced to make. Take, for example, the case of Charles Jarvis' translation of the famous Spanish text *Don Quixote* (1742) which appeared after Jarvis passed away. There was a malicious theory (which apparently Pope had initiated, that Jarvis translated *Don Quixote* without knowing Spanish. Notice that this was a comment on a translation which has been reprinted innumerable times since its first appearance. In fact, it was this translation that had made Cervantes' masterpiece known to so many generations. The comment, obviously wholly untrue, was only a reaction against the changes and modifications made by the translator.

But in spite of such remarks, one need not be apologetic about 'manipulations', because quite often translated literatures have been responsible for major literary movements. They have also been the backbone of development of many literary languages in India and elsewhere. To take an example of such influences, one could recall the influence of Ibsen in translation which had changed the dramatic method of the modern stage in the European context. The translations and adaptations of such authors as Brecht into different Indian languages and their resultant influence on our theatre movement are well-known illustrations of this point.

In several chapters, we return to important questions on changes, manipulations and modifications in translated texts and idioms inasmuch as they contribute to the general theory of language development and planning. In particular, we will see how deviation can become a tool for innovation, and the model of translativity a strategy for developing underdeveloped languages.

5

LOSSES AND GAINS

HOW MANY TIMES have we had this experience where the joy of reading of a literary text in translation is lost! Lost, either because the resultant text has fallen far short of expectations or because, in a zeal to replicate the source text, the translators have overdone theirs. The zeal can be put on hold. But what about our 'expectations' from a transfigured work? We would be lying if we said they were never fulfilled, because at times, a given rendering or 'adaptation' may achieve a rare structure or status that might not have been associated with the original. Not that there is a fixed formula for such successes. Whatever method we may try—literal or literary—neither one is bad, because in each case one must 'appreciate', 'evaluate' or 'analyse' a literary text. As we all know, literary appreciation depends crucially on 'reading'. It turns out then that reading is the real thing.

Today we have obviously moved away from the practice of reading for a 'perfect understanding' of a literary text, as I. A. Richards (1929) would have liked us to do. The moment we begin to read literary translations, particularly if we also happen to know the original work, the deviations stand out before us very clearly. Have we not met authors who remain upset with their own (re-)creations or (re-)writings that have undergone a thorough metamorphosis?

A translator is often apologetic, too. He would sometimes point to unavoidable operations or changes performed on the body of target texts that are rooted deeply in a very different cultural tradition. Such changes are also a part of the strategy to circumvent a virtually 'untranslatable' portion, the knowledge of which may or may not come with the brush one had had with the writings on translation theory. On some occasions, however, translations may appear to be sheer ingenious manipulations. But then, not all translators are apologetic about manipulations. As a result, many authors still remain upset about recreations or rewritings of their own texts, which they find have undergone an irrevocable alteration. Of course, there is another extreme where some translators take it as their divine duty to 'improve' upon the original texts. One cannot forget the arrogant remark of Fitzgerald, the well-known translator of Omar Khayyam, who had once commented that 'it is an amusement to me to take what liberties I like with these Persians who (as I think) are not Poets enough to frighten one from such excursions and who really want a little art to shape them (Fitzgerald to Rev. Cowell)' (Trivedi 1992: 37).

Quite in contrast is the position on translation taken by an Indian poet who tries to define the tremendous responsibility of the translator through these lines on poetic translation. They are obviously true of other kinds of texts, too:

> Poetry translation is
> a transmigration.
> As a fish dives through water
> the translator moves through
> minds. On the bank of each
> word, in the thick sand,
> he kneels, studying
> the colour of each shell,
> blowing each conch.
>
> Poetry translation is
> the embarrassing head-
> transposal of the Vikramaditya
> tales. The translator
> supports another poet's
> head on his trunk. Each line

is a lane worn out with
war, misery and boredom.
A bylane of music along which
parade immortal men, gods
and trees. An abyss opens
where a line ends. The souls
of the dead quench their thirst
in that pool of silence.

O, Those who come this way,
please remove your footwear
and leave your garments here.
You must sneak through naked,
like the wind in the valley.

One day I dreamt of myself
translating my poetry
into my own language.

All of us translate each poem
into my own private language
and then we quarrel over the meanings.

It seems to me that the Babel
will never be complete.
(Satchidanandan 1984: 39–40)

TRANSLATION AS REWRITING: ACCOLADES AND BRICKBATS

The moot question is not whether translators have any right to deviate by deliberately undertranslating texts or by bringing in 'suppletions' or substitutions. Rather the question is whether such deviations can also lead to literary innovations in its own right, and if so, must it involve rewriting inevitably. Recall what Bassnett-McGuire and Lefèvre (1993: ix) had said:

> Translation is, of course, a rewriting of an original text. All rewritings, whatever their intention, reflect a certain ideology and a poetics and as such manipulate literature to function in a given society in a given way. Rewriting is manipulation, undertaken in the service of power, and in its positive aspect can help in the evolution of a literature and a society.

In fact, Dryden (1711 [1800]) very clearly identified the ideal aim of a literary translator in the following words:

> A translator that would write with any force or spirit of the original must never dwell on the words of his author. He ought to possess himself entirely, and perfectly comprehend the genius and sense of his author, the nature of the subject, and the terms of the art or subject treated of; and then he will express himself as justly, and with as much life, as if he wrote an original; whereas he who copies word for word loses all the spirit in the tedious translation.

Whatever we may say about Edward Fitzgerald's attitude to the original Persian writing (see earlier discussion), it is still a fact that he would be remembered not as a translator of Sophocles into English, but as someone who transfigured, if we may say so, through his version of *Rubaiyat* (1859), Omar Khayyam—a medieval Persian poet—to an English genius of the nineteenth century. Another translator, Arthur O'Shaughnessy, in his rendering of *Lays of France* (1872), follows suit, and charts an independent course as he elaborates, paraphrases and embroiders rather than translating the 'Lais' of Marie de France.

Notice that translated literatures have sometimes been responsible for major literary movements. We have earlier discussed (see Chapter 4) the influence of Ibsen and Brecht in translation. But a more apt instance can be found in the powerful impulse provided to the romantic movement in the continent by Voß's translation of *Odyssey* (1781) and Iliad (1793) and A. W. von Schlegel's renderings of Shakespeare over a 13-year period (1797–1810).

THE TEXT AND THE WORK

Some structuralists interpret the reading of a literary text as a productive and creative activity. Rather than viewing the reader of a text at the end of the line, waiting to 'receive' a text or a work and 'receive from' it pleasure, pain, fun, directions, advice or even responses to questions that she always wanted to ask but dared not ask, the reader is viewed as reading to produce 'interpretations', to create histories, ideas, mores, sciences and systems that are as valuable as the text itself. A reader always rewrites the texts, and she comes back to do so again and again, because every time she writes it, the text appears ever more 'writable'. She does so because she is able to mimic the creative process that was the cause of the writing of a given text in the first place, without worrying about the accuracy or otherwise of the reproduction or rewriting. Thus, texts are scriptible by definition. Here the reverberations available in a text are more important than the thing itself, as the French poet and critic Stéphane Mallarmé had put it long ago.

In comparison, works are extremely 'readable' objects that are not written again and again. They are only to be read and enjoyed. They are only to be consumed, as it were. Words in these works move from a definite point to another definite or 'appointed' end, and hence they captivate the readers. That means that all literary works of certain standard or value are extremely 'lisible', but rarely 'scriptible'. Obviously, another important point of difference between the text and the work is that the latter fades more rapidly than the former. The text lives through different ages and generations and gets manifested through works of different authors, merged with different philosophies and outlooks, and, at times, even written in different languages. The RaamaayaNa text provides one of the best examples of this. All the works that are responses to the text of the Raama–Siitaa or the Raama–RaavaNa story written in Awadhi, Bangla, Maithili, Telugu, Tamil, and a host of other languages, including languages used outside India (e.g., Thai) are works as well as different readings of the same text. Just as these can be interpreted in one sense as translations or as 'transcreations', in another sense they have provided us with a kind of creative response from readers with extraordinary literary skills (such as Tulasiidaasa, Krttibaasa, Kamban, etc.).

TRANSLATION AS INTERPRETATION

It is important for us to understand the ways in which literary translators are capable of positively contributing to literary appreciation and criticism, sometimes more than the conventional monolingual critic. More often than not, the typical critical analyst believes in a set of moral and formal values of the texts and works to be interpreted—values that are supposedly 'eternal'. In contrast, the translator, in trying to go through the twin processes of 'comprehension' and 'formulation', first tries to examine, not the morality or the formal structure of the text, but a series of questions about its origin, function, and future. In particular, he would like to know who wrote the text and under what socio-political conditions; who were and are its readers and their social compositions; and at which point of time the text emerged. A typical critic will look for holistic meaning in a text, that is, look for 'the' meaning, not caring to appreciate that language (and consequently, literature, too) is essentially ambiguous.

Second, although critics may consider as futile the search for alternative or supplementary meanings, or although they may, restrict themselves to only a few apparently legible and self-evident interpretations from several cues that the author has provided, literary translators are not bound by any of these guileless and simplistic interpretations. This is because they are not only interpreting the original text, they are reading it to re-read and re-create. They are finding meanings in a text in relation to the world of meaning of the target language as well as in terms of its possible readings (that each one of them thinks is possible) in the source culture and community.

Third, since ten different translators are likely to give ten different translations, based on many differing interpretations, this appreciation of ambiguity is ingrained in the approach of a literary translator. In fact, it is now increasingly realized that one can interpret a literary text only if one dare attempt to render it interlingually, inter-semiotically or even intra-lingually, although the third approach is usually uninstantiated. Some of the best critiques of a literary text have come from their cinematic renderings (hence, inter-semiotically).

READING OF LITERARY TEXTS : THE ANOMALY

When we discuss the problem of reading of literary texts, an interesting anomaly comes to the fore. Consider, for instance, what the well-known fiction writer Jorge Luis Borges (cf. Tirumalesh 1990) tells us about the fictitious language of the Tlonans. He paints the Tlonans as people from another planet who talk without nouns, because the world for them is a 'heterogenous series of independent acts' (Borges 1976: 33). Equivalents to nouns in the language of the Tlonans are impersonal verbs modified by monosyllabic suffixes with adverbial function. For instance, here as a word 'translation' will be an impossibility, but as an action, 'to translate' is perfectly possible. That is the kind of confusing situation that translation theoreticians have to deal with. The example used by Tirumalesh (1990: 1) from Borges was of course different: 'moon' (being an impossible construction) versus 'to moonate' (being perfectly possible). As we have seen with various paradoxes in the theory of translation, it applies to the verb ('to translate') we are interested in, too.

At this point, it is educative to recall what is known as the Sapir-Whorf hypothesis, which claims that language acts as a grid, or a *ventana*, to look at the world outside. That is, it will structure, classify, assign truth values, determine presuppositions or colour our perceptions of the world, just as our culture would determine what kind of language we will have or what its various categories, derivational mechanisms, sentential rules, or sound laws or constraints on them will be. Even if we leave out the question of lack of falsifiability of such a hypothesis, and even if it is partly true that 'the world in which different societies live are distinct worlds, not merely the same world with different labels attached' (Sapir 1956: 162), English and Hindi may be languages quite different from the world of the Tlonans. In our world 'to translate' may be semantically void; otherwise, how can one explain the fact that while there is an enormous literaure pointing out the difficulties, if not the impossibilities, of translating, while there is also a huge repository of actual translations existing in our languages?

Add to that the examples that anybody can produce to show how different two languages can be in terms of their expressive power. An impossible, illogical and ungrammatical structure in one language becomes a perfectly possible structure in another. The more we discover such linguistic differences, the more remote seems the possibility of our reaching the declared goal of building a universal grammar (UG). Some have learnt the art of getting around this problem by emphasizing that rather than talking about laws that are purported to be 'universals', one should view language structures or such seemingly opposing grammatical constructions in terms of language typology. Others have taken it as evidence of the impossibility of translation.

It is not difficult to understand the frustration of the universalist. Just when everything seems to be going well with her theoretical predictions about UG or with her universal hypotheses, there seems to appear, with devastating effect, a Malayalam, Maithili, Dyirbal, Malagasy, Middle Mongolian or a little known Brazilian language that upsets all generalizations of linguists and universalists. However, to draw a negative inference from the above events or from the mythical episode of Narcissus and Echo is to give up all hope of reaching any meaningful explanation of the phenomenon. It is not enough to state that languages defy all generalizations. Such defiance must also be explained.

THE SOURCE AND THE TARGET

In the context of transference between source and target texts, it is very difficult to be precise. As I have already shown in Chapter 2, nonsense fables of authors like Sukumar Ray will always be regarded as a challenge for anyone who would dare to translate it into English or any other non-Indian language.

A COMPARISON

Consider the following example of Ray's *fables bilge* or 'malarkey', as they are sometimes called:

> It was terribly hot. I lay in the shade of a tree, feeling quite limp. I had put down my handkerchief on the grass; I reached out for it to fan myself, when suddenly it called out
>
> 'Miaouw!'
>
> Here was a pretty puzzle. I looked and found that it wasn't a handkerchief any longer. It had become a plump ginger cat with bushy whiskers, staring at me in the boldest way.
>
> 'Bother!' I said. 'My handkerchief's turned into a cat.'
>
> 'What's bothering you?' answered the Cat. 'Now you have an egg, and then suddenly it turns into a fine quacky duck. It's happening all the time.'
>
> I thought for a while and said, 'But what should I call you now? You aren't really a cat, you're a handkerchief.'

> 'Please help yourself', he replied. 'You can call me a cat, or a handkerchief, or even a semi-colon.'
> 'Why a semi-colon?' I asked.
> 'Can't you tell?' said the cat, winking and sniggering in a most irritating manner. I felt rather embarrassed, for apparently I should have known all about semi-colon. 'Ah!' I said quickly. 'Now I see your point.'

There is no doubt that the passage reads very well if it is treated as an independent text, freed from the original. But to seriously consider the text as a translation, let us look at the original text now in order to determine the strategies used:

> bejaay garam. gaachtalaay dibyi chaayaar madhye cupcaap
> shuye aachi, tabu gheme asthir. ghaaser upar rumaalTaa
> chila, ghaam muchbaar janya jei seTaa tulte giyechi
> amni rumaalTaa balla, 'myaao!' ki aapad! rumaalTaa
> myaao kare kena?
>
> ceye dekhi rumaal to aar rumaal nei, dibyi moTaa-soTaa
> laal TakTake ekTaa beRaal go~ph phuliye pyaaT pyaaT kare
> aamaar dike taakiye aache!
>
> aami ballaam, 'ki mushkil! chila rumaal, haye gela
> ekTaa beRaal.'
>
> amni beRaalTaa bale uThla, 'mushkil aabaar ki? chila
> ektaa Dim, haye gela dibyi ekTaa pyaa~k-pyaa~ke haa~s. e to
> haameshaai hacche.'
>
> aami khaanik bhebe ballaam, 'taa hale tomaay ekhan
> ki bale Daakba? tumi to satyikaarer beRaal nao, aasale
> tumi haccha rumaal.'
>
> beRaal balla, 'beRaalo balte paara, rumaalo balte
> paara, candrabinduo balte paara'. aami ballaam, 'candra-
> bindu kena?'
>
> shune beRaalTaa 'taao jaano naa?' bale ek cokh buje phyaa~c
> kare bishriirakam haaste laagla. aami bhaari aprastut
> haye gelaam.
>
> mane hala, ai candrabindur kathaaTaa nishcay aamaar
> bojhaa ucit chila. taai thatamata kheye taaRaataaRi
> bale phellaam, 'o hyaa~ hyaa~, bujhte perechi.'
>
> (Ray 1921[1986]: 125)

If we compare the original passage with the translated texts, certain semantic and structural losses become evident. The first noticeable thing is that the translator had violated the norms for the use of space and silence as in the original text. The first paragraph should have ended after the sentence 'Here was a pretty puzzle', although this sentence itself was not enough for the original 'ki aapad! rumaalTaa aabaar myaao kare kena?' A more literal rendering of the original would have been: 'What is happening? Why does the kerchief say: Miaouw?' But that is besides the point here, as we are not merely considering truthfulness but are trying to pinpoint losses.

Second, '"Why a semi-colon?" I asked' should have been a part of the earlier paragraph, if it was to be like the original.

Now let us look into losses, both lexical and semantic. Expressions such as '*dibyi*' (leisurely), '*cupcaap*' (quietly), '*tabu*' (still), '*ghaam muchbaar janya*' (to wipe out the perspiration), etc., in the first paragraph are missing in the English version. Also, '*rumaal to aar rumaal nei*' could have been replaced with 'the handkerchief was no more a kerchief' but the translator, for reasons that had to do with the naturalness of English syntax, opted for 'it wasn't a handkerchief any longer'. '*moTaa-soTaa laal TakTake ekTaa beRaal*' became 'a plump ginger cat', which was indeed the best in this situation. But how on earth does one translate '*pyaaT pyaaT kare ... taakiye aache*' ('staring at me in the boldest way')? It is not mere 'boldness'; add to that 'mischievousness', 'repudiativity', 'inquisitiveness' and 'plainness', because had it been mere 'boldness', a back translator (from English into Bengali) would render it as '*kaT kaT kare ....*' Also missing in English is the alliterative '*chila rumaal, haye gela ekTaa beRaal*', even though '*ki mushkil*?' has been aptly converted into 'bother!'

In considering these changes, however, we find a number of significant alterations—some required because of linguistic and cultural differences, some others not so necessary. For instance, in the first text, the alternative name offered by the ginger cat was not 'semi-colon'. The pedantic nasalization mark '~' or less scholarly 'nasal accent' does not come anywhere near the original word, 'candrabindu', indicating a letter of the Bangla alphabet, which carries a lot of associative meaning because of the way it looks in the Bengla writing system (ँ). Such connotations are difficult to render.

In what follows, we present to you a number of lexical constructions that pose enormous difficulties for any translator who wishes to re-create the ambience of the original through intelligent twists and turns in the target language, not by following the source language construction literally but, often, by going beyond them. Some of the examples given here appear in the texts I have quoted and some elsewhere in the same book by Sukumar Ray. A close look at these will confirm that the translator had to take hard decisions on a large number of original expressions by Ray.

	Expressions in Original	*Choices Made*
a.	moTaa-soTaa laal TakTake ekTaa beRaal	ginger cat
b.	pyaa~k-pyaa~ke haa~s	quacky duck
c.	candrabindu	semi-colon
d.	gechodaadaa	Cousin Treehooper
e.	gechobaudi	Treehooper's wife
f.	daa~Rkaak	Jungle-crow
g.	baRamantrii	the Head Vizier
h.	paatra mitra	pastors and masters
i.	Daaktaar makkel	doctors and proctors
j.	gechobaajaar, kaageyaapaTTi	Raven Row, Woodmarket
k.	paatikaak, he~Rekaak, raamkaak	House-crow, Gor-crow and Carrion-crow
l.	udho ... budho	Other ... Brother
m.	hijibijibij	Higgle-Piggle-Dee
n.	shriibyaakaraN shing	Grammaticus Horner
o.	nyaaRaa	Smoothpate
p.	jholaa paraa hutam pe~caa	Screech-owl in a long, black gown
q.	baaduRgopaal	Bat
r.	mejamaamaa	Uncle
s.	baRamaamaa	Uncle

The last two 'uncles' have entirely different roles to play but one finds it very difficult to translate kinship terms from Indian languages into English anyway. As we can see on pages 56 and 57 '*pishe*', '*maamaa*', '*khuRo*', '*mesho*' in the dialogue of Higgle-Piggle-Dee were avoided by the translator. Instead, he chose 'uncle', 'uncle', 'nephew', and 'cousin', respectively. This is a typical problem with a culturally different text. The translator was obviously aware that '*khuRo*' (= father's younger brother) and '*mesho*' (= mother's sister's husband) cannot be equated with 'nephew' and 'cousin', but there had to be different kin words (other than the generic 'uncle' for all) to make this part of the text effective, and there aren't that many terms in English. Similarly, while the transfer of '*nyaaRaa*' into 'Smoothpate' was smooth, '*baaduRgopaal*' cannot be adequately covered under a simple 'Bat'.

The above discussion makes one point pretty clear, namely, that even if one takes the translations of very high quality, there is bound to be a semantic loss, a gap of mismatch. That takes us to the next section which is intended mainly as a practical section with multiple texts showing different kinds of losses. The discussion here is very minimal, because as students of translation, the losses would easily be perceived by any attentive reader.

MEANING LOSS

Let us begin by considering some typical examples of possible losses. The texts given here are from the *Sumatishataka*, written in Telugu (a part of *Niitishatakas*, others being *Kumaarashataka, Amarushataka, Kantashataka, Suniitishataka* and *Vemanashataka* by Baddenna (of the twelfth century?). The original line is followed by word-for-word gloss and then come the renderings.

SOURCE LANGUAGE: (TELUGU)

adharamunu	*kadala*	*niyyaka*	
the lip	without	letting move	
madhuraamruta	*bhaaSaa*	*ludigi*	*maunasthundai*
nector-like-sweet	speech	having died down	keeping silent
yadhikara	*rooga*	*puurita*	
authority	sick	filled	

badhiraandhaka	*savamu*	*juuda*	*paapamu*	*sumatii*
deaf and blind	corpse	to see	sinister	O man with good sense

'He moves not his lips! He refrains from words flowing with honey and nectar; he is a solitary
A deaf and blind corpse swollen up with the disease of authority is indeed a shocking object'.
(Brown 1842)

Feigning speech but tight-lipped
withholding sweet word in stony silence
he is a power-swollen corpse—
deaf and blind, to sight him is sin, O Sumathi!
(Srinath and Subbarao 1987)

The lips move not
Speech-sweet as nectar, die down; is mum.
O man with good sense! It is indeed sinful
to see a deaf and blind corpse—
filled with the disease of authority.
(translation mine)

PROBLEMATIC AREAS

As Newmark (1981: 7–8) rightly points out, the translator is a victim of a constant tension between the acts of overtranslation and undertranslation. A lot of semantic gaps in translated texts come because of this tension.

Yet another set of possible problems arises if the SL text has a situation peculiar to the nature and culture of the SL speech community. A translator, then, has to decide whether she should (i) transcribe, (ii) translate, (iii) substitute with something similar from the TL, (iv) naturalize by making minor modifications (be they grammatical or phonological), (v) loan translate, or (vi) paraphrase. If the SL and TL differ lexically, grammatically and phonologically, at both *langue* and *parole* (Saussure 1916) areas there is bound to be a loss, especially at the lexical level.

Again, individual uses of language (although SL and TL are different) of the author and the translator may not coincide. Idiosyncrasies and private meanings may cause losses. Further, the author and the translator may have different theories of meaning. Differences may occur in what each one of them values more than anything else: (i) denotation or connotation; (ii) symbolism or realism (any other -ism related differences); (iii) multiple versus single interpretation.

The other possible source of loss is in such pairs of languages that are different in *langue* as well as *parole,* that is, in both structure and use. Such differences may occur at any level. For instance, at the lexical level, the differences may be in different dimensions, such as follows:

(a) Formality of styles available (frozen to completely informal)
(b) Affectivity that any given text can achieve in the two languages (no reaction to over-reaction)

(c) How general or technical these languages can be/become
(d) How are the texts evaluated in these languages (in terms of morality, pleasure, intensity or coverage?)

Let us consider the problem of style first. We will take a few texts to show that it will not be an easy decision for a translator in any one of our Indian languages to decode the particular style used in them and accordingly decide as to how best to convert it into our languages.

> 'But I am Tortoise,' said Slow-and-Solid. 'Your mother was quite right. She said that you were to scoop me out of my shell with your paw. Begin.'
> 'You didn't say she said that a minute ago', said Painted Jaguar.... 'You said she said something different.'
> 'Well, suppose you say that I said that she said something different. I don't see that it makes any difference; because if she said what you said I said she said, it's just the same as if I said what she said she said. On the other hand, if you think she said that you were to uncoil me with a scoop, instead of pawing me into drops with a shell, I can't help that, can I ?'
> 'But you said you wanted to be scooped out of your shell with my paw', said Painted Jaguar.
> 'If you'll think again, you'll find that I didn't say anything of the kind. I said that your mother said that you were to scoop me out of my shell', said Slow-and-Solid (Kipling 1902: 70).

> On the doorstep he felt in his hip pocket for the latch key. Not there. In the trousers I left off. Must get it. Potato I have. Creaky wardrobe. No use disturbing her. She turned over sleepily that time. He pulled the halldoor after him very quietly, more, till the footleaf dropped gently over the threshold, a limp lid. Looked shut. All right till I come back anyhow.
> (Joyce 1922: 56–57)

Anyone who dares translating similar authors who wrote in Indian languages into a Western language would soon realize the difficulties in deciding what should be the nearest equivalent to the style used in these texts.

This also brings us to the fourth point: even if we neglect the private meanings, the text writer and the translator may have completely different value systems and different semantic maps with which they operate. Therefore, there are bound to be losses or gains in the domain of semantics of the text(s) being subjected to any translating activity. We are reminded of the translation of the following verse from the *Amarushataka*, 49:

SOURCE LANGUAGE: SANSKRIT

nabhasi jaladalakSmiim saasrya viikSya drSTyaa
pravasasi yadi kaantey ardham uktvaa kathamcit
mama paTam avalambya prollikhanti dharitriim
yad anukrtavatii saa tatra vaaco nivrttaaH!

This verse was translated by W. S. Merwin and L. Moussaieff Masson in the following way:

Lush clouds in
dark sky of tears she saw my love
if you leave me now she
said and could not say more
twisting my shirt
toe gripping dust
after that what she
did all words
are helpless to repeat and
they know it and give up

(Merwin and Moussaieff Masson 1981: 89)

It is obviously a very difficult task for any translator to do justice to these lines in Sanskrit. It may also be difficult for TL readers to appreciate these sentiments because of a huge difference between the way the man–woman relation unfolds in our culture and the way it works in the West. But one must still appreciate the strategy used by the translators in attempting to render the piece into English, where they made several changes:

(i) They altered the line divisions
(ii) They opted for a free verse style

(iii) They took recourse to italicization/underscoring to identify the incomplete sentence spoken by the woman
(iv) They made lexical adjustments, such as 'paTam' > 'shirt', etc.

OVERTRANSLATION

Let us take up a few typical examples of the two dangers that confront a translator all the time—the dangers of overtranslation and of undertranslation. The first instance we give is a poem (or song) from Tagore's *Aruup ratan* (in Bengali) which goes like this:

mama citte niti nritye ke je naace
taa-taa thai-thai, taa-taa thai-thai, taa-taa thai-thai.
taari sange kii mrdange sadaa baaje
taa-taa thai-thai, taa-taa thai-thai, taa-taa thai-thai.

haasi-kaannaa hiraa-paannaa dole bhaale,
kaa~pe chande bhaalomanda taale taale,
naace janma, naace mrtyu paache paache
taa-taa thai-thai, taa-taa thai-thai, taa-taa thai-thai.
kii aananda, kii aananda, kii aananda
dibaa-raatri naace mukti naace bandha,
se tarange chuTi range paache paache
taa-taa thai-thai, taa-taa thai-thai, taa-taa thai-thai.

While rendering these lines into English, Father C. F. Andrews overdid the translation (as noticed quite early by Surendranath Das Gupta in 1916):

In my glad heart, in my mad heart, who is dancing?
  Ding a ding dong, ring a ting tong, ding a ding dong
Where no fears are, joy and tears are ever glancing,
  Ding a ding dong ...
Where the music rises higher, like a fire,
Now advancing, all entrancing, joy enhancing
  Ding a ding dong ...

Pain and gladness, smiles and sadness, toil and leisure
Night and morning, light and dawning, full the measure
  Ding a ding dong ...

Oh the pleasure, oh the pleasure, oh the pleasure
of our dancing, ever glancing, all entrancing
  Ding a ding dong ...

Like the Ocean in its motion waves are
Fears are groundless, freedom boundless, life is waking
With our dancing, ever glancing, joy enhancing
Ding a ding dong ...
(quoted in Lal 1987: 100)

Consider what a serious translator of Tagore such as Ananda Lal (ibid. 101) had to say about such overtranslations: 'Such a translation can only provoke laughter. The meticulous attention paid to rhyme and metre replicates the original Bengali technique but does not possess any vitality of its own, and the jejune refrain kills whatever little life the song had.' The translation that Lal himself provides of this song is free from this tension:

Who dances in my heart the dance eternal?
What mridanga beats with it incessantly?

Smiles and tears, emeralds and diamonds, swing in fate,
Good and bad vibrate to the rhythm, keeping time, Birth and death dance at one another's heels.
What happiness, what happiness, what happiness,
For freedom and confinement dance all day and night
I flow with those waves, joyful, at their heels.
(Lal 1987: 101)

UNDERTRANSLATION

An example of undertranslation comes from Thomas Fitzsimmons' translation of a ghazal of Ghalib as given in Aijaz Ahmad's book (1971: 25), which was an experiment in getting poems translated by monolingual poets through a well-defined mechanism of using an intermediate literal translation plus a detailed commentary forming the bases. The original ghazal of Ghalib in Urdu reads like this in its first two couplets:

ishrate qatraa hai daryaa me~ fanaa ho jaanaa,
dard kaa had se guzarnaa hai dard kaa davaa ho jaanaa.

jaa~ fase gariye mubacchal badme sard huaa
baavar aayaa hame~, paanii kaa havaa ho jaanaa.

The original explanation or the philosophical import is not difficult to understand, although like any truly great text, it is also open to interpretations. The basic meaning, however, seems to be the following: the first couplet means that to be consumed by the whole can be the ultimate joy of the part, just as pain becomes its own medicine. The second one tells us that we can only sigh and not weep at our weakness once it crosses certain limits, which is why one can now believe that water (tears) can indeed become air (sigh)—comparable to the process of cloud-formation.

The literal translation of Ahmad, though not claiming to be poetic, seems to capture the above meanings aptly:

> The happiness of the drop is to die in the river;
> When the pain exceeds bearable limits,
>   the pain itself becomes the medicine.
>
> Our weakness is such that tears have turned into mere sighing
> Now we really believe that water can turn into air.
> (Ahmad 1971: 22)

Let us now consider a target language poet's translation of this important poetic text:

> Waterbead ecstasy: dying in a stream;
> Too strong a pain brings its own balm.
>
> So weak now we weep sighs only;
> Learn surely how water turns into air.
> (Fitzsimmons in ibid.: 25).

First, the text may describe a situation peculiar to the natural environment of the particular speech community or its 'peculiar' social setting, which to us may seem peculiar and odd but may not actually be so. In such contexts, whatever strategy one adopts (transcription, substitution, naturalization or translation), the translated text is bound to leak in one respect or another.

GENETICALLY UNRELATED LANGUAGES AND TRANSLATION

Translation presents special problems for languages that are genetically unrelated or typologically different. The reason is very obvious. The constraints that crop up when one contrasts two such languages constitute the real problems in the process of translation. These problems heed to be tackled by any comprehensive theory, particularly if one believes Jakobson's (1981: 262) words that equivalence in difference is the cardinal problem of language and the pivotal concern of linguistics. There is no doubt that total translation is the replacement of SL grammar and lexis by an equivalent TL grammar and lexis with consequential replacement of SL phonology, graphology by (non-equivalent) TL phonology/graphology (Catford 1965:22). Catford's hypothesis may be validated only when differential bilingual dictionaries with careful comparative definition of all the corresponding units in their intention and extension become handy. Likewise, referential bilingual grammars should define what unifies and what differentiates the two languages in their selection and delimitation of grammatical concepts.

A scientific investigation is warranted to study the typological differences and peculiarities in translation. Nama (1990: 81) observes that the translator or mediator between two different linguistic systems is compelled to resolve a good number of obstacles. The success or failure of a translation mainly depends upon how far and how best the translator resolves these obstacles. Translators themselves do not find that the notion of equivalence can be achieved through various replacement processes between pairs of languages. In *Language, Structure and Translation*, Eugene Nida (1975: 180) remarks:

> ...a careful analysis of exactly what goes on in the process of translating, especially in the case of source and receptor languages having quite different grammatical and semantic structures has shown that, instead of going directly from one set of surface structures to another, the competent translator actually goes through a seemingly roundabout process of analysis, transfer and restructuring. That is to say, the translator first analyses the message of the source language into its simplest and structurally clearest forms, transfers at this level, and then restructures it to the level in the RECEPTOR language which is most appropriate for the audience which he intends to reach.

IN CONCLUSION

The main purpose of this chapter was to make one aware of the fact that it is a comaparable set of things that happen when one creates new literary texts vis-à-vis when one translates such texts. The chapter also discussed the need to identify the problem areas in translation, and underscored the differences between the text and the work to relate them to translation. The translator was viewed as an interpreter here, and was shown as someone who would suffer from the tension between over- and undertranslation, choice of styles, cultural differences as well as the genetic and structural relationship (or a lack of it) between the source and target languages.

6

THE BACKGROUND

In the modernist debates on translation, one often uses the metaphor of governance to decide which text will rule the roost in the TL culture. Others also use the metaphor of disease (for instance, 'uncontaminated' versus 'contaminated' texts) as well as that of warfare ('win'/'gain' or 'loss' of meaning or translator), besides raising the issue of whether 'translated texts' are to be described as 'partly inherited' and 'partly made up'. The 'tacit contract' among the members of both source and target texts is, of course, not easy to conclude, because no community is pressureless and apolitical. In each, members are often vying with each other and competing with one another's group to agree or disagree on all such contracts.

Interestingly, Mufwene (1998) raises an important question, which I shall restate here: 'Are the norms of [expression] set in every speech community by native speakers?' He tries answering it partly and also argues that native speakers' intuitions do not have the same privilege in all texts, and that this is a highly variable entity. Recall Saussure's (1916[1966]: 14) claim that no individual can ever 'create or modify [speech] by himself'. The literary histories of our languages have shown that the greater the prowess and power of the individual, the better are the chances of these innovations surviving.

It is not that there are no interesting ideas on the theory of translation emerging out of other theoretical positions. In a paper titled 'Intercultural Hermeneutics and Literary Translation', for instance, Pramod Talgeri (1988a) draws an interesting parallel between the way sentences are embedded into other sentences, which are themselves embedded, and the kind of 'embeddedness' of a literary text in a cultural context. Viewing 'word' as an inseparable 'agent' of cultural memory or viewing it as a 'patient' of social history, the hermeneuticians underline the participatory experience of the source language culture which the translator is expected to recontextualize following the grammar of the target culture. Since the text has to be given a new garb, a novel locus, a virgin name and thus, a new identitity (and new 'references', as Talgeri would like to call it), here is an opportunity for the readers of the source text to find newer and as yet undiscovered layers of meaning through its translation.

We are often told about 'language purity' and 'linguistic corruption'. Students of sociolinguistics as well as translation studies are familiar with such thoughts. The popular belief is that the ancient or early formation of speech is pure and it becomes corrupt and 'vulgar' as the days go by. Look at the parallel in the field of translation: the original text is pure, and it tends to get corrupted as it travels from one language to an other, and then to another, etc. At a given point of time in South Asia as well as in Europe, it was commonly and tacitly agreed upon that the purity of the 'original' must be maintained at any cost—if necessary, by artificially inducing a certain degree of prescriptive planning or by opting for grand plans in the form of 'Sanskritization', which we could roughly equate with 'purification'. The modernists responsible for the spread of this particular theory believed that this was a highly desirable activity, and is actually possible. Thus, while everybody agreed that 'Prakritization' (often read as 'degeneration') of languages and texts was inevitable, it was to be arrested to create a platform of discourse that is widely acceptable, easily teachable and learnable so that it defies aging.

High modern language is thus a higher value speech in comparison to all those which, for some reason or the other, did not get the chance of undergoing appropriate changes to qualify for this epithet. Now this clearly creates a 'caste' distinction among speech groups. Some are declared as 'twice-born', not only 'standard' but 'modern' as well, whereas a large number of BhaaSaas are expected to remain even below the first level. What is taken for granted is that there are a large number of speech groups that do not get the desired push to end up as acceptable forms of literary expression.

For the sake of argumentation, one could even turn the tables and say that what is unmodern is chaste, consecrated, inviolate and inviolable, whereas what is modernized is impure, contaminated and mixed code/text, tainted with a purpose. There is a connection of all these to the issue of linguistic empowerment: who or which group 'owns' (or decides the destiny of) a form of speech becomes an important question to resolve so that we can decide who are the 'other' (and hence, 'foreign') and consequently who are 'native' to a speech, and thus are a part of the 'self'. Those human aggregates who are a part of this construction of self will of course watch with ever-increasing alarm that what they have always taken for granted as their own have slowly become an acreage of only some among them. This forces a certain kind of cleavage among all those who were expected to be a part of the 'self', but who now suddenly find the ground slipping from under their feet. All this may have happened because some class, or caste, community or group wants to capture the position of power, at the cost of others, to decide who should be othered.

Namvar Singh (1970), in his own critique of modernity, had once stated that beginning in 1936, of the four protest movements in Hindi against the poetic tradition of aristocratic gentility ('abhijaata shaaliinataa'), namely, *pragativaad*, *prayogavaad*, *laghu-maanavavaad* and *akavitaavaad*, in each such instance 'de-Sanskritization' was the aim of those who initiated the protest. He called the 'great' poetic tradition often upheld aloft by poetic giants 'false courtesy' (*chadma bhadrataa*) and such protestations instances of 'false discourtesy' (*chadma abhadrataa*) because every time there is a protest, slogans are raised to drop a few words to allow the entry of some other expressions. Poet-critics like Sriram Verma (1970) have argued that poets have suffered a terrible erosion of language, and their poetry in Hindi is stuck with only ten words—conspiracy, ruling class, blood-sucking, shoes, gun, violence, repair, march, wall, and preparation—with which they seek to change the entire society.

If modernity is a product of civilization, if it is a characteristic of our crisis, *uttar-aadhunikataa* allows us to realize—in the words of Jean-Pierre Mileur (1985)—'our post-enlightment dilemma' and that makes it possible to appreciate that 'the burden of our modernity involves the apparent necessity of a choice between the best interests of the past and those of the present and the future'. Postmodern philosophers too claim, to quote Berel Lang (1986), that 'there's a sharp gap between the past and present'.

Before talking about paradigms such as *uttar-aadhunikataa* and/ or *aadhunikataa*, their connection with translation must be made clear. By way of a footnote, let me add here that it is important to remember that '*uttar*' here is not 'post-something'. Also important is to recall that in our philosophical tradition, we have already had positions such as *uttar-miimaangsaa*. The elliptical bohemian rootless *aadhunikataa* that we are all familiar with is transcended in *uttar-aadhunik* writing. *Uttar-aadhunikataa* will then have to be viewed as a serious attempt to destabilize our neat demarcation of known versus unknown, to challenge the theory of information and redundancy. The question is: does this paradigm allow us to look at the act of translating differently from the way we are accustomed to view it? As sociolinguists, we are interested in finding out whether 'translation' allows an alternative model of development of our bhaaSaas.

AADHUNIKATAA AS A PARADIGM

Let me begin from the beginning. In Bengal, *aadhunikataa* as a paradigm descended, like the proverbial saint Naarada often did, from the predictable and expansive heaven of Europe during the early nineteenth century, when Bengali critics like Hur Chunder Dutt and Kailash Chandra Basu had first made out a case for the supremacy of the Western over the Oriental. In a lecture on Bangla poetry at the Bethune Society in 1851, the two had stated that there was no Bangla poetry worth discussing as whatever was available was brazen and vulgar. Kailash Dass, who moderated their talks, held the same view.

It was no coincidence that this attempt to negate one's own poetic tradition should misguide poets like Michael Madhusudan Dutta (as quoted in Guha-Thakurata 2001:74) to write in 1853 (to a friend) that 'it is my intention to throw off the fetters forged for us by a servile admiration of everything Sanskrit'. Regrettably, he begins these lines by saying, '... Remember that I am writing for that portion of my country-men who think as I think, whose minds have been more or less imbued with western ideas and modes of thinking'.

Around the same time we find critics like Ishwar Gupta (consider his voluminous autobiographical treatise titled *Kavijiivanii*) arguing that in the context of Bangla poetry he would rate spontaneity and employment of *deshiiya* or colloquial collocations and expressions much higher in poetic value than poetizing with pedantry—a poetic talent which could be acquired by making compromises with what was 'natural' and 'unmarked'. The counter-position offered by Ishwar Gupta was emboldened by perceptive poet-critics such as Rangalal Bandyopadhyay (1852) who, in a subsequent meeting of the same Bethune Society on 13 May 1852, put forth his 'Proposal on Bangla Poetry' (*Baangaalaa kabitaa biSayak prastaab*). Here Rangalal had perhaps sown the seeds of comparative literature in India when he critically compared Shakespeare with Bharatchandra Raygunakar, but more importantly, he denied that one must sever one's umbilical chord to achieve modernity.

Further, Rangalal (1852) made a prognosis that in a colonial context a dominated and subjugated race could also author great poetry but that it would usually have the tendency to drift towards anarchy and sexual fantasizing. (It is needless to say that in the poetry of the decadent modernist after another 100 years we do notice such debasement in abundance.) We notice the sarcasm hidden in the epilogue of Rangalal in his *Padminii Upaakhyaana* (1858), where he identified the limitation of his time—the introduction of Western education, consequently the inculcation of Western values, resulting in a possible poisoning of our race but at the same time the inevitability and unavoidability of this influence. Translated into English (as was done by this author), his words would read like this:

A 'great' luck for India portends
Her night full of sorrows ends
Would she still remain asleep, o friends?

By the grace of the British kind
in the horizon of our mind
knowledge as sun will spread far 'n behind!

In the lake of peace petus
resides the happiness-lotus
let the learned mind bemuse us

O morn of kindness lords
if revolting cloud accords
a poison-rain,
let them not send!
Her nights full of sorrows end.

(Bandyopadhyay, 1858, translation mine)

Here I would like to draw the attention of readers to what is popularly known as the nineteenth-century 'awakening' in Bengal (often described as a 'renaissance', obviously because even historical tools and categorial labels employed are often derivative—we are only engaged in plumbing and fitting them) which made it possible for the making of literary and social reformists like Ishwar Chandra Vidyasagar. But what did they say about this 'inevitable' Western education to which Rangalal had referred? Vidyasagar takes a vow as he says: Whatever else I may do with my children, I shall not send them to English schools—there isn't a better and surer way of becoming *rootless* and *hollow.* (He used the words *aSaar* and *de~po.*)

Dwijendranath Tagore also joins the debate as he is credited to have argued:

> If these (British) schools and colleges are done away with, I do not think there will be a great harm for the indigenous education (*lokashikSaa*) in our society. Rather it may have a more positive result in our society if socially/contextually relevant education is introduced. The way today's Bengali child is growing up within the constraints of a foreign model of education, how is he expected to contribute to our nation-building?

Much later, in 1928, philosophers such as Krishnachandra Bhattacharya would say the same thing: 'Our mode of thinking is thus a hotch-potch and is necessarily barren. Servility has made inroads into our innermost consciousness'. Independent thinking seemed to be the first casualty of Westernization which, to my mind, seems to be the precondition for modernization. It is this modernity that seemed to be increasingly driving the subsequent generations towards consumerist and materialistic Western models of social organization, ensuring a permanent intellectual and economic slavery.

While this was happening, not surprisingly, an insipid romanticism in both tone and tenor had been smuggled in stylistically in the writings of many, getting rid of which was a problem even for an erudite BhaaSaa writer such as Bankim Chandra Chattopadhyay. Bankim complained that neither the English neo-romantics nor their nineteenth-century Bengali replicas in Hemchandra and Navin Chandra Sen could satisfy him until he could rediscover the everlasting charm of oralcy of the poets like Ramprasad Sen (refer to Pramatha Chaudhury's criticism of *aado-aado bhaav* and *gado-gado bhaav* in poetry).

A reflection of this critical reference can be seen in Vivekananda's negative assessment of the young and juvenile Tagore's initial dabbling in the construction of his own poetic diction. Of course, fortunately for us, Tagore changed, just as Madhusudan had. As time went by, Tagore became more and more engaged in his own reading of his time and space and in presenting a critique of his environs. He vigorously differed from proponents of the borrowed glow of Eurocentric modernity and charted his own course, digging out his own style from under his roots. Whereas the modernist would argue that the past must be stilted and stunted at some point so that one could grow beyond it (Brecht, cited in Sen 1993: 65), here is what Tagore (1894) had to say about looking back at one's own roots:

> jakhan baahire raudrer kharatara taap, aakaash haite brSTi paRe naa, takhan shikaRer prabhaabe aamraa atiiter andhakaarer nimnatama desh haite ras aakarSaN karite paari.
>
> (When the sun shines mercilessly, raising mercury in the world outside, when there is not a drop of rain from the sky, at that time, thanks to our roots, we can draw upon *rasa* from the dark innermost chamber of our past.)

Madhusudan, on the other hand, first struck fetters of all kinds—end-rhyming, conventional metrics, thematic treatment, lexical coinage—and then synthesized European and Indian trends to evolve his own inimitable diction that demanded (but failed to get in his lifetime) a new yardstick for evaluation. For that lack of appreciation Madhusudan was saddened. That was also when he defined a poet as 'the proud, silent, lonely man of song'. By 1881, he wrote to Rajnarayan Bose:

> Some of my friends as soon as they see a drama of mine, begin to apply the canons of criticism that have been given forth by the

> masterpieces of William Shakespeare. They perhaps forget that I write under very different circumstances. Our social and moral developments are of a different character.

CANONIZATION AND UNIVERSALS

This then brings us to another characteristic of *aadhunikataa*, namely the creation of, or rather, the universalization of literary canons. Contrast this with the well-known Sapir-Whorf hypothesis which argues that no two languages reflect the same social reality and that human languages simply do not have different labels attached to the same/similar set of categories, or else translation would be reduced to a search for mere equivalence.

Now whether one believes in the linguistic relativity principle (where language diversity has the focus) or in inherent semantic diversity à la Hirsch (1967) and Husserl (1939[1973]), or even in the reader's liberation movement led by Barthes, while looking back at the nineteenth-century history of critical discourse in the BhaaSaa literature, monism seemed to be a dominating force. There were writers like Bankim who tried to shrug it off by distancing themselves from all attempts at standardizing a language. Bankim's revolt against the archaic or *saadhu* Bengali in his novels or his idea of synthesizing what his detractors called *guruchaNDaalii* (classicalized colloquials) was a case in point. Among Tagore's contemporaries in the field of poetry such as Biharilal Chakraborty, Dwijendranath Tagore or Govindachandra Das, the last two also favoured the colloquial and down-to-earth (rural) style in their poetry, which had been reflected in Tagore's own poems especially after *Sonaar Tari* (1894). To conclude this point, the forces of modernity contributed to our languages more towards what one can call 'Sanskritization' of literature (by that we refer not merely to the introduction of classical lexis or syntax but also to unifications/standardization tendencies), whereas the counter-force in Bengal was always in favour of retaining diversity of style and diction and not divorcing it from roots—something I called 'Prakritization' of literature elsewhere (cf. Singh 1989b).

Interestingly (and this brings us to the another point), we must remember that on the theoretical plane, it was again Tagore who opposed 'modernity' in a lecture to fellow writers and poets in May

1927. We must also note that by the 1920s, the modernist agenda had been firmly established among the post-Tagore poets who began writing in derivative forms and styles following French, German and English poets. This is not to undermine the poetic prowess of poets like Bishnu De and Sudhindranath Datta, as they often challenged and changed our poetic syntax and enforced pattern shifts. But a careful analysis of their work will show that their poetic diction was replete with verbs of intellection, comprehension, affectation and volition, a resonance of which we could see even in current modernist poets like Alokeranjan (cf. Singh 1994b, a statistical study of his award-winning anthology *Marami Karat*). Modernity, then, also promoted intellectualization of our theme and treatment.

Not all the modernist poets in Bengal wrote about poetry or writing but we find some of them announcing, as Buddhadev Bose did in 1938, that the 'Tagore era has met its doom' or as Sunil Gangopadhyay would do in the 1960s, in his oft-quoted lines—*tinjoRaa paayer laathite rabiindra-racanaabalii luTaay paaposhe* ('three pairs of legs kick Tagore volumes/make them roll on mattresses'), the fourth characteristic of *aadhunikataa* becomes clear: demolish all that is institutionalized. But what did Tagore say in 1927? He argued that the main purpose of literature and art was to innovate and to create new forms, where the role of content was limited. Let me now extend his argument. Since content here mattered only so far as it helped creating a neologue or neotaxis, the European modernity enterprise which was built upon the loss of cultural cohesion and which was largely elliptical and denied all previous content, mattered very little to the contemporary Bengali litterateur.

IMAGING *AADHUNIKATAA*: DECAYING 'MODERNITY'

When Tagore voiced his first concern about the agenda of the modernists in 1927, he also claimed that 'modernity depends not upon time but upon temperament', and in what we consider to be a crucial exemplification of his statement, Tagore had analysed Eliot and Pound and rejected their 'attitude of aggressive disbelief and calumny towards the universe' as modern. Of course, he went one step more than was warranted to call this attitude 'a personal mental aberration'. But

Tagore was not being merely critical as he set up a different definition of what is 'eternally modern', which is a point of beginning for the *uttar-aadhunik* in Bangla:

> Pure modernism, then, consists in looking upon the universe, not in a personal and self-regarding manner, but in an impersonal and matter of fact manner.... In the same dispassionate way, that modern science analyses reality, modern poetry looks upon the universe as a whole; this is what is eternally modern.

But Tagore refused to attach any importance to the label 'modern' here as a tool for literary historians because by his logic the vintage Chinese poet Li-Po was also modern.

Here was then the first postmodern attempt to divorce 'modernity' from time and space, but the modernists in Bengal in the 1930s would have more of them. Thus wrote Buddhadev Basu in 1948 in his 'An Acre of Green Grass', once again trying to use Tagore to legitimate his position 'Rabindranath made Bengla a part of Europe. The rest of India, in those early days of disorder was hostile, cold, crustaceous, only Bengal absorbed Europe (a lofty claim indeed: UNS) with speed and thoroughness that should be marked as a record of human relations.'

Here was a clear equation between *aadhunikataa* and Europeanism or Westernization. About these derivative and initiative exercises in discovering one's routes of transplantation (as against the search for 'roots' among the 'eternally modern'), Sisir Kumar Das (1991: 229) made an interesting observation:

> The imitations of British modernists had one salutary effect: the new poetry that was born with Eliot and his contemporaries came as a challenge to the ideals considered by the English educated Indians—those ideals were also derived from the English poetic tradition.... It was a borrowed experience, nonetheless it gave a courage for experimentations. Even imitations can create the awareness of the original.

This emergence of 'new poetry' in different Indian BhaaSaas came at a different time. In Hindi, we find its impact quite early by 1941–44 in Ajneya's writings, although in Bengali it all started with the *Kallol* era poets—Premendra Mitra, Achintya Sengupta and Buddhadev Basu (with his *Bandiir bandanaa* [1930], *Kankaabatii* [1937],

Damayantii [1943] and *Draupadiir saaRii* [1948]) and with Sudhindranath Datta's first anthology, *Tanvii* (1930), and later with his *Orchestra* (1935) as much as with Bishnu De's *Urbasii o AarTemis* (1933), *Puurbalekhaa* (1941) and *Sandviiper car* (1947). In Hindi, it all began with the replacement of *chaayaavaad* by the poets owing allegiance to *prayogvaad* and *pragativaad* in the early 1940s. Later, with the *taar saptak* poets (1943), many others (esp. Muktibodh [1964, 1984], known for his posthumous works) came into the forefront. In Punjabi too, the change began in the 1930s with Mohan Singh's (1931, 1945) writings and was consolidated with Baba Balvant's voice of protest in his *Mahaanaac* (1941) and *Bandargaah* (1951). Marathi, with Mardhekar's *KaaMbii kavitaa* (1947) and P. S. Rege's *Dolaa* (1950), entered the modernist bandwagon a little late but it still preceded Gujarati where the revolt against past traditions began with Suresh Joshi's *Upajaati* (1956) and with Niranjan Bhagat's poems (1949). In comparison, Kannada was a much later entrant with Adiga's 1952 anthology and contributions by B. C. Ramachandra Sharma (1952, 1953).

While the second phase of *aadhunikataa* in Hindi began with magazines like *Pratiika* (1947) and *Nayii Kavitaa* (1954) led by Ajneya, the corresponding development in Bangla began with the publication of *Krttibaas*, which threw out the neo-modernists like Shakti Chattopadhyay, Sunil Gangopadhyay and Sankha Ghosh. The denigration of the classical has, however, been a recurrent theme of all the modernists. Consider what Sunil had to say, writing under the pseudonym 'sanaatan paaThak' (1971: 991), about Bankim, who 'cannot but be described as anything other than a second or third-rate writer'. Smear campaigns such as these continued for some more time. Thus wrote Shakti (1976: 4), unfortunately though, that 'In the present times only four percent people read his novels, and he would have been an obscure and tenebrous entity had his pieces not been included in the school text-book'.

So far, I have talked about only three generations of modernist poets in Bengal, represented by Michael, the *Kallol* poets and the *Krttibaas* poets in the 1850s, 1920s and 1950s respectively, and have identified certain characteristics of their writings that together create an image of 'modernity' in our minds. This image is of severing of links with one's tradition, identification of modernity with Westernization or Eurocentrism (in the dimension of space) and as a trend that can emerge only after pre-modern traditional phase of literary productivity (in the dimension of time), insipid romanticism, obscurity, standardization of the expression system while at the same time taking liberties with it, and establishment of a universal (read 'Western') canon of critical appreciation, etc.

There was one line of writing which begins with the alternative poetry of Bishnu De (1933, 1941, 1947) and which flowered in poems of Samar Sen (1937, 1939) and Dinesh Dash (1942). This writing found the most convincing voice of protest first in the legendary single-anthology poet like Sukanta Bhattacharya (1948a, 1948b), who wrote the famous lines '*KSudhaar raajye prthibii gadyamay, puurNimaar caa~d jena jhalsaano ruTii*' (In the land of hunger the earth appears prosaic; the full moon in the sky looks like a burnt chapati), and later in Subhash Mukhopadhyay's (1946, 1950) poems, like '*priya phul khelbaar din nay adya*'. This poetry of protest emerged in Bengal in the 1940s with the communist movement.

The decay of modernism began in Bengal with the third generation of modernists who gathered themselves under the umbrella of a periodical called *ShatabhiSaa* in 1951, where the new modernists admitted that the techniques used by the poets of the 1930s (meaning the first generation modern poets of the *Kallol* era) became 'obsolete' because their 'social consciousness' and 'liquified poetizing' was of no use any more. *Krttibaas* succeeded in this endeavour, but the first thing it tried to do was to break the backbone of criticism. Here was the initiation of what I would like to call an 'adjectival' style of criticism. Appreciation became a matter of personal whim and fancy. As time went by, *Krttibaas* revolted against any scholarship, which was why Sunil Gangopadhyay wrote in 1971 reminiscing about those days: 'All those essays about poetry were impenetrable and dry, full of artificial and thorn-like verbose expressions. Most of those essays were intellectual exercise, or an attempt to look for an avenue in apparent philosophization. The purity of poetry got burnt out in its explanations'.

In 1976, the *uttar-aadhunik* criticism first raised its head in the writing of a group of poets, writers and painters in *Gaangeya patra*. Predictably, the war of words between the decaying modernists and the *uttar-aadhuniks* continued for another 20 years. But by 1986, with the publication of the anthologies *Kabitaar bhaaSaa* and *Myth, saahitya o sangskrti*, the curtain put up by the modernists was already raised. Dipak Majumdar (the founder-editor of *Krttibaas*) had declared null and void

> ...the semantics of words like pain, grief, satan, ultimate, empty, sin, chastity, blood, song and God (= *yantraNaa viSaad, shaitaan, param, shuunya, paap, shubhra, rakta, gaan and iishvar*)—all those expressions which continued from the end of last century until yesterday.

Does it not find a parallel with the pattern of thinking of Namvar Singh and Sriram Verma?

It reminds us of a similar predicament of the Hindi modernists in the late 1960s when the document entitled *Siidhii lekhak shivir ke dasta-vez*, was brought out—where (on 14–16 March 1970) a group of Hindi poets and critics had raised the issue of the 'debasing' of poetic language. The specific term used by them was *avamuulyan*. One can read it in two ways, one where it is synonymous with 'atrophy' or degeneration, meaning thereby that the words and expressions of today's language have lost their edge, as a consequence of which they have become gyrandical and genderless. In this interpretation, syntax gathers dust due to perfunctory invariance and vivacious content leaves the tattered form of language way behind in its pilgrimage to poetry. The other possible reading is that like our currency, our language today has also been devalued, where our possible stock of sounds, words and structures far outweigh our plausible stock of ideas, imagery and semantics (cf. Singh 1990: 28). We do not know which meaning to accept but this parallel development of modernists who could even decree a language no longer fit for great poetry seems interesting to us.

The first and foremost characteristic of decadent modernism of the 1980s was this rejection of language, the search for an 'otherness', which is ever elusive. Quite related to this was their anti-scholasticism. There have always been exceptions like Sankha Ghosh or Alokeranjan Dasgupta. Even when poets like Alokeranjan draw from Western myths and look for novelty in metrics or in concatenation of expressions, there is neither rejection of language nor any trace of scholastic aptitude.

Obviously, for the third generation modernists of the 1950s and 1960s, the second generation had set a precedence in bringing in Western poetry through translation, transplantation (of ideas/myths/imageries) or through imitation. To mention an instance of the former type, we could see the tremendous influence of Buddhadev Basu's transcreation of Baudelaire—which had practically acted as a manual for budding modernists of the kind of Shakti Chattopadhyay and Pabitra Mukhopadhyay (Gupta 1989: 22).

Contrast the third generation modernists with those that have emerged today as their successors and who have called themselves *e~Rigopaal ge~Rigopaal*. They warn you, dear reader, that you would get answers to all your ills. (All subsequent texts are my translations from original Bengali poems.)

> If your nerve is weak, let us know
> If your girl-friend finds you frigid 'n leaves,
> let us know
> If you have constipation, do let us know
> We'll tell you the way out
> We'll tell you all.
>
> (Chakraborty 1994: 59)

Their modernity lies in their dependence on the resonentia—on sexual power, and not on words:

> Like a peacock in the rain
> gobbles up drops of clouds
> to spread its wings in plumage—
> like it draws upon power from its
> urge for sex,
>   in the same way
> it's the voice which is crucial
>   in any love-sentence
> not the words that make them all.
>
> (Pal 1995: 89)

These poets seem to enjoy their own debasement by negative portrayal of themselves:

> They tell me I am a piggy tail of a homely hound
> it is very easy to chop me off—

And me too think I am a piggy tail of a ...
They tell me I am the crow
in the story of the crow in the guise of a peacock ...
(Bhowmick 1995: 89)

The second typical feature of the latest generation of modernists lies in their agenda of debasing women—in the imagery they choose to depict women. They paint a world where 'in the midnight/we might/meet a foolish woman/who's just aborted again' (Samad, 1995: 83). When the poet sings a song of sixpence, enamoured by the display of a woman's bare legs, in a pseudo-discourse with her dress which is eager to reveal, he is obviously viewing gender only as a saleable category. For instance, the modernist writes:

O you coloured saree! Don't you fly up to show your leg
it is a leg beyond compare—an intoxicating leg it is
it is a leg shaven off—carefully nurtured and borrowed leg it is!

What a way to describe a woman who, the poet claims, understands only spices and not poems. Literally,

She is in the pressure cooker, empty rhetoric and rain
She is in the science—proton, electron, profane
She is in the faith inspired as fired force
She is in the jungle, also in the intercourse
She is in the warmth of a knee
in the field of love is she!
(Acharya 1994: 111)

UTTAR-AADHUNIKATAA: LESSONS FOR A NEW TRANSLATION THEORY

In a keynote address to a Seminar on Translation at the Central Institute of English and Foreign Languages (CIEFL, now EFLU, or the English and Foreign Languages University) (16–20 March 1998), I had talked about 'Speech as Chaos: Translation as Cacophony', trying to draw a parallel between theories of language and translation. Speech, I said, has a chaotic existence, and chaos like speech has a unique pattern occupying a three-dimensional space. I said it requires three different kinds of semantics to understand them:

First, chaos can be understood in terms of semantics of confusion—the universe of which ranges from a mere befuddlement to a fierce fracas. This confusion can be a mix-up, malady or even an anarchy, the natural offshoot of it being 'disorder' of various kinds—personal, political, socio-cultural, literary and even linguistic. Any text which defies our own logic of understanding will appear to us, the uninitiated, as a mere medley of cacophony. It is perfectly possible that interpretations defy the author, too, a theme that translates easily:

> Why are the letters
> that float in the sky so bitter?
> can the fiery weather
> mellow them?
> ('Conspiracy', Singh [with Raj] 2006: 26)

Second, there is this semantics of amorphism, under which chaos can be understood as something which happens and evolves and, therefore, has a form and is yet a formless, indeterminate, indefinite and an obscure entity. The contradiction which is evident in the above statement is in building a theory of translation. I am not surprised to find that while 'translation' seems to be an 'impossible' nominal construct, it is still a perfectly acceptable verb. Chaos, and all that goes in that class—language, image or text, thus defy forms, and are yet amenable to rule—governs explanations to different degrees.

Third, chaos can also be understood as standing for the void—for a space—something that symbolizes not an object or entity, but the interrelationship between them. It is this intermediary space unspoilt by grammar, where the creative resides. The subject of her discourse, who is more a 'potential' than a 'real' communicator, provides the much needed hiatus between one man and another, between man as an individual and society, between an organism or substance and its environs. A translator seems to be twice removed from this scene often trying to negotiate between two worlds, and thus becomes the link between two cultures.

Let me give two examples here, one each from poetry and prose in Maithili, of how such negotiations are made. The deviations and obligatory innovations have been underlined here:

1. Her name was Kanchan, but they call her Kanchaniya. She was poor and untouchable, which was why everybody would call her Kanchaniya, and not Kanchan. She has been a silent witness of fourteen springs. Her father Harjanma was a farm labourer of Bauku Choudhury. Last year, during the summer, he fell down from a rose-apple tree and died. He left behind, like other labourers, the only property he had—the two earning hands of her daughter and the legacy of a loan in her lame mother...

   Her hut was away from Babhan-toli. It wasn't really a hut. It was only a shanty shed which has somehow been made livable by affixing a door. The lamey had been having fever for over a month now. And besides, she had a large spleen in her stomach. Where will she get money from to buy the medicines she needs?...

   With a wolf in the stomach, Kanchaniya sat motionless in a corner of their courtyard the whole day, placing her head on her knees.

   ... Where are you? she heard the feeble voice of her mother from inside the room. But even this fervent call of the sick woman could not break her inertia....

   When Digu too left, Balo remained seated without any movement in the semi-dark early evening hours for a long time. Much later, he probably remembered the festival of Sukrati. He lighted the German lantern with big glasses and hung it from the hook hanging down the roof.

   ... Babu! a feeble voice could be heard from back of the outer house. But his drunken eyes were so blurred in bibbery that they were unable to make out the hazy figure from the darkness of that corner.

   Who's that? Balo asked in awe. When the shadow came nearer he could recognize Kanchan.

   From whatever she said he could understand everything—the old woman was sick and hungry, so much so that she was hungry the whole day. There was nothing at home ... but all along his eyes were elsewhere ... they were watching Kanchan. She was looking quite beautiful. The torn old saree was unable to hide her sharp features. Noboby knows when Kanchan blossomed like that! Bounder me, she's snappily grown up lickety split.

   (Singh 1996)

2. From with
the sound of silence
and the intimate word
emerge painfully.

Within, sitting in a cave,
someone weeps

Within, sitting on a peak,
someone laughs aloud

Within, you hear someone walk
with cautious steps

Within, you catch the sound
of an envelope opening

Within, words froth in
the cauldron of each line

Sister, it pains a lot
to fathom your tears:

('Sounds Growing Within', Singh [with Raj] 2006: 30)

If texts have a geometry that is not so well understood, but which clearly have both pattern and chaos inherent in them, it should be interesting to see how the theorist try to understand them. The linguists propose to understand them in terms of a duality of patterning that is twofold: vertical and horizontal. Vertically, the idea is that language is basically a layered construct which is organized in some sort of a hierarchy of syntax and morphophonology. In this sense, as a construct language is viewed as having two levels of patterning—one on top of the other. In an essay entitled 'Nativity of Language', Annamalai (1998: 148) hints at another kind of double articulation: Language has double existence: grammatical and social. They are not a priori existence, but they come to exist through human construction. He then goes on to elaborate the other pattern of language:

> The social existence of a language comes about through its social construction by the community of speakers. The social construct may be about the boundary of the language.... It may be about the norm of the language.... It may be about the propriety over language.... It may be about what the language stands for; that is, about its cultural and political symbolization (ibid.: 149).

Notice that both the grammatical and social existence of language shows such patterning as are beyond individuals and idiosyncrasies, because what is grammatical must also bear the stamp of being social. In other words, language is as much general as it is specific, no matter how contradictory that may sound. It is this language within and over which an author dwells, and weaves her text, and yet must be readable to others. Since variation and stratification are bound to be there in its social aspect, grammar cannot be a monolithic entity. But is grammar a convenient metaphor?

Returning to the question of development of languages, I had argued elsewhere (Singh 1994a) that languages that develop on their own are said to have undergone primary standardization and those that are developed consciously are supposed to be under the category of secondary standardization. We could now see that those days are gone when language modernization followed language standardization, because there could be third/developing world communities where both may go hand in hand. Alternatively, we may find languages which can chart out new courses of development not generally talked about or known. There it seems to follow either of these courses: (i) Policies that worked elsewhere which have to be modified and re-implemented; or (ii) there could be models, policies and options that could be invented rather than being translative. These are known to have different models, being translative versus being innovative.

If language development is a 'homogenizing' process bring in linguistic uniformity rather than encouraging the blooming of a large basket of varying styles and such other speech varieties, one must also see whether any one of the above strategies could ensure development without sacrificing the inherent heterogeneity of our languages.

One might be surprised to hear about 'inherent heterogeneity'. How can a text have such layers? While in the original texts, descriptive texts and dialogues could show the variations, they seem to get sufficiently neutralized in their English rendering. In the poetic translation, the changes may not seem so obvious, but in the prose texts (especially in fiction), they are clearly visible. Consider the following translations (done by this author) from texts originally written in Bhojpuri:

1. They are watching
   the dew-drops;

They know these weren't drops—
This was the sky weeping silently
All night—
These were her tears!
And yet people trample on them
And walk ahead!

Times do not remain the same!
Season changes
And the day comes
When the whole world dies in thirst,
And yet
The sky
Does not shed even a drop of tears!
(Singh 2000b: 83)

2. Once again, there was a Panchayat meeting in the village today. Autar Baba was seated on the highest seat. The seat was nothing but a pendulant cot with bamboo straps tied below and woven with ropes made out of seasoned grass. As Autar Baba settled down on it, the ropes of the cot bent down unusually. Baba was wearing a half of five yards cloth below, and tied the rest across his legs behind his back from where it was swinging in the air, back and forth. The Panchayat there would also swing along. Dangling his dhoti like this, only God knows how many cases were handled by Autar Baba. One has lost count of them....

   Gojar Chowdhry would then appear mixing khaini and chuna on his palm and would instantly begin shooting his cryptic comments, 'What's the matter Pundit Baba? The members of the Panchayat haven't come yet?' In a few moments, they would arrive anyway. Autar Baba would until then lie baring his back and legs. He would now rise and sit up straight. As he did that, that piece of cloth tied around his back and legs would begin dangling once again. Spitting his betel water in a corner, he would thus begin by looking up at Gojar Chowdhry, 'Yes, tell me Gojar-bhai! Why are we assembled here?'....

Those half-naked middle aged fellows sitting on the ground in a semicircle suddenly livened up. Some faces became pale in fear. Some had hiccups. Some began coughing nervously. Some became speechless for a moment. That was when Satua Kaka burst out, 'Why don't you speak up, bastard? What stops you from speaking? Is your mouth paralysed?' A fear gripped everybody like a black cloud covers the entire sky. A middle-aged dark fellow began inching towards the cot of Autar Baba. Everybody was watching him intensely. He wanted to say something but wasn't able to speak up. It seemed all his words were stuck in his laryngeal groove. Kisnu gathered some courage to say, 'Why don't you speak up, brother? Why do you keep quiet?'....

Satua Kaka, Birju Baba, Autar Baba and a host of others started asking the same question at the same time, 'Tell us! Why wouldn't you dine at Mangal's house?' All those sitting on the ground got their voice back. Everybody had the same thought, 'Why? Why?' That was when Girgitwa laughed aloud. All started looking at him. Girgitwa was still laughing trying to hold on to his laughter but was unable to do so when Birju Baba asked him angrily, 'What's this Girgitwa? Why did you begin dancing like a joker in the middle of all this? Just keep your mouth shut!' Autar Baba now looked at Girgitwa carefully. He asked, 'What is it, Girgittu? You must be trying to hide something you know! What's that? Why don't you tell us all?'

Girgitwa now began laughing more loudly. After a while, he controlled himself and said, 'Hey Baba! You too are aware!' Now everybody's eyes moved toward Autar Baba.

(Singh 2000a: 51–53)

CONCLUSION

In a few recent essays on translation, Otto Ikôme (1994a, 2001) appears to take the view that an author/speaker is a 'foremost political predicate for social empowerment' which make such concepts as any other social stereotype. In the chain of communication, (i) who is the initiator when we are dealing with a text in translation? (ii) how do we decide who will become the initiator?

If we consider the function of the given target text, it may seem that whenever and wherever there is a translation, it will be the source language, often with power, determining the nature and extent of superimposition or transplantation of a text over another, or a language over another.

Further, when a text has already travelled across linguistic and cultural barriers, it may be of little importance to know what it was in its previous incarnation or whether or not it was an 'original' text. We recall here Sukanta Chaudhuri's (1987, 1997) excellent translation of *Ha-ja-ba-ra-la*, a Bengali text by Sukumar Ray we all grew up with and which we took as impossible to recreate in another language.

Let me then misquote, add to and modify Ikôme's (2001) statement here:

> Where many languages [= *interpretations*] compete for space, functions, speakers [= *readers*] and power [= *grip*] in very close quarters [= *over a very large number of readers*], 'native' qualities <*ADD: of a text*> would come to the forefront only when society and politics must resolve the ensuing problem of brokering linguistic [= *interpretive*] power '*equitably*' [between source and target versions, as also among the various sincere interpretations of the same in either of the communities].

Let us see how it reads with my modifications and manipulations:

> Where many interpretations compete for space, functions, readers and grip over a very large number of readers, 'native' qualities of a text would come to the forefront only when society and politics resolve the ensuing problem of brokering interpretive power 'equitably' between source and target versions, as also among the various sincere interpretations of the same in either of the communities.

That is clearly a position an *uttar-aadhunik* scholar would also take.

7

ON IMAGINATION

WRITING TAKES US far away from what we hope to write about. Should one be apologetic about it? I guess not, although there is some scope for disagreement. It is not necessary that one has to compare the author with the extremes in the triangle of the 'lunatic', the 'lover' and the 'poet' as Shakespeare had done in his *A Midsummer Night's Dream* (v. 1, 7):

> The lunatic, the lover and the poet,
> Are of imagination all compact:
> One sees more devils than vast hell can hold,
> That is, the madman: the lover, all as frantic,
> Sees Helen's beauty in a brow of Egypt:
> The poet's eye, in a fine frenzy rolling,
> Doth glance from heaven to earth, from earth to Heaven;
> And, as imagination bodies forth
> The forms of things unknown, the poet's pen
> Turns them to shapes, and gives to airy nothing
> A local habitation and a name.
> Such tricks hath strong imagination.

There is a point in what Shakespeare says here about imagination. All images are instances of double articulation, and in each lies a part that is born out of the 'manipulation' of reality. The author does not stop at such manipulation; she also tries giving it a name and a context. She is easily excused for such excursions from truth and text.

However, we are not so kind with translators who deviate from the original, and try to 'transcreate'. We should rather try to find out under what circumstances one opts for the strategy of 'transcreation', which the poet calls 'tricks' in the above lines, or what kind of changes could be (or, should be) brought about when one transcreates. To start with, one has to admit that neither the author nor the translator can assume a distinct identity vis-à-vis the text, and this fact has been noticed by many already. In a letter to Richard Woodhouse dated 27 October 1818, John Keats writes: 'A poet is the most unpoetical of anything in existence, because he has no identity; he is continually [informing] and filling some other body.' There are sometimes references to delusion vis-à-vis creativity:

> What stately vision mocks my waking sense?
> Hence, dear delusion, sweet enchantment, hence!
> (Smith and Smith 1841[2003])

Some would, of course, describe their products as pieces of fiction or fictition, as in *The Tempest*, where the author describes all characters that he weaves into the story with the following words:

> Our reveals now are ended. These our actors,
> As I foretold you, were all spirits and
> Are melted into air, thin air:
> And, like the baseless fabric of this vision,
> The cloud-capp'd towers, the gorgeous palaces,
> The solemn temples, the great globe itself,
> Yea, all of which it inherit, shall dissolve
> And, like this insubstantial pageant faded,
> Leave not a rack behind. We are such stuff
> As dreams are made of; ...

As against this position, there is a school of thought, which believes that poets and authors owe their 'imagination' primarily to their surroundings, and therefore, their writing must grapple with all problems that life presents—political, social, religious, scientific, or even personal. In that, they should at least follow the example of poet-sages like Homer (cf. Gunn 1971). But they lament that what was happening was the opposite. One such position has been aptly summarized by J. Robert Barth:

> While no one would claim an identity of religion and poetry, a relationship between them has often been affirmed, even as new theories of poetry have emerged. Today, views of this relationship range from the dedication of poetry to the service of religious doctrine to the affirmation that a poem exists for its own sake and in a world of its own, whose values are irrelevant to religion or philosophy or even human life. Between theses two extremes, however, there is a room for an enormous range of other views: Poetry as an expression of human aspiration and faith; poetry as an exploration of moral dilemmas posed by religious quest or commitment; poetry as a manifestation of human concern for ultimate realities; poetry as a surrogate for a belief that has been lost–man's refuge from the chaos around him (1987: 371).

Some would go to the extreme of bringing in a comparison of literary creativity and magic. This is not merely because both depend heavily on the power of words, but because the logic of a creative person may be very different from the rational logic. Both poet and magician see links and connections between things not easily perceived by a common person. No wonder, therefore, that in the Celtic tradition, poets were not clearly separable from druids. Similarly, Bo Almqvist, in his studies on old Nordic tales, tells us about at least 200 poets who had supernatural power. Many may thus bring in certain equations between the magic of poetry and the poetry of magic.

But that apart, there are scholars like Humphrey Jennings (1987) who would take the position that while poetic vision and imagination are a part of life and their importance cannot be belittled, a distinction should be made between means of production and means of vision. He laments that the function of the poet has been historically limited to a division of labour, in such a way that poetry becomes more and more specialized, until at last it has no subject but itself. Moreover, the industrial revolution has wrenched the means of production and means of vision further apart from one another. (It must be pointed out that in Jennings, the means of production is the determining force in literary history too but the difference is that he does not include culture as a part of superstructure, as for him it is a part of the base.)

So this question will always be an important issue to debate whether the hope of poetry lies outside poetry. Some like Eliot or Arnold would of course argue that the hope of creative writing lies in pitting it against civilization. Eliot (1932: 459) had gone to the extreme of painting a bleak future of this relationship when he wrote:

> When every theatre has been replaced with 100 cinemas, when every musical instrument has been replaced by 100 gramaphones, when every horse has been replaced by 100 cheap motor cars, when electrical ingenuity has made it possible for every child to hear bed-time stories from a loud-speaker, when applied science has done everything possible with the material on earth to make life as interesting as possible, it will not be surprising if the population of the entire civilized world rapidly follows the fate of the Melanesians.

But the question is: is culture anti-technology, anti-modern, or even anti-popular? (Hartley 1990: 1100). That is not easy to answer. Many may take the position that culture and civilization are in a kind of antonymic relationship. And that civilization has on its agenda an undeclared writ to subvert culture. This reminds one of the relationship between *sangskrti* and *prakrti* on the one hand, in the realm of culture, and between Sanskrit and Prakrit, in the field of language on the other. The distancing that, say, poetic language will naturally achieve without even consciously attempting it will not necessarily be appreciated by all. In disgust, Charles Darwin was credited to have written (as quoted in Jennings 1987: 343–44): 'But now for many years I cannot endure to read a line of poetry: I have tried lately to read Shakespeare, and found it so intolerably dull that it nauseated me …', but he did admit that 'the loss of these tastes is a loss of happiness, and may possibly be injurious to the intellect, and more probably to the moral character, by enfeebling the emotional part of our nature' (ibid.).

The point is that whenever we read a literary text, we derive a pleasure that is neither nameable or measurable. This unquantifiable reaction touches a chord where one feels a rare kinship with its progenitor, because this pleasure, in greater or lesser form, must have been his or hers, too. For an author who himself tries to recreate his own text in another tongue and feels constrained, finds his hands tied by the lack of equivalent idioms, collocations and metaphors, the frustration lies in not being able to re-live the same pleasure. Where an original author fails, a sensitive and a seasoned translator may succeed. But this success cannot be ascribed merely to his having been able to find the correct correspondences, nor to his achievements in capturing the meaning intended by the original author but to his ability for what Abhinavagupta would probably call *anukiirtana* in Sanskrit—something that allows one to churn, munch, taste, sing and understand the *kiirtana*, the text. All poetry is *anukiirtana*, according to Bharata. In English, we would, therefore, say that all writing is double articulation.

The intense feelings that result in a poem witness their first translation when a poet pens them down. Ask a poet and she will tell you that the words in her possession are woefully inadequate for the feelings that envelop her at the time of, or at a time preceding, her writing. All original writing is, therefore, a kind of paraphrasing—something that goes through the usual painful process of looking for the 'right' expression, and in settling for a syntactic 'fit'. That means that the language of literature is bound to become a little different from the rest of its application. A reader can understand and appreciate a text, provided he 'reads' and 're-reads'—not only the lines in the text, but also what lies between the lines.

But are there some conditions of reading? Abrams (1953: 6–29) had suggested long ago that there are four coordinates in any act of critical reading when one approaches a work of art: the subject of the work, its audience, the artist and the work itself. In different periods of history of reading which, to a large extent, overlap with the history of written literature, one or the other of these factors was given prominence.

From Plato's time to the Renaissance, the mimetic theory emphasized the reference of a work to the subject-matter it imitates (ibid. 10). Although Plato, in his *Republic*, rejects the imitation of the temporal world, he does advocate imitation of the ideal, transcendent ideas. For Aristotle, imitation is of immanent human actions, and not of transcendent ideas.

The Renaissance marks a shift from this situation to what is called a 'pragmatic view' by Abrams. Here the focus shifts from the subject of the work to its audience. It was during this time that this idea was floated by Dryden and Samuel Johnson that the ultimate goal of creative writing is to doctrinate potential readers into a particular mode of action.

In the 'expressionist' theory, which emerged during the Romantic period, the artist himself is foregrounded. The artist's feelings, aspirations and language become crucial. The search for transcendence assumes great importance because the search is carried out here through exploration of the inner self, or through the interaction of the self with the nature.

Finally, there was this 'objective' theory which focused on the work itself. The French symbolists or the Chicago school as well as the new critics led by I.A. Richards, William Empson, John Crowe Ransom and Cleanth Brooks—all lay emphasis on the inner structure of the poem to the exclusion of any external reference. Note that all the four stages are a matter of relative emphasis, rather than of exclusive concern.

In today's context, packaging of the text for the consumers, including its presentation for the audience of translations becomes the most important thing. Time is what is the least available element for reading now. It is, therefore, most apt to say, following William Blake:

> To see a world in a grain of sand
>   And a heaven in a wild flower.
> Hold infinity in the palm of your hand
>   And eternity in an hour.
> ('Auguries of Innocence').

Obviously, nobody has time to read, and there is no question of re-reading. So if a text or a point of view has to be emphasized, one has to talk about what was once called *anuvaada* in *Kaadambarii* where the word stands for repetition or *punarukti*. Literally, *punarukti* means 'saying it again'. Even in the famous medieval Bengali text, *Caitanya-caritaamrta* by Vrndaavanadaasa, translation or *anuvaada* has been described only as *anukiirtana* (literally, 'singing after'), or *anukSaNa kathana* (or 'repeating all the time'). Here, the word *vidheya* was used for something that is yet unknown, whereas *anuvaada* was that which crossed the realm of unknown to known. This position was also independently taken in a religious text, *Ekaadashii-tattva*, where statements such as the following are made: *anuvaadamanuktvaa tu na vidheyam udiirayet*. The word *anuvaada* is at times interpreted as 'saying the opposite' (as in CanDiidaasa or even in Jnaanadaasa). Not surprsing that the same technical word also means 'opposite'.

Accordingly, we could classify translation into three different types: (i) *anukathana*, or imitation where the original text is followed quite closely, and is rendered into the target language text, word-for-word

(ii) *punarkathana*, or 'paraphrasing' where the meaning is accepted as an invariant and accordingly a text is transferred into another language, by meaning transference, and (iii) *adhikathana*, or complete rendition of the source text where adherence to the semantics of the original, or its structure, is not essential. When Popovič, in his *Dictionary for the Analysis of Literary Translation* (1976), talks about five kinds of *shifts* in translation, similar things were covered, except that there were add-ons, especially the *constitutive* shift where the differences in the two texts are traceable to the structural differences between two languages, and the *generic* shift where genre changes or changes in trends influence translations. The *individual* shift in his scheme covered the grounds touched upon by both imitation and paraphrasing, whereas his *topical* shift takes care of the cases that come under metaphrasing. His *negative* shift, of course, takes care of all misadventures in translating particular texts or parts thereof. But whatever typology we may float to describe the nature of this activity, our aesthetics of translation will derive from our language, and from our understanding of the language. It is only rarely that authors make a conscious attempt to de-contextualize their poetic texts. Some even go to the extreme of internationalizing their allusions as in this Assamese text in translation:

Wherever you
Sigh
There grows
My
Sal tree of
promise.
Wherever
You feel helpless
You will find
My voice —
'I am there'.
Disshang
Rhine
Mississippi
Thames
Everywhere
You will find me

(from Bordoloi, 'I Am There', tr. in Sarma 1984)

AESTHETICS OF TRANSLATION

More often than not, we understand our own creative urge in terms of images that derive from such an aesthetics. Take for instance, the use of an interesting image by Roland Barthes (1978) from the life around us to explain the nature of understanding texts. He says that ideas cleave and cohere to the body of language like a 'leech' does (cf. Barthes 1986: 352–54). In the process of 'de-leeching' of texts, in order to be able to transcreate in the contemporary Indian languages, we also come to know in detail about the crises of our time in literature. It is now evident that if one has to try and build a theory of aesthetics of translation that is relevant for transcreators in Indian languages, it can derive only from our categorization of languages. In other words, I would claim that our understanding of texts which is important for our decision on interpretation and translation of these texts depends heavily on our identification of images depicted in the text. It is not surprising that a linguist looking at texts is likely to look at them in terms of the images he has received from the legacy of grammar. Similarly, a creative person will view the same text differently.

In fact, one can extend this position further and say that 'our aesthetics will derive from the canon of our worldview', which in turn, is 'determined by our own languages' (Singh 1990). If we argue that our languages and cultures (stated in plural because more often than not an oriental person is split between at least two cultures and almost surely two languages) constrain our perception as well as are constrained by it, building a 'standard' critical theory can only be viewed sceptically as a new way of establishing hegemony.

In fact, if we are to believe that 'there is no magic land of meaning outside human consciousness' following semanticists like E. D. Hirsch (1967), it will follow from there that all attempts at building a monolithic critical discourse are to be viewed as attempts to level up this magic land of meaning by obfuscating all uneven terrain and by precluding any future corruption of space. Cognitive psychologists like Edmund Hussler would even go one step further and state that 'meaning' may be conceived as a self-identical schema whose boundaries are determined by an originating speech event, while 'significance' may be conceived as a relationship drawn between that self-identical meaning and something, anything, else. Compare this position with Barthian idea of signification which argues that ideas cleave and cohere to the body of text like a leech does and that 'criticism' is a system of demystification or de-leeching language. Also, in Rosenblatt's (1984: 123–28) view, poetry is defined as an event of reading poems (i.e. poetry 'happens' only when one 'reads' poems). The claim is that literature is that thing which a reader discovers in a text.

TRANSLATION AS LITERATURE THREE

Here I would suggest that we view translated texts as another kind of originals, accepting what Tirumalesh (1990) calls 'Translation as Literature Three', in addition to the indigenous literary traditions of literature one (SL) and literature two (TL). It is clear that by taking this stand, we are not suggesting that a comparison of the translated text with the original must be stopped. But it has to be realized that at times, a given translation or an 'adaptation' may achieve a rare status or a beauty that might not have been associated with the original. Or, it may gain a literary fame on its own merit. Let me give an example of a recent rendering of such quality from Bangla into English.

The following is a difficult poem I had translated from Bangla into English (published in *Indian Literature,* the journal of Sahitya Akademi), where the changes begin from the way one chooses the title to many other aspects:

> When the tamarisk called me, surprise surprise,
> Who was it that I recalled at the dead of night
> When the waves kept up their game with the shores,
> When the moon swam along and washed her hands sinuous
> And the lighthouse lit up the tumult of spring water in the sky,
> Try n' recall—was it not me who came last year,
> Placed you in my heart, and loved aloud.
> Now my room is dark—the descent of evening
> Now my day is gone in cloud after cloud after cloud
> Now it is dark as the night stands still;
> Near the shore plays water alone,
> Absent smile of yours gets into the leaves of tamarisk,
> And when the night deepens, it calls me aloud …
> 'Nirupam, O Nirupam! Nirupam!'
>
> (Singh 2006b)

The same text—*Jhaauer Daake*—in original, reads like this (in Roman transliteration):

> jhaauer Daake takhan aamaar haThaat mane paRlo kaake
> raatribelaa ...
> upakuler sange cale sroter khelaa
> saa~taar kaaTe sroter jale caa~der naram dukhaani haat
> *lighthouse* dekhaay aalo duur gaganer jala-prapaat
> gata bachar esechilaam, buker bhitar besechilaam
> tomaay bhaalo
> ekhan sandhyaa hayeche ghar,
> kebal meghe, meghe, meghei din phuraalo...
> ekhan nithar raatribelaa
> jaler dhaare kebali hoy jaler khelaa,
> abartamaan tomaar haashi jhaauer phaa~ke
> aamaay gabhiir raatri Daake, ...
> o nirupam, o nirupam, o nirupam!

As one would notice, there could obviously be many ways of rendering the text into English. The original title of the Shakti Chattopadhyay poem was *Jhaauer Daake* in Bangla, which literally means, 'At the Call of the Tamarisks'. The choice before me was to opt for a slightly modified tag such as 'When the Trees Call!' or something similar, but I went for the actual call of the tree, rather than the description in the third person, and the result can be easily seen. Further, if one were to render the first two lines of the original differently and literally, they would read as: 'When the tamarisks called, I don't know who I remembered that night...' In contrast, what we see in the English version is the foregrounding of time in the second line. '*raatribelaa*' ('lit at night') in the Bangla original is missing but there are gains in the overall structure of the lines and concepts, with some interpolations (such as 'dead of night'): 'When the tamarisk called me, surprise surprise/Who was it that I recalled at the dead of night...'

One could argue that the lines such as '*upakuler sange cale sroter khelaa*', by virtue of use of a simple present expression by the original poet, we get an impression of timelessness of this game between the 'waves' and the 'shores'. But this was not going to be a strong point of the text in translation, because here the iteration and universality are attempted to be captured by structured and layered wh-clauses. Thus, this line, which literally means, 'The waves keep playing games with the shores', was transformed into: 'When the waves kept up their game with the shores ...' This happens not as a chance but as a result of the syntactic commitments the translator makes in the English rendering (which we underscore here):

> <u>When</u> the tamarisk called me, surprise surprise,
> <u>Who</u> was it that I recalled at the dead of night
> <u>When</u> the waves kept up their game with the shores,
> <u>When</u> the moon swam along and ...

One could go on endlessly on these two texts. Lines like the following would perhaps make the most proficient translator think for a long time on how to handle them: '*gata bachar esechilaam, buker bhitar besechilaam/tomaay bhaalo.*' Once again 'love' is foregrounded by a twisted syntax, where the complex verb '*bhaalobesechilaam*' is fragmented and sent to another line with the second person pronoun. It is clear that this facility of syntactic violation is absent in English, and hence one has to tackle the concepts with a novel set of lines, with unavoidable deviations: 'Try 'n recall—was it not me who came last year/Placed you in my heart, and loved aloud.'

Alternatively, two such texts—one original, and the other, its translation or transcreation—may both achieve such feat for entirely different reasons. If this is so, this phenomenon calls for our serious attention, because there is something to learn for prospective translators from these instances.

Let me give another concrete example here. Here is a Ghalib text with an overall translation as well as a transcreated version.

> vah firaaq aur vo misaal kahaa~?
> vo shaabo rozo ma husaal kahaa~?
> fursate kaarobaar-e shaokh kise
> zao ke nazaara jamaal kahaa~?
>
> thii vo ek shaks ke tasavvur se
> ab vo raaNaa ye xayaal kahaa~?
>
> aisaa aasaa~ nahii~ lahuu ronaa
> dil me taaqat jigar me~ haal kahaa~?
>
> mujamhil ho gaye ko vaa Gaalib
> vo anaasir me~ etadaal kahaa~?

Compare and evaluate the three versions and what I have stated earlier will become obvious, as each of the two transcreations not only become important renderings of Ghalib but go beyond that. They are 'literature three' in their own right. I shall first give the overall translation based on the principles of 'glossing':

VERSION 1 (Closer to text—overall)

Where are (no more) those meetings, those separations!
No more those days and nights, months and years!

Who has the leisure to indulge in matters of love!
No more is the delight of beholding the beautiful things!

It was from the imagination/vision of someone;
No more is the youth/grace of thought now!

Weeping (tears of) blood is not so easy;
No more strength in this heart, stability in our condition!

Ghalib! My limbs are now feeble;
No more is any balance/temperance/equilibrium in the elements!
(Ahmad 1971; Ghazal XII: 62)

VERSION 2 (Transcreation)

No more those meetings, partings, tears!
No more those days, nights, months, and years!
Who has time for love, its lore?
Delight in beauty? - now no more.

All that was from the thought of someone,
a grace that's taken, now long gone.

Tears now hurt more, they flow deep.
Heartsick these days, it's blood we weep.
Oh, Ghalib—weak limbs, no hope, disgust:
no balance now, even in this dust.
(Translated by William Stafford in Ahmad 1971: 64)

VERSION 3 (Transcreation)

Where is now the separation,
And where the joy of union?
Whither have fled those days,
And nights and months and years?

Who has now the leisure
For the transactions of love?
Where is the former yearning
To behold the form of beauty?...

Once it was inspired
By the idea of a person;
Where is now the graceful
Charm of thought?

It is no longer easy
To shed tears of blood;
Where has the heart's strength faded,
And the steadfastness of the liver?
O Ghalib, the limbs
Of my body have become so weak;
The former balance of the elements,
Tell me—where has it vanished?

(Translated by Hussain 1977: 119)

POSITIVE ASPECTS OF DEVIATION

When we see that the early translation scholars have been concerned with 'literariness' of a given text or with 'primary' and 'secondary' sources of translation, we become aware of the assumptions they make even before they actually begin to 'appreciate' or 'analyse' a literary text in translation. In reading and understanding a literary text in translation, we cannot afford to repeat their mistake. But we still have to decide on our goal. If our goal is to achieve a new theory of literary appreciation based on both original writing and translated literature, it has to be a theory that can hopefully accept both kinds of 'creativity' as its initial input or data.

NO APOLOGIES FOR MANIPULATION

The first question that comes to one's mind is: should translators be apologetic about the changes and deviations they have to opt for? As we see in real-life situations, some are themselves visibly upset with their own recreations or re-writings, while there are others such as Fitzgerald (as dicussed in Chapter 5), who give the impression that they take it upon themselves as their divine duty to 'improve' upon the original.

Susan Bassnett-McGuire and André Lefèvre (1993: ix), in their preface to Edwin Gentzler's (1993) *Contemporary Translation Theory*, write to reassure those engaged in literary translation activity that although deviation is an inevitability, it can also lead to literary innovations in its own right:

> Translation is, of course, a rewriting of an original text. All rewritings, whatever their intention, reflect a certain ideology and a poetics and as such manipulate literature to function in a given society in a given way. Rewriting is manipulation, undertaken in the service of power, and in its positive aspect can help in the evolution of a literature and a society. Rewritings can introduce new concepts, new genres, new devices, and the history of translation studies is the history also of literary innovation, of the shaping power of one culture over another.

There are times when an original genius accepts, quite voluntarily, a 'subordinate' role in accepting the responsibilities of transposing and creatively presenting an original author in his or her language.

In the following section, we deal with important questions on changes, manipulations and modifications in translated texts. In particular, we will see how deviation can become a tool for understanding the inner meaning of a text.

THE TEXT AND THE WORK: SCRIPTIBLE VERSUS LISIBLE

Let us begin our discussion on deviation and transcreativity by taking a second look at the example given in the earlier section. Consider different transcreations of the Ghalib text already quoted earlier. If we compare William Stafford's rendering with the following two translations, it will be obvious that they are not of the same merit:

> VERSION 4 (Transcreation)
>
> Gone are those meetings, these separations!
> Those days and nights, months and years!
>
> Who has time for dwelling on love!
> Gone is the pleasure of looking at beautiful things!
>
> It seems like a dream of another life.
> Gone are those youthful turns of thought!
>
> Gone are the tears of blood that used to come easy!

The heart is weak; the world cannot be trusted.

Ghalib! Your limbs have become feeble;
Gone is any justice in the scheme of things.
(Translated by Mark Strand in Ahmad 1971: 65)

VERSION 5 (Transcreation)
All those meetings and partings!
Days, nights, months, years gone!

Falling in love takes time;
So enough of desiring and gazing.

It all took a certain force of vision
and the youth of the mind is over.

Shedding tears of blood is no game,
A strong heart, a steady nerve, are wanted.

I'am too old for an inner wildness, Ghalib,
when the violence of the world is all around me.
(Translated by Adrienne Rich in Ahmad 1971: 63)

Some structuralists interpret the reading of a literary text as a productive and creative activity. Rather than viewing the reader of a text at the end of the line, waiting to 'receive' a text or a work and 'receive from' it pleasure, pain, fun, directions, advice or even responses to questions that she always wanted to ask but dared not ask, the reader is viewed as reading to produce 'interpretations', to create histories, ideas, mores, sciences and systems that are as valuable as the text itself. A reader always rewrites the texts, and she comes back to do so again and again, because every time she writes it, the text appears ever more 'writable'. She does so because she is able to mimic the creative process that was the cause of the writing of this given text in the first place, without worrying about the accuracy or otherwise of the reproduction or rewriting. Thus, texts are scriptible by definition. Notice that here the reverberations available in a text are more important than the thing itself, as Mallarme had put it long ago.

In comparison, works are extremely 'readable' objects which are not written again and again. They are only to be read and enjoyed. They are only to be consumed, as it were. Words in these works move from a definite point to another definite or 'appointed' end, and hence they captivate the readers. That means that all literary works of certain standard or value are extremely 'lisible', but rarely 'scriptible'.

Obviously, another important point of difference between the text and the work is that the latter fades more rapidly than the former. The text lives through different ages and generations and gets manifested through works of different authors, merged with different philosophies and outlooks, and, at times, even written in different languages. The RaamaayaNa text provides one of the best examples of this. All the works that are a kind of response to the text of the Raama–Siitaa or the Raama–RaavaNa story written in Awadhi, Bangla, Maithili, Telugu, Tamil, and a host of other languages, including languages used outside India (e.g., Thai) are works as well as different readings of the same text. Just as these can be interpreted in one sense as translations or as 'transcreations', in another sense they have provided us with a kind of creative response from readers with extraordinary literary skills (such as Tulasidaasa, Krttibaasa, Kamban, etc.).

It is important for us to understand in what way the literary translators are capable of positively contributing to literary appreciation and criticism, sometimes more than the monolingual conventional critic. More often than not, the typical critical analysts believe in a set of moral and formal values of the texts and works to be interpreted, values that are supposedly 'eternal'. In contrast, the translator, in trying to go through the twin processes of 'comprehension' and 'formulation', first tries to find out—not about the morality or the formal structure of the text—but about a series of wh-questions on its origin, function, and future. In particular, she would like to know: who wrote the text and under what socio-political conditions; who were and are its readers and what were their social compositions; and at which point of time the text emerged. Second, a typical critic will look for a holistic meaning in a text, that is, look for 'the' meaning, not caring to appreciate that language (and consequently, literature, too) is essentially ambiguous.

Next, although critics may consider the search for alternative meanings or supplementary meanings futile, or although they may, at the most, restrict themselves to only a few apparently legible interpretations self-evident from several cues that the author may have provided, the literary translators are not bound by any of these guileless and simplistic interpretations. This is because they are not only interpreting the original text, they are reading it to re-read and re-create. They are finding meanings in a text in relation to the world of meaning of the target language semantics as well as in terms of its possible readings (which each one of them thinks is possible) in the source culture and community.

Further, since ten different translators are likely to give ten different translations, based on many differing interpretations, this appreciation of ambiguity is ingrained in the approach of a literary translator. In fact, it is now increasingly realized that one can interpret a literary text only if one dares to attempt to render it—interlingually, inter-semiotically or even intra-lingually, although the third approach is usually uninstantiated. Some of the best critiques of a literary text have come from their cinematic renderings (hence, inter-semiotically).

VIEWING TRANSLATION AS AN ACTIVITY

Consider, for example, the most widely known definition of translation by Catford (1965:20): 'Translation is the replacement of textual material in one language (SL) by equivalent textual material in another language (TL)'. In the above definition, certain defining concepts have been assumed. For instance, the terms 'textual material' and 'equivalent' are not elaborated. Here, the term 'textual material' is expected to refer to both linguistic and non-linguistic properties of the SLT or the source language text, viz. theme, sense, socio-cultural factors, and economic background. The term 'equivalent' here assumes that TLT would convey almost the same meaning as that in SLT. But if 'replacement' is indeed a key concept in translations of all kinds, it has to be elaborated. One can probably conjecture that while translating, replacement by an equivalent material takes place at three levels: lexical, grammatical and semantico-pragmatic levels.

1. At the lexical level, whatever may be considered to be the equivalent material or element may theoretically be a complete or a partial replacement. Given a choice, a translator would prefer to observe an economy of expression and opt for one lexical item in TL for a single item in SL, ideally with broadly overlapping semantic range of at least principal meanings.
2. At the grammatical level, equivalent expression may be similar or dissimilar in terms of syntactic structure and word order.

Replacement by a similar (or exact in some cases) grammatical equivalent means following the SL grammatical pattern in the TL text, ignoring the actual differences that may be there between the two languages in allowing this pattern to be available or reasonably frequent in the TL. An ideal replacement at the grammatical level may involve the use of an available grammatical pattern in TL which has the same or similar range of grammatical functions. A change of word order in the TL may create a problem of acceptability in certain cases.

3. At the semantico-pragmatic level, replacement by an equivalent expression may refer to exact sense surrogation, which will make it a denotative equivalent, or to attainment of the closest possible sense of the SLT, which will make it a suggestive equivalent. Here, a translator sometimes may not give primacy to retaining or recreating the linguistic features but may instead concentrate on preserving the sense of the SLT into the TLT explicitly. A standard or an ideal translation is an outcome of a balance maintained between the two.

One is not always creative in finding the three kinds of equivalents given above. Consider the following non-literary prose-text with two translated versions. If we compare them and critically evaluate, we will find that none of these attempts has been very imaginative or creative, although they are somehow able to convey the general sense of the original, which—although it is a journalistic text—is a well-written piece:

ORIGINAL TEXT: 'THE DISINTEGRATION OF THE JANATA DAL (JD)'

Sri V. P. Singh can draw only small comfort from the fact that the denouement in Lucknow of the War of Attrition between his faction and that of Mr Ajit Singh has gone in his favour. The Janata Dal is dying. The recognition given by the Speaker of the Uttar Pradesh Assembly to both the factions as separate Dal groups formalizes the schism in the party's most critical bastion. It is only a matter of time before the impact of the breach in Lucknow seeps into the parliamentary party.

TRANSLATOR A'S VERSION

shrii V. P. sinh is tathya se thoRii raahat anubhav kar sakate hai~ ki Lakhanauu me~ unake guT tathaa Ajit sinh ke guT ke biic calanevaale sangharS kaa faisalaa antataH unake pakS me~ huaa hai. Janataa dal naSTa ho rahaa hai. Uttar Pradesh vidhaan sabhaa ke adhyakS dvaaraa dono guT ko prthak dal ke ruup me~ maanyataa dene se dal ke sabase mahatvapuurN gaRh me~ usakaa aupacaarik vicched ho gayaa. Lakhanauu me~ dal ke is vicched kaa prabhaav der aber sansadiiya dal par paRanaa hii hai. Lakhanauu me~ shakti pariikSaN me~ shri Ajit sinh Janataa dal ke un vidhaansabhaa sadasyo~ se burii tarah paraajit hue.

TRANSLATOR B'S VERSION

shrii V. P. sinh aur shrii Ajit sinh ke biic hue sangharS par Lakhanauu me~ hue vaad vivaad kaa pariNaam yah huaa kii V. P. sinh kaa palaRaa bhaarii rahaa. srii V. P. sinh ke pakS me~ rahaa. Janataa dal kaa patan ho rahaa hai. Uttar Pradesh sabhaa adhyakSo~ dvaaraa dono~ pakSo~ ko alag-alag dalo~ ke ruup me~ dii gaii maanyataa hii dal ke sabase sankaTaapanna durga kaa vighaTan hai. Lakhanauu me~ is pariNaam ke prabhaav kaa sansadiiya paarTii par paRanaa samay kii baat hai.

Translation as an activity is an attempt to replace, rewrite or recreate a message or a text of a given SL into a TL. Obviously, it involves taking decisions on a number of alternatives to reach the ideal goal of 're-creation' of the appropriate equivalent of a given text. Moreover, it will require one to explore the appropriate use of linguistic and non-linguistic information as given and implied in the SL text or about the text, depending on the conditions, environment, and language(s) used in a given instance. Therefore, the decisions on alternatives should be taken carefully. In this respect, the activities of the translator can be classified into two types of actions : the source-oriented-activity (SOA) and the target-oriented-activity (TOA). SOA gives an account of the task of the translator as a member of the community of SL speakers/readers. They are expected to demonstrate their understanding of the SL text which they may choose to interpret either in SL or in TL, or merely render into TL or paraphrase it in SL. Broadly, the SOA component revolves around the tasks of reading, comprehension, and interpretation. TOA is an outcome of the SOA related to the drafting of original thought in TL. It is thus an activity of thought-representation carried out with critical appreciation and self-reliance. Here the translator has to update his knowledge that enables him to preserve the ideal target of re-expression. It is actually a writing-based activity. Obviously, it assumes one's competence in the TL with respect to various types of expressions, styles and registers.

An ideal translator will not only worry about proper expressions in TL, she will also have to see that the way she has created/drafted/written the TLT makes its meaning coherent. For achieving this goal, the translator will have to take a number of crucial steps that are enlisted here:

1) identification and clarification of the original theme;
2) selection of an appropriate language structure and language use according to the context;
3) precision in utilizing the non-linguistic factors such as socio-cultural background and pragmatic values; and
4) intelligible reproduction of the fullest possible 'signifi' or sense structure in TL.

Since translation deals with the formal replacements of structures from SL to TL, the replacement does not only mean physical replacement of graphic form (by transliteration to various other strategies including various types of borrowings) but also of some supra-graphic features, i.e. the social, economical, cultural, and political information either demonstrably loaded in or clearly implied through the text. In this respect, too, translation becomes a multi-dimensional art. It varies according to (*a*) the quality of text, (*b*) its function, (*c*) its coverage of the subject-matter, and (*d*) the degree of perfection required to maintain a balance in the act of finding ideal 'replacements'. A translator is then a multifaceted genius, not only saddled with the difficult task of large-scale substitution, but also playing the roles of a mediator, reader, thinker, evaluator, intrepreter, as well as a recreator of a creative process.

AESTHETICS OF TRANSCREATION VIEWED LINGUISTICALLY

We have already mentioned that a linguist will be looking at a literary text differently from a creative writer. The question is whether in terms of the images he has received from the legacy of grammar, one can indeed consider a literary text profitably. The answer is an overwhelming 'yes'. But we must remember that this is not the only point of view.

We know that a linguist categorizes his segments or his data in terms of certain broad categories, such as noun, pronoun, verb, adjective or adverb, etc. Accordingly, he can also read a nominal imagery in a literary text as an interpreter, although the original author may not have done this consciously.

NOMINAL IMAGERY

To take a concrete example of a nominal imagery, let us take a text or two in both original and translation versions. That is how one explains the use of images based on 'sentential construction' and 'discourse semantics':

TEXT A

kathaaraa chinnabhinna haye aache
ki aar balbe
haavaay duuSaN anugandha
baakye duuSaN
baakya bhiiSaN jaRa haye jaay
jaRajaiba haye mare
ekhan maRak kathaar maRak calche ekhan
ebang pacan jeman dhaarer sangskrti.
ki aar balbe
kathaa sab jena kata kaal aage balaa haye geche
kSiiN kathaa praaN
phuTe oTho baak
bishaal sphoTan bhaabchi aami.
('Kathaa', Sen 1988: 16)

TRANSLATION A

Discourses tear asunder
What shall they speak
Air pollutes smells of atoms
Sentences infected
Sentences get terribly stiffened
Die stillborn grisly
Now is a drought—epidemic of words now
And putrid becomes the borrowed culture.

What will they speak
Words galore have already been said long ago
Slender life and words
Ascend O Vak
I cerebrate a large 'plosion.
(Author's translation)

The poet finds his space, his private world polluted, so much so that his sentences are now born crippled. The existing ones get stifled. The forthcoming ones die a repulsive death. The piece is a part of Anjan's larger text in Bengali: '*Tin bishve din raatri*' ('Days and Nights in the Three Worlds'; also see Singh 1989c), and has to be read closely with transcreation of his another piece, called 'AakaraN' ('The Structure') as given here:

Text B	Translation B
bhese uThche samasta kaal	Time eternal emanates
sakal ebang sarba	All and entire time
bhese uThche aadim astra	The ancient arms too appear
jibaashma aar pratna	Fossils and antiquaria
aakaar nicche barnaguli	The letters are taking shape
shabdamaalaar paak	In the cauldron of lexis
aakaar nicche agnikanaa	The fireballs are shaping up
ebang taahaar jvaalaa	And their blaze
janma nicche rupakalpa	Metaphors in the making
ekTi shishu aakaar nicche	A child is taking shape
samasta kaal kholaa	All times are open
maraa gaange mrter bhaasaan	Immersion of the corpse in the dead river
kSiiN Taaner bhaaSaa	Drifting through sluggishly
janma ebang mrtyumaalaa	The alphabet of birth and death

('AakaraN', Sen 1988: 15, author's translation)

The text 'AakaraN' is a history of sentential construction and creation of 'sign'. The earlier text, 'Kathaa', seems to be showing the degeneration and decadence of the 'sentence'. Let me borrow the words of Malcom Bradbury (1983: 151–52) to describe the degeneration that the poet talks about, where, it seems that the 'conditions of crisis are evident: language awry, cultural cohesion lost, perception pluralized'.

OTHER IMAGERIES

Language can, of course, also act as a pronominal in the vernacular of imagery and be viewed (Barthes 1978) as a field of *pomme frites* (French fries) on a frying pan. I would like to call this Barthian imagery pronominal because here 'language' stands only as an object which is not the real thing but without which nothing real or substantial can be stated.

Now, let us begin using the qualifying words or adjectivals in characterizing 'language'. Like the duality of patterning that characterizes human language, 'image' is also subjected to another kind of duality which has been called the dynamics of 'reverberation' as against the energetics of 'causality' (cf. Minkowski in Bachelard 1958: xii). The poetic image has the quality of 'transsubjectivity', even when it shows variations as against the other concepts that are constitutive and which are, therefore, open to causal relationship. A poet creates his own language, and even when 'the poet does not confer the past of his image upon ... [us], yet his image immediately takes root in ... [us]' (Bachelard 1958[1964]: xii). At the level of 'reverberations' then, a poem possesses us entirely. Knowing that the image in the text has been given by another person, the image that we as readers derive makes us feel so involved with the text that we begin to feel that we could have created it. The twists and the turns that we, enliving such texts, give in speaking, repeating, singing or enacting the oral poetry derive precisely from this confidence that the poem has become 'really our own'.

The question is what the creative writer does with language in order to actuate such images or such qualities. One idea seems to be that she distorts the world of words, corrupts vocabularies, cripples the syntactic norms of the canonical language, and introduces an unprecedented grammatical violence. She bends and mends language to accommodate the images. And the task of the translator is to transfer this violence into another community, into another language. To the extent that this is true, the literary interpreter and the translator as the 'subjects' of the given texts begin to qualify and quantify their dual 'objects'—the direct (text) as well as the indirect (SL or TL reader).

Let us now move on to yet another kind of imagery. In order to contextualize our translator/interpreter, or to take an adverbial approach, one must appreciate that the source and target texts quite often refer to completely or substantially different space and time or that the encoder is 'manipulating' the message form to achieve a certain kind of unreadability/incomprehensibility. In such cases, it becomes crucial for us to know the where, when and how of the given text. In particular, we must know whether the manipulation was done because the author wanted to write in a private language and wished to be unreadable or because the cultural differences between the two times, two cultures or communities is such that author now seems to be unreadable. As I have shown elsewhere (cf. Singh 1990), the translator has to know the answer to such questions if she has to chalk out his strategy of dealing with a particular text. Surely, it is not the language that becomes unreadable (or unspeakable); it is either the ideas put in certain adverbial domain or the 'ideators' (a neologism) who lived and wrote in a particular condition that might be responsible for this 'mysticism'.

THE NATURE OF CREATIVITY

Given this position from which an integrated view on aesthetics is born, it should not be surprising that in the subsequent parts, I shall view transcreation in a broad manner. Translation for me and to many like myself would be transference of form and function from one code to another. In this chapter, therefore, the aim will be to draw certain generalizations on the nature of creativity that would be true for different kinds of transferences, and which would qualify to be described as a transcreation.

The first problem we face is the problem of innovation. At the outset it must be noted that innovations as such do not have to do only with translation, but with creative writing, too, because innovations result from the creative urge of the innovator and from social and intellectual necessity. It is used as a recourse or a way out, when one faces problems of lexical choice or word combination in the absence of particular form or content, or when one wants to create an entirely novel concept by giving it a new name or expression. A translation is usually more likely to favour a semantic extension of an existent form, rather than opting for a neologism.

At the same time, we may be dealing with a text where there are already lots of new coinages. A translator in this case cannot shut his eyes to these. If he too decides to bring in new words and expressions either by creating or by promoting an element from a sub-language, or by naturalizing a borrowed expression, we must look at it as a part of legitimate translation activity which, in effect, may bring the TL and the SL closer to each other in terms of their structure.

Languages vary in terms of the extent they can assimilate innovations. There can be languages that resist borrowing on a large scale. The reasons for this resistance could be many: language pride resulting in a superiority complex, constraint coming from the way the cultural institutions are organized in the society (i.e., the ratio of indigenousness and borrowing), a false desire to retain 'purity' of one's language, or even a myth which does not allow one to fill one's world with words which are all supposed to be divine creation, etc.

Again there may be differences between the degrees of allowance that the society gives the translators. That is, it is possible that the society at large allows the translators to innovate (because otherwise a transfer of knowledge would be impossible), while it may not encourage its creative writers to do this in a big way. Thus, innovation can either be a tool or a technique a translator uses, or it can be an activity restricted to original writing where it is viewed as permissible only in the expressive function of the language.

Now there is a limit up to which this proximity can be achieved. Ideally, no two languages or cultures would either like to be the same or tolerate an extreme convergence. There is thus a kind of compromise that is brought about by the translator between the SL and the TL, and this leads us to the next point, viz., that the translator also brings about a compromise between overtranslation and undertranslation by innovating. The innovation may range from a complete novelty to simple transpositions or borrowings. Innovation thus may not always mean creation of new lexical items or novel constructions.

In this context one has to agree with Hartmann's remarks:

> the trouble is that translation theorists have not managed so far to explain what motivates the choice and appropriateness of

> particular interlingual equivalence, and whether (and how) the directionality of the process might be crucial to its success. In any case, translator and interpreter training practice seems to proceed without much reference to an explicit set of principles derived either from an adequate theory or from empirical data (1990: 47).

CONCLUSION

Most people have some misgivings about translation. Some identify it only as a classroom exercise. Some others find it merely as a tool used to introduce popular literature of an alien language into one's own language. Some will of course take it as a means to convert certain legal and governmental documents into other languages in a more or less routine manner. It is yet to be realized by many that translation is no longer a hit-or-miss pursuit, that it is an equally creative and dynamic activity in every respect, and that it gives us an entirely new perspective in creating a theory and aesthetics of interpretation.

8

AIMS AND OBJECTIVES

THE PRESENT CHAPTER is a modest contribution to mutual illuminations where a theory of literary translation draws from an otherwise unutilized repository of knowledge that goes by the name of common sense. It aims at understanding the nature of intralingual translation of texts. As a literary critic and teacher of literature, one is used to paraphrasing, but there is hardly any literature available on its methods, conditions, constraints, and its place in the politics of creating literary styles and linguistically standardized forms of expression. At the same time, it is a well-known fact that all practising translators derive help from basic conversational strategies such as 'paraphrasing', used by both monolinguals and bilinguals. Here, particular emphasis is put on paraphrasing as a strategy of literary translation, where both interlingual paraphrasing among bilinguals and paraphrasing between two or more styles and speech varieties in a monolingual situation are discussed.

PARAPHRASING AS TRANSLATION

It is often seen that an author—especially a fiction writer or a playright and sometimes ever legal luminaries—re-word the same statement by a changed set of vocables or by a modified syntax. This is something an oral interpreter—both a teacher of literature and a simultaneous translator—must learn to master. This is because quite often in the course of quick-speed translation, his or her break-neck attempt to transfer dialogues or texts carry over the same SL syntactic structure, making it difficult, if not impossible, for the readers/viewers/authority or the person employing/using the interpreter to grasp what was said. An immediate paraphrasing can save the situation.

Translation as paraphrasing is very different from translation as a plain interlingual transfer in many ways. While interlingual rendering is a product of history (Lilova 1993: 6), and is constrained by the politics of a given period, paraphrasing is a response to one's requirement at a particular point of time. At a given moment, when your interlocutor (or, the person you are engaged with in conversation) is unable to follow you or is unable to get the full import of your statement, you cannot but try to say the same thing 'in other words', which is what 'paraphrasing' is. Let us consider a few texts of both types to instantiate the two kinds of activity—paraphrasing and translation on the one hand, and inter- and intra-lingual paraphrasing on the other.

Consider first a case of intralingual paraphrasing where we begin with a text which is itself an extremely readable and admirable translation of a Bangla text into English, where the translator had to take certain liberties but which still captured the mood of the original:

TEXT 1A: COME RAIN, COME!

There's the cluster of flowers on the face
And the whirling fiery steam all around.
Such a chilly stream those flowers are
Such brimming ripples,
The train of words floating in the sky
And getting withered in the wind,
Now the terminal honour,
Come rain, come!

(Mitra 1990)

Now, suppose if the text in translation has to be rephrased so much so that it eventually becomes a different version of the SL original, but not necessarily as a direct translation from Bangla. Suppose if all this is achieved through paraphrasing of its English version, how does one react to it? So that this discussion does not remain a hypothetical proposition, in what follows, an attempt at paraphrasing Text 1A has been made by this author:

TEXT 1B: SHOWER O RAIN, BESHOWER!

The array of corsage on the face of flowers—
the purl and spin of flaming virility.
What a nippy tide you are, my flowers
and your brimming burbles!
A string of words gliding in the sky
and getting shrivelled in the squall.
Here's my last salute,
Shower O rain, beshower!

Now, we could look into an inter-lingual paraphrasing, where a conscious attempt has been made to use the strategies available in the TL tradition (English in this case) to render a poetic text of Bhartrhari from an unrelated language (Sanskrit). Consider the following example from Merwin and Moussaieff Masson's (1981: 89) anthology of ancient Indian love-poems, 'The Peacock's Egg':

TEXT 2A: THE ORIGINAL (SANSKRIT)
nabhasi jaladalakSmiim saasrya viikSya drSTyaa
pravasasi yadi kaantey ardham uktvaa kathamcit
mama paTam avalambya prollikhanti dharitriim
yad anukrtavatii saa tatra vaaco nivrttaaH!

TEXT 2B: TRANSLATION
Lush clouds in
dark sky of tears she saw my love
if you leave me now she
said and could not say more
twisting my shirt
toe gripping dust
after that what she
did all words
are helpless to repeat and
they know it and give up

If we have to paraphrase this particular literary text, where we have the authoritative original tagged to it, we have the advantage of re-creating which could do one up on what is regarded until now as an excellent interlingual paraphrase. Here is the version I have come up with, and it goes without saying that there is scope to improve it further:

> Lusty clouds in the dim colours of sky
> make her see 'My love!', she says in sigh,
> 'If you went at once', can't say more,
> coils and curls my shirt writes on floor
> with her toe on dust and what she must
> have done afterwards you know, I trust
> words are scanty skimpy mirror on the sly;
> Lusty clouds in the dim colours of sky!
> (Paraphrased by the author)

It is obviously a very difficult task for any translator to do justice to these Sanskrit lines in a linguistically distant tongue. It may also be difficult for the TL readers to appreciate the sentiments as well as the musicality of the original. This could be because of various reasons. The huge difference between the way the man–woman relationship unfolds in the ancient Indian culture and the way it works in the West is surely one of them. But a larger share of the blame has to be borne by the translators who adopt a particular strategy in attempting to render the piece in English by making several strategic changes as they paraphrased the text: (i) by altering the linearity or line divisions, (ii) by opting for an unfettered syntax, untangling oneself from the binds of metrics (iii) by taking recourse to italicization/underscoring to show the broken sentence spoken by the woman, (iv) by making readjustments in finding lexical equivalents, such as 'shirt' for 'paTam', etc.

ASSUMPTIONS

TRANSLATION AS AN EXTENSION OF SPEECH ACTIVITY

While detailing a few psychological problems in teaching the theory and practice of interpretation, Pegacheva (1959: 138) defines translation as a 'peculiar instance of speech activity in course of which a number of psychological difficulties have to be overcome'. Most of us learn to get over such difficulties based on our common sense and experiences and not on any formal training. Zimnyaya (1993: 88–89) too contends that

> Translation is essentially [an] activity. My aim is to show that translation is a complex, specific, secondary type of speech activity. This statement holds good for all forms of translation ... Translation is a type of speech activity that can be studied alongside other types such as listening, speaking, reading and thinking.

All serious students of translation would notice that viewing translation as a kind of speech activity has many interesting consequences.

First, a common sense approach to translation lets us take it for granted that every native speaker of a language has an intrinsic competence in translating, just as it has been claimed that she has linguistic competence as a speaker-listener of her language. Reading and writing are acquired as secondary skills, and therefore one only 'knows' these applications of 'speech' through a conscious training, preferably through a formal method of learning. The question that arises at this point is the following: is translation comparable to secondary speech activities, or is it like a primary speech activity?

IS TRANSLATION A SECONDARY SPEECH ACTIVITY?

If it is like reading and writing, it must be an acquired craft. If it is not, it must be something that one learns unconsciously. We would like to claim that all native speakers constantly paraphrase themselves or redraft their statements (potentially all statements, but practically at least some). Therefore, everybody takes recourse to intralingual translation or paraphrasing. At the same time, when we learn our mother tongue as a school subject, we have to master various extensions of both written and spoken skills that have something to do with 'paraphrasing'—letter-drafting, elaborating upon a story-line, and preparing an essay are a few of them—all of which require paraphrasing. Here, we are indeed putting our paraphrasing technique to excellent use, as we are learning to 'translate' intralingually through a formal method.

We can return to the same question raised earlier and rephrase it in the following manner: can translation be comparable to secondary speech activities or can it be a kind of primary speech activity? Our answer is that it can be both. Even when we take paraphrasing as a natural instinct which all native speakers possess, it is nevertheless a skill which needs polishing and a greater degree of perfection, which is what any formal education system does. In this sense it is equally comparable to 'speaking' which everyone knows how to do. But one will have to learn many common sense extensions of it, for example, to speak on a topic for which no planning is done (extempore speech), to present—through structured speech—arguments for or against a motion (public debate), to speak on solemn occasions ('condolence speech') or in formal meetings ('introduction', 'presidential remarks' or 'vote of thanks'), etc.

Interlingual Paraphrasing Among Bilinguals

The second consequence of viewing translation as a speech activity is that when someone is a born bilingual or when one acquires a language other than one's mother tongue, one is expected to know how to express the same feelings in different languages. There are exceptional bilinguals, however, who know how to use another tongue in limited domains, or who use two (or more) languages mostly in mutually complementary contexts. Except in such instances, a bilingual person is a 'natural' translator, too. Once again, she will have to sharpen her translation abilities if she is to qualify as a 'professional' translator. Even in this respect, translation is a kind of natural ability. Therefore, any theory of translation arising out of a multilingual and multi-literary Third World context must take paraphrasing seriously.

Paraphrasing Between Speech Varieties and Styles

The third consequence is that a large number of speakers in each community is born to speak a particular speech variety, which in their later life may be used mostly at home and in the family domains, i.e. in a limited circle; whereas what is used in most other contexts (both spoken and written) is the standard speech variety. Obviously, the nature and quality of this standard will differ from person to person, although ideally it should not. The fluctuation or variation will also depend on one's dialectal or sociolectal background. There are cases when one thinks and dreams in a non-standard speech variety and gives one's thoughts and dreams words in the spoken standard, thus adopting a strategy of paraphrasing intralingually almost simultaneously.

TRANSLATIONAL CRITERIA

TOTAL AND PARTIAL TRANSLATION

It is in this context that we can appreciate the definition of 'translation' given by Crystal (1987: 344) who views it as a 'natural term used for all tasks where the meaning of expressions in one language (the 'source' language) is turned into the meaning of another (the 'target' language), whether the medium is spoken, written or signed'. The main question is whether this task involves what some people call 'total translation'. Catford (1965: 21) regards the latter term as misleading, for total translation involves a complete replacement of SL grammar and lexis. Consequently, one may even have to replace SL phonemes/graphemes by non-equivalent or not necessarily fully equivalent (or say, 'comparable') TL phonemes/graphemes.

Compare this with 'partial translation' where some parts of the SL text are left untranslated: they are simply transferred and incorporated into the TL text. In the latter case, even if an equivalent emerges at all or is found or created, they are either based on chance similarities or on the phenomenon of convergence. An interlingual paraphrasing will be closer to partial translation, whereas an intralingual paraphrasing has some in-built advantage of the same script and is generally similar in respect of phonological device, and at least comparable at the word level. Hence it will be closer to total translation.

RANK-BOUND AND UNBOUNDED TRANSLATION

Similarly, recall that Catford makes another kind of distinction, namely between rank-bound translation and unbounded translation. The former is one in which the selection of TL equivalents is deliberately confined to one particular rank in the hierarchy of grammatical units, while an unbounded translation is one in which equivalents shift freely up and down the rank scale. Word-for-word translation is rank-bound, which is generally considered to be bad translation. Although there can be a debate on how bad it is, and whether it is actually so bad, particularly for literary or religious texts, paraphrasing of the stricter and more conventional kind is closer to rank-bound translation. On the other hand, oral paraphrasing bordering on interpretation is closer to unbounded translation, because paucity of time or saving time is an important factor here. We know that good literary translations are something between a rank-bound translation and a free rendering (Catford 1965: 25).

COMMUNICATIVE AND SEMANTIC TRANSLATION

Newmark (1981 and 1988) had come up with an important distinction between communicative and semantic translation which too could be compared here with paraphrasing as a strategy. Let us try to understand their difference in terms of literary renderings. The most important difference between communicative and semantic translation of texts is that the former attaches greater importance to the performance factors such as message, receiver, utterance, etc., whereas semantic translation stresses on meaning, sender or author, or on thought processes inherent in the original text. Both interlingual and intralingual paraphrasing will have to draw equally from these two different kinds of factors because they put emphasis on the message as well as the meaning on the one hand and on both addresser and addressee, especially in an interpreter's work, on the other.

Where there is a conflict, communicative translation and interlingual paraphrasing must dwell on the 'force' rather than the content of the text. It also addresses itself completely to the TL reader, who does not anticipate difficulties or obscurities, and would expect a generous transfer of foreign elements into his own language. But in intralingual paraphrasing, like a semantic translation device, one remains within the original culture and assists the TL readers in understanding its connotations if they constitute an essentially human (non-ethnic) message of the text.

Generally, like communicative translation, paraphrasing of both kinds are likely to be smoother, simpler, clearer, more direct, and conforming to particular conventions and canons of the concerned language and literature, tending to almost undertranslate. They both contrast with semantic translation on this point as the latter strategy tends to produce a more complex, more awkward, more detailed, and probably a more faithful text. It pursues the thought processes rather than the intention of the transmitter.

These different strategies are to be taken as general guidelines. A translation can be more or less semantic, even when a particular section or sentence is treated more communicatively than semantically. It means that if a translator approaches a particular text semantically in its totality, and in doing that if some parts of a sentence or a paragraph need communicative translation, heavens will not fall. Similarly, the whole text could also be approached from both communicative and semantic points of view, to provide alternatives.

In interlingual paraphrasing and communicative translation the translator has the freedom to improve upon the flavour of the original in the TL, where he can re-create, modify, and adopt certain things to give it a near-precise flavour and tone of the original. This freedom is totally absent in semantic rendering, as the the words become 'sacred' due to the importance given to the form and content of the SL text. In the case of intralingual paraphrasing, the sacred nature of the lexis is not at play, and yet the freedom is missing here, because there are certain inherent limitations of intralingual transfer when one is confined to the same language community.

TEXTS

Having discussed various theoretical issues that help our understanding of paraphrasing, let us now consider an instance of paraphrasing of an Indian language text into English. The source language in this case is Telugu, and the text is dated several centuries ago. Consider the following where the first level of paraphrasing is provided by us through glossing word for word:

TEXT 3A: *SUMATI-SHATAKAM* (TELUGU)

aakonaa kude-yamrutamu
When hungry food-itself nectar

taakimpaka icchuvaade daataa dharitrin
without hesitation who gives donor in the world

sookoorchuvaade manasari
who tolerates hardships wise-man

teekuwa galawaade vamsatilakudu Sumatii
courage one-who-has ornament of-the-clan O Sumati.

Now, there are several versions of the text in English, including a version created by this author for the sake of paraphrasing. The first version is a prose rendering which falls in the category of plain-prose translation:

TEXT 3B: Translation 1

> To the hungry man dry bread is ambrosia. He that bestoweth without reproving is the greatest benefactor on earth. He who puts up with an attack is the sound-hearted and the man of spirit is the ornament of his race.
>
> (Brown 1842)

If we consider this text carefully, we will find a number of manipulations to suit the cultural context of the reader. Otherwise, 'dry bread' could not have been used for 'food' (of any kind), nor would the translator use the expression 'put up with an attack' for 'withstanding hardship'. Is *manasari* 'sound-hearted'? And then, where is the refrain? Consider another version, which is an attempt to retain the poetic structure:

TEXT 3C: Translation 2

> Food got in dire hunger is heavenly nectar
> donor is he who has an out-stretched arm
> only he who sustains distress is manly
> a man of valour is the jewel in the family crown.
>
> (Srinath and Subbarao 1987)

Several questions would come up the moment we put this translation to close examination: how do the translators get 'dire' and 'heavenly'? Where does the expression 'out-stretched arm' come from? Is *manasari* 'manly'? Is the phrase 'jewel in the family crown' better than C. P. Brown's 'ornament of his race' (= *vamsatilakudu*). Consider another version which is a mere paraphrase done without necessarily possessing a sound knowledge of the original language:

TEXT 3D: Translation 3

> When hungry any food is delicious.
> In charity, unsuspecting oblation makes you
> the almoner in the world.

In hardship, one who withstands
becomes the prudent—O Sumati—
One who has courage becomes the paragon of his people.
(Author's translation)

CONSEQUENCES

When we hear about 'literariness' of a given text or about 'primary' and 'secondary' sources of translation, we become aware of the assumptions that are taken for granted even before one 'appreciates' or 'analyses' a literary text in translation. In reading and understanding a literary text in translation, we have to decide on our goal. If our goal is to build a new theory of literary appreciation—based on both original writing and translated literature and drawing heavily from what is known as 'common sense' or what sometimes goes by the name 'world knowledge'—it has to be a theory that can hopefully accept both kinds of 'creativity' as its initial input or data. However, the moment we begin to read translations, particularly if we also happen to know the original, the deviations appear before us very clearly. A more thoughtful attention to these points of deviation tells us that sometimes they are unavoidable changes rooted in target language, culture or literary tradition. In some other cases, they are a part of a strategy to circumvent a virtually 'untranslatable' portion, the knowledge of which may or may not come with the brush one had had with the writings on translation theory. On other occasions, they may simply appear to be announced or undeclared subtle manipulations.

It is important for us to understand in what way literary translators are capable of positively contributing to literary appreciation and criticism, particularly from a comparative angle—sometimes more than the monolingual conventional critic. Notice that more often than not, the typical critical analysts believe in a set of moral and formal values of the texts and works to be interpreted, values that are supposedly 'eternal'. In contrast, the translator, in trying to go through the twin processes of 'comprehension' and 'formulation', tries to find out—not about the morality or the formal structure of the text—but about a series of questions about its context and about its logical structure.

Second, although critics may restrict themselves to only a few apparently legible paraphrases, or, call them 'interpretations,' self-evident from several cues that the author may have provided, the literary translators are not bound by any of these guileless and simplistic interpretations. This is because they are not only interpreting the original text, they are reading it to re-read and re-create. They find meanings in a text in relation to the world of meaning of the target language semantics as well as in terms of its possible readings (which each one of them thinks is possible) in the source culture and community.

Third, since ten different translators are likely to give ten different paraphrases, based on many differing interpretations, this appreciation of ambiguity is ingrained in the approach of a literary translator. In fact, it is now increasingly realized that one can interpret a literary text only if one attempts to paraphrase it interlingually, inter-semiotically or even intra-lingually. Obviously, some of the best critiques of literary texts in the twentieth century have come from their inter-semiotic cinematic renderings.

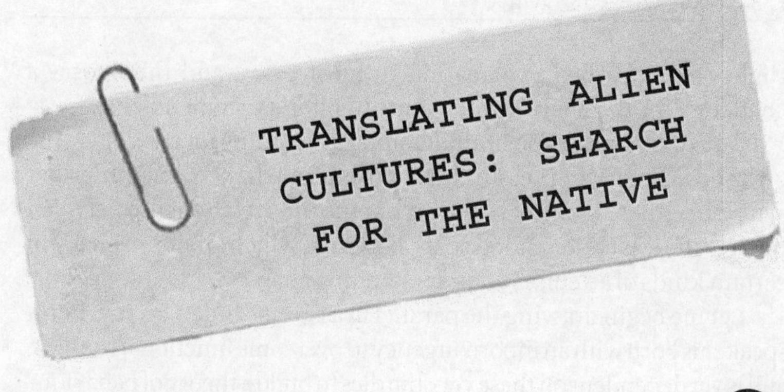

9

SPEECH AS CHAOS: TRANSLATION AS CACOPHONY

I HAVE CLAIMED EARLIER that speech has a chaotic existence, and that chaos, like speech, has a unique pattern occupying a three-dimensional space (Singh 1998). In fact, it requires three different kinds of semantics to understand them.

First of all, chaos can be understood in terms of the semantic of confusion, the universe of which ranges from a mere befuddlement to a fierce fracas. This apparent confusion can be a mix-up, malady or even an anarchy. The natural offshoot of this anarchy is disorder. This disorder can be of various kinds—personal, political, social, cultural, and even linguistic. In each case, the victim would be man and his ability to create systems.

The second semantic to understand chaos (or speech, if you may like) is that of amorphism. Under this, chaos can be understood as something that happens and evolves and, therefore, has a form and is yet a formless, indeterminate, indefinite and an obscure entity. There is obviously a contradiction here. But isn't there this contradiction in building a theory of translation, which I called an impossible nominal construct and yet a perfectly acceptable verb? Chaos, and all that goes in that class—language, image or text—thus defies form, and tries to slight rule-governed explanation in most cases, and thus poses a challenge for the analyst who wants to offer a commentary.

Third, chaos can also be understood as standing for the void—the great cosmic space, pressureless and intermediary, something that symbolizes not an object or entity, but the interrelationship between them—the least understood space between, which attains primacy in certain kinds of attempts at understanding chaos.

Let me begin drawing the parallel in a reverse order. First, when a speaker is born with an inborn urgency to overcome functional hurdles, and is yet dependent on these very hurdles to build a theory of behaviour (personal, political, social and cultural, and hence, also linguistic) and when he has the capacity to use his tool with which he may initially fumble or fiddle but not err for long—it is this intermediary space, formless and unspoilt by grammar, that he appears in. The speaker who is still a more 'potential' than a 'real' communicator, provides the much needed hiatus between one man and another who may happen to be his progenitor, between man as an individual and the society, between an organism or substance and its environs. There can be many mismatches between each of these in a given pair. For instance, members of a speech community may be divided by language, taste, character, behaviour and ethnicity, and it is the author or the translator who often negotiates between their worlds, and become the hiatus.

When we as speakers step into this world, our faculty or ability will also have a rare flexis which allows us to bend our senses in whichever way our immediate and not-so-immediate environments may require. We have got to do this every moment to understand any object—our interlocutors, our environment, and even ourselves. It is this flexibility which allows us to prevaricate, prognosticate, and interpret. Thus, although our 'interpretive competence' had not assumed any shape by then, and was, therefore, not governed by any rule or pattern, it was still not outside the realm of reason and rationality.

Furthermore, there is no doubt that much of speech is chaos in the first sense of the term anyway. Any human language or any text which defies our own logic of understanding will appear to the uninitiated as cacophony. Further, scholars have argued with conviction that human creativity knows no bounds with shape, length, organization and variety of any intellectual construct being open-ended, thus making any cataloging of permissible permutable and potential texts as an impossible task. All these go on to point out that it makes sense to talk about all semiotic constructs, including human language as having a chaotic existence. We are also told that because speech crucially depends on world knowledge, which both philosophers and psychologists as well as natural language understanding (NLU) specialists find it as the least understood phenomenon, the pragmaticians spend a long time approaching linguists with their analytical account of this chaotic universe although it is difficult to make use of their logic of common speech.

DUALITY OF PATTERNING

If chaos, and with it also speech and consequently texts, have a geometry that is not so well understood, but about which it is clear that there is both pattern and chaos inherent in them, let us see how the theoreticians try to represent speech in their characterization. The reactions of linguists who tried to understand this duality were twofold: vertical and horizontal.

For a long time, the expression 'duality of patterning' as a description of human speech has dominated the theoretical scene. However, as I see it, it has been accepted only in one sense which is basically a vertical interpretation of the concept of duality. In this sense, it is commonly understood that language is basically a layered construct which is organized in some sort of a hierarchy.

In this sense, as a construct language is viewed as having two levels of patterning, one on top of the other, the first of which is the level of words where the building blocks are units of phonation or sounds, and the other being that of sentences, where what is patterned to make them are themselves the product of the first level of patterning. This neat-looking scheme joins language analysis with the physics of speech at the first level, and the semantics of utterance in the second. Together, they present an aligned recursive picture of the process of speech construction.

The justification for viewing grammar as a multiply layered object usually derives from this vertical representation. One should not be surprised if the psychological theories claim that human beings speaking language are viewed as having layered compartments in that part of their brain which is responsible for speech production as well as comprehension. Besides one may even have to say that from a sociological point of view too, language is a layered object with a certain kind of hierarchy.

There is, however, another way in which the expression 'duality of patterning' could be understood. Take, for instance, an essay by Annamalai entitled 'Nativity of Language' (1998), which does not state about this duality in so many words, but from which one can interpret his understanding of language as a human construction only in terms of horizontal structure. Annamalai opens his piece with these words:

> Language has double existence. One is grammatical existence and the other is social. Both are not a priori existence, but they come to exist by human construction. The grammarian constructs the grammar of language, which is a manifestation of its grammatical existence. His construction of the grammar is founded on his theory of grammar. This makes the grammar a theoretical construction....

He goes on to elaborate the other pattern of language:

> The social existence of a language comes about through its social construction by the community of speakers. The social construct may be about the boundary of the language.... It may be about the norm of the language.... It may be about the propriety over language.... It may be about what the language stands for; that is, about its cultural and political symbolization.

Notice that both grammatical and social existence of language show such patterning as are beyond individuals and idiosyncrasies, because what is grammatical must also bear the stamp of social decision. In other words, language is as much general as it is specific, no matter how contradictory that may sound. It is this language which I as an author lord over, and weave my poetry, and yet it is I who must also be understandable, acceptable or readable to others of my kind. Let me elaborate this point further.

First, although Annamalai argues that as a theoretical construct, 'there can be as many grammars of language as there are theories of grammar', this potential multiplicity is applicable to any societal and intellectual construct. Further, he does not specify how different these two kinds of grammars are—those that are created as a theoretical enterprise, and those that are mental products of a large number of speakers.

Second, no theory can spring up as an arbitrary modelling device because it is usually a product of the knowledge base the society has generated and stored, and it draws heavily from this base as it undergoes testing, modification and 'patterning'. I shall go one step further and say that I tend to believe that a society gets the grammars it deserves. It also gets the theories it deserves. So watch out for the texts! In other words, what we will do about our theory-building activity in translation will depend on the kinds of texts that we create (and re-create).

Third, as a claim, 'as many individuals that many grammars' may apparently seem logical, but it is frankly a preposterous position. Can there be as many theories of a text as its interpretations? If that is so, we are only taxonomizing, and not building explanatory theories. Further, 'language' may vary from person to person, as any field investigator would easily testify; but that does not lead one to necessarily conclude that 'grammar' also varies from person to person. It does not mean either that grammar is an invariable monolithic entity.

Fourth, although Annamalai requires that speakers' mental grammars and the grammarians' theoretical grammars should ideally match, this matching is problematic as there are many versions of these constructs. Does anyone want to claim that the logical text that a translator-interpretor constructs as a proto-element, following Newmark's 1981 model of translational processes, must match the metatext that lies in either the culture, society, or any such heritage, or with the deep text that motivates an author to write a given piece? When one claims that an ideal translator should not be constrained by any of these things—author, reader, source language, target language, etc., and not even by the 'text'—how can one expect there to be such perfect matches? The answer to me seems obvious.

THE ORIGINAL TEXT AND THE METAPHORS

The history and politics of science have taught us that unbridled theoretical power always brings in unequal and hierarchical categorizations that might lead to untruth and the establishment of wrong models. And it is from here that the journey of the political construct called the 'translator-interpretor' begins. Those who played this theory-building game so far have always created a verticalis so that there is always very little space on the vertex, and most theories keep falling off the peak because they are disqualified on some count or the other.

In some recent essays on translation, Otto Ikôme (1994a) appears to take the view that an author/speaker is a 'foremost political predicate for social empowerment', which makes such concepts as any other social stereotype. In the chain of communication, who is the initiator when we are dealing with a text in translation? If a scientific answer is what one is looking for, we have got to consider the function of the given target text. Otherwise, whenever and wherever there is a translation, it will always be the language of the colonizer that would determine the superimposition or transplantation of one language over the other(s). When a text has already travelled the distance so as to cross linguistic and cultural barriers, it may be of little importance to know what it was in its previous incarnation or whether or not it was an 'original' text (as if its derived nature makes it unreliable/untouchable by definition), and which one is the 'native' text. In fact, these reactions will also depend on a number of other factors: the extent of language contact between the source and target communities or culture, their mutual ratings, and the linguistic mobility of a text.

TEXTS AS BOTH GRAMMATICAL AND SOCIAL CONSTRUCTS

The equation between grammatical and social constructs of language is not one-to-one. Let us see how far one can go.

The first social construct relates to what is known as the question of what is a 'standard' language vis-à-vis what are 'non-standards'. Corresponding to this, the theoretical construct is what Saussure would like to call the theoretically invariant form of language, or the 'synchrony' of a text, whereas what the philologist actually works with are its various diachronous forms or dated fragments of linguistic samples that time has preserved. Note that both concepts—standardization and synchrony—may fulfil very important practical and metaphysical roles, but are essentially 'hypothetical' concepts as far as we are concerned.

Next, we are often told about 'language purity' and 'linguistic corruption'. The sociolinguists working on linguistic attitudes of speakers are quite familiar with such thoughts. So are the students of translation studies. The popular belief is that the ancient or early formation of speech is pure and it becomes corrupt and 'vulgar' as the days go by. Look at the parallel in the field of translation: the original text is pure, and it tends to corrupt as it travels from one language to another, and then to another, etc. At a given point of time in South Asia as well as in Europe, it was commonly and tacitly agreed upon that the purity of the 'original' must be maintained at any cost—if necessary, by artificially inducing a certain degree of prescriptive planning or by opting for grand plans in the form of 'Sanskritization', which we could roughly equate with 'purification'. Those responsible for the spread of this particular theory believed that this was a highly desirable activity, and is actually possible. Thus, while everybody agreed that 'Prakritization' (roughly, 'degeneration') of languages and texts is inevitable, it has to be arrested to create a platform of discourse that is widely acceptable and easily teachable-learnable, and so that it defies aging.

Let us see whether this has a parallel in the theoretical construction of language. To my mind, the 'logical structure' of language (i.e. 'deep structure' of sentences in syntax and 'logical or underlying structure' of texts in translation theory) is expected to be beyond individuals, incorruptible and immutable but which still gets modified into a series of intermediary structures to end up as surface constructions. It is supposed to happen every time we actually speak or even write, and it has a puritanical angle, except that the time-frame here is not significantly great. One can still work on this parallel by assuming that the sum-total of all logical structures is what is the pure and unmodified metatext/language. The latter has a one-to-one relationship with the semantic interpretation of text/speech because this takes care of both synonymy and homonymy.

Further, the next social construct worth taking seriously is that language can be and needs to be made 'modern', a step which makes a given speech capable of being used in a much larger number of domains and in many manifestations (written, printed, computational and in various electronic media). This modern language thus has a higher value speech in comparison to all those which, for some reason or the other, did not get the chance of undergoing appropriate changes to qualify for this epithet. Now, this clearly creates a class distinction (or shall we say, 'caste' distinction?) among speech. Some are declared 'twice-born'—not only 'standard' but 'modern' as well—whereas a large number is expected to remain even below the first level. What is taken for granted is that there is a large number of speech which does not get the desired push to end up as modern forms of expression.

Note the consequences of this lack of push: although in terms of status, achievement of modernity raises the prestige of a speech, in practice it can give rise to many 'uncharacteristic features' (such as adjustments in the writing system or spelling rules to suit the technological constraints), 'untypical expressions' (such as large-scale borrowing of technical terms, loan translations, clipping and blending of various kinds, besides the introduction of many novel syntactic patterns or changes in the frequency of occurrence of the rare structures), and 'admixed styles' (sudden spurt in code-switches and mixture of many codes, typically observable in both written style and in public speaking besides the pattern used in the mass media). In short, modernization leads to many apparently anomalous and atypically contrived compromises, not all of which are taken kindly by the 'native' human subjects in the role of speakers and readers for whose benefit it is expected to be done.

From a particular social angle then, what is unmodern is chaste, consecrated, inviolate and inviolable, whereas what is modernized is impure, contaminated and mixed code/text, tainted with a purpose. The nearest theoretical construct that has some parallel to it is the competence–performance distinction, where 'linguistic' and 'communicative competence' form the primordial rudiment of speech—whereas all the distortions and distractions or numerous adjustments and compromises get into the actual 'performance'. But where speech 'performance' has an inevitability factor associated with it, when 'competence' is a highly conjectural abstraction, language 'modernity', howsoever desirable to some (or many), is not an inevitable destiny of this social product. So, the parallel has some limitations.

The fourth and the last social construct that many of us can think of is based on the ideology that links it to linguistic empowerment: who or which group owns a form of speech or has propriety over language becomes an important question to decide who are the 'others' (and hence, 'foreign') and consequently, who are 'native' to a speech, and thus part of the 'self'. Human aggregates that are a part of this construction of 'self' will, of course, watch with an ever-increasing alarm that what they have always taken for granted as their own have slowly become an acreage of only some among them. This forces a certain kind of cleavage among all those who were expected to be a part of the 'self', but who now suddenly find the ground slipping from under their feet. All this may have happened because some class or caste or community or group want to capture the position of power, at the cost of others, to decide who should be othered.

REFLECTIONS ON LITERARY TRANSLATION

Language had been an expression of both the 'free' self of man as well as that of man as a social animal. It was the responsibility of scholars working in the interface of language, society and culture to reconstruct the nature of and potential for this 'freedom' and 'bondage'.

I also believe that in the name of globalization, 'culturalization' of the political and the economic in the context of developing world can forestall our enquiry into the relationship between language and society. As interpreters, we must try to explore to what extent it is possible to unmask the pretence of the colonizers of the mind. In other words, we must try to differentiate between the discourse emanating from the 'underprivileged' speech communities and the 'learned discourse' on language in the centres of cultural power. Scholars working on the language and culture interface, and naturally on translation, function as catalysts of discourses that could contribute to convergence between theories of language, literature, society and culture, and consequently provide us with new grounds for studying the transition taking place in them.

An important but rarely discussed question has to do with the 'psychological perspective' in translation studies. It is particularly important to ask to what extent the translation theorists can learn from what happens in the translators' psyche—where they establish the relationship between the units or segments of the original text as they perceive it. Similarly, the fundamental questions that a psycholinguistic theory of translation raises are: to what extent is the model of listening and reading that underlies all human communication applicable to the act of translation? Or, can there be a unified model of the processes of translating and interpreting, particularly when translators process 300 words an hour outside 'real-time', whereas interpreters in most cases have to process at the speed of 9,000 words an hour without getting any chance or time to weigh different alternatives?

Similarly, one could also raise questions on relating the translators' psyche and the problem of meaning derivation of a text with reference to the Universe of semantic representation? Or, to what extent could one use the Information Theory models developed primarily for intralinguistic communication for an interlinguistic transfer? Is translation essentially an act of recodification'? To my mind, this opens up another line of enquiry that the students of translation are yet to pursue. For instance, are we not recodifying even as we are at the stage of semantic processing of thoughts, ideas and themes at the first level of creativity?

At the opposite end rests the question of what saves a translation. Do apparent structural identity and even a large percentage of shared vocabulary necessarily mean that the translator's task would be easier? Since linguistic universals are conceived as absolutes, and since translation is at best a probabilistic if not a particularistic phenomenon, can there be a theory of translation that is universally uniform? Or, can it at best be a set of eclectic checklists of techniques and strategies? Can the practical translator pitch his tent somewhere between the Quinian notion of 'untranslatability' and Keenan's 'exact translation hypothesis'?

In a paper by G. J. V. Prasad entitled 'The Untranslatable Other', the author, himself a creative writer, starts with a quote from Kamala Das: '"Don't write in English", they said, "English is not your mother tongue"'—which, in one sentence sums up the dilemma before the creative writers actively engaged in writing in an 'alien' variety of English which has had more nicknames than 'proper' names. This raises a very important question for all those who write creative texts in other tongues. Should they view their own pieces as attempts to 'subvert' the other tongue or as a discovery of space between two cultures? Does this special variety allow the author to think in her mother tongue but express in a different language—as has been admittedly done by Mulk Raj Anand, among others? Is there a parallel with translation when she is working on such a text? Is this choice political or is it because one has, due to the special multilingual and pluricultural set-up in the developing world, grown up in a milieu that allows him the luxury of oralcy but denies the knowledge and requisite intuition for the written style in the mother tongue? How far are the criteria of 'honesty' and 'humanness', which Kamala Das had extolled of her own styles valid? Is it true that 'English enables' Indo-Aglian writers 'to explore terrains which could be spiked with mines in mothertongue'? I am sure many of us among translators from Indian languages into English would be interested in these questions.

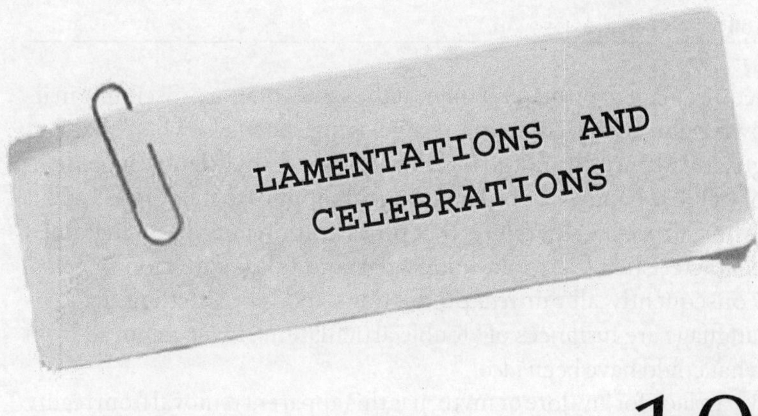

10

PURITY OF LORE: THE ABSENCE OF PURE FOLKLORISTICS

One often hears the grumble that there has not been a pure folklore studies, like pure mathematics. I have often asked myself why it is that in our long tradition, no one has talked about an autonomous discipline of folklore. It was once considered to be a part of literary studies where it has had the same fate as it had later at the hand of linguists. Linguists tried to subsume it (or, rather, consume it) under the broad discipline of language sciences. Anthropologists, too, behaved in a similar fashion, as stated by Handoo (2000: 7):

> … each discipline armed with the imperialistic concept of annexing as much as possible, began trying to bring the other discipline under its own umbrella.… Similarly, when non-literary artefacts of cultures were studied by folklorists, anthropologists behaved exactly in the manner, scholars of literature had in the case of studies carried on text-based folk literature.

There have been, however, saner voices willing to view this enterprise in a twofold manner—first, as an inter-disciplinary endeavour where each participating discipline sheds the apparently pristine requirement of purity, and then, at the same time, as a discipline in its own right. In this context, I recall having stated elsewhere that language and purity do not go together. And since the essential ingredient of folklore happens to be language, this applies to folklore as well. It is not surprising, therefore, that prevarication must be an ingrained characteristic of our folk-knowledge and folk-expression systems. Consequently, all our *real* productions and reproductions vis-à-vis language are instances of 'double articulation', twice removed from what could have been *ideal*.

In fact, for any lore or myth, it is this apparent removal from reality that adds colour to what one says or does with language even when a given text is not as pretentious as to be scoring a point or sending a message. Our folk-narratives, or folk-drama, or our folk-poetry cannot be a mere mirror of reality. And yet, they draw heavily from our context, our environs and our vision of space and time.

For that matter, even when we talk about apparently more respectable modes of text-generation in different genres that also reflect our life and living, the imprint of a folklore on them is often undeniable. Whether in the journalistic writing or programmes in the mass media, the same creative uncertainty (the same prevarication?) gets reflected. No wonder then that what we are expected to do scientifically under the oath of honesty and truthfulness is not what we actually do, whether we stand as witnesses or when we sit in judgement on others, because there is this general uncertainty in all instances of speech. It is from this uncertainty, the removal from reality, and this double-articulation that all modern folklore flows and enriches our existence.

MYTHS AND LORE AND THEIR SOCIO-CULTURAL ROLE

Myths as ensconced in folk-texts, as we all know, perform different functions. But in addition, they play a critical role in how a culture constructs its sense of time. They are distinguished from other forms of popular, often orally transmitted, literature. Some may like to classify this kind of literature according to its functions: *fables*, which instruct; *etiological tales*, which explain; and *folktales*, which entertain. According to some other scholars, myths are contrasted both to history, which concerns recent and well-documented events, and to poetic epics and narrative legends, which deal with historically important persons, places, or with incidents from the distant past. Take for example, the story of Lady Godiva's naked ride through Coventry, as in the legends of Norwegian and Icelandic kings (recorded during the period of the twelfth to fifteenth century). Folklore, however, often tells us stories that are situated in an imagined, remote, timeless past and dwell on themes such as the origin of living beings and the supernatural. This fine distinction between folklore on the one hand and epics and legends on the other, is not often easily made.

In all fairness, one must admit here that myths have enriched Western literature since the time of Aeschylus and have been used by many major English poets such as Milton, Shelley and Keats. The influence of Puranic stories on playwrights and authors of *kaavyas* in the Indian tradition is also well-known and documented. Interestingly, many literary greats, especially William Blake, Franz Kafka, Tagore, James Joyce, W. B. Yeats, T. S. Eliot, and Borges have consciously and continuously created and constructed new myths, sometimes using the old materials and newly constructed symbols.

Studies of the folklore and folk-legends of North and South American natives, Australian aborigines, the peoples of South Africa, and others have revealed how widespread our mythological elements and motifs have been. As we all know, many themes and motifs recur in various cultures and ages, the commonest being the myths of the creation of the world. The origin myths begin with the story of a god fashioning the earth from an abstract chaos to a specific animal, and take us to the one where god is seen as creating it from a handful of mud. Other origin stories refer to cyclical creation and destruction, in parallel with never-ending seasons of birth, death and rebirth. In Greece, the concern with renewed fertility was seasonal. Certain other cultures, such as that of the Mesopotamians, focused on longer periods of vegetative death through prolonged drought. Another well-known idea is that of a golden age in which humanity is viewed as having degenerated from an earlier perfection. Hesiod's Golden Age and the Garden of Eden in Jewish and Christian traditions are examples. Then, the flood motif is extremely widespread too, and this group of myths also lead us to other myths treating the origin of fire, or its retrieval from someone who has stolen it. The relation between the living and the dead is another common theme.

FOLKLORISTIC UNIVERSALS

There have been many theories as to the reasons for similarities among beliefs, lore and myths of such diverse peoples. In other words, could there be *folkloristic universals*? Many have, however, viewed them as poor reflections of history, and have attempted to analyse them in non-sacred ways to account for their apparent absurdity. Such opinions have been expressed in all ages. For instance, the Greeks explained myths as allegories, and looked for a reality concealed in poetic images. Theagenes of Rhegium (sixth century BCE) was an early supporter of this interpretation, which was later developed by the Stoics, who reduced the Greek gods to mere moral principles and natural elements. Euhemerus, for instance, considered the gods to have been renowned historical figures who became deified through the passage of time. The animists see myths as developing from an improper separation between the human and non-human.

A later allegorical interpretation claims that at one time myths were invented by wise men to point out a truth, but that after a time myths were taken literally. One example of this can be seen in the myth involving Kronos, who devoured his children. Kronos is the Greek word for time, which is said to destroy whatever it brings into existence. Philologists like Max Müller, on the other hand, saw myths evolving out of corruptions of language. There is a similar theory that myths, including scripture, are corruptions of history.

The great modern advances in the study of the folk and the myths began in the nineteenth century, when scholars like Sir James Frazer and Sir Edward Burnett Tylor argued for the study of mythology and folklore not as bad histories but as social institutions, and called attention to the myths of contemporary simple societies. The coinage of a name for the discipline of 'folklore', however, had to wait until August 1846 when William Thomas used it in a communication to a fellow scholar and editor, as reported by Alan Dundes (1965).

Today, the initial evolutionary theories of Frazer and Tylor may be discredited as simplistic and ethnocentric. The current theories instead posit a common psychological or emotional basis and relate these narratives to universal religious impulses. In *The Golden Bough* (1890), Frazer had argued that all mythical narratives were originally connected with the idea of fertility in nature, with the birth, death and resurrection of vegetation as a constantly recurring motif. Psychoanalysts like Carl Jung believe that there is an inherent tendency in all people to form same or similar mythic symbols.

On the other hand, Indologists and the religious scholar Mircea Eliade (1987) contend that myths are recited and reflected in lores, where the main purpose is that of ritually re-creating the beginning of *time,* when all things were initiated. This, he argued, allowed one to return to the original and successful creative act. Sigmund Freud (1900) believed that the apparent irrationality of myths arises from the same source as what he called the disconnectedness of dreams. He thought that they are both symbolic reflections of the unconscious and repressed fears and anxieties which are universal aspects of the human condition, or which characterize distinct societies.

Most contemporary students of mythology and folklore, however, have turned away from attempts to explain similarities in content or the universalistic texts by calling attention to the different contexts in which these cultural texts occur. They believe that folklore functions in a variety of ways within a single culture, and at the same time differs in function from one culture to another.

Malinowski (1957) considered all myths to be validations of established practices and institutions, whereas Claude Lévi-Strauss (1955) focused on their formal properties. He pointed to the recurrence of certain kinds of structures in widely different traditions of folk literature, and took recourse to Saussurean binary opposites by highlighting oppositions such as nature/culture and self/other. He argued that the human brain organizes all perceptions in terms of contrasts and concluded that certain oppositions are universal. Further, he advocated the interpretation of these texts as culturally specific transformations of certain universal structures. From those days until the present postmodern times, innovative studies have enriched our general understanding of various aspects of culturation, especially in areas such as ethnomusicology, performing folk arts, folk customs and beliefs, and have added newer dimensions to our understanding of folklore studies.

THE VARIATIONISTS

To my mind, both folklore and linguistics share one major concern, namely, that of the primacy of speech over writing. Let us not forget that Saussure himself had treated writing as a parasitic form, the representation of a representation. This may seem to some like a relatively innocent move, but in fact it was probably a part of the politics of theory-building that he had engaged in. Recall that he had warned us that linguists could 'fall into the trap' of attending to written forms that could eventually 'usurp the role' of speech. If writing was set aside as dependent and derivative, accounts of language could take as the norm the experience of hearing oneself speak, where form and meaning seemed given simultaneously.

In fact, the privileging of speech is not only a weighty matter, it is also very nearly inescapable. It is so because whether in linguistic analysis or in folklore studies, and by extension, in semiotic analysis of any kind, everything depends upon the possibility of identifying signs, for which it is necessary to grasp or identify signifieds. It is, therefore, not an accident that semiotic theory should find itself implicated in phonocentrism and logocentrism. This is neither an accident nor an error, as pointed out by Derrida in *Of Grammatology*:

> The privilege of the phon has dominated the history of the world during an entire epoch, and has even produced the idea of the world, the idea of world-origin, that arises from the difference between the worldly and the non-worldly, the outside and the inside, ideality and non-ideality, universal and non-universal, transcendental and empirical, etc. (1976: 7–8).

These are, of course, large claims. These new binary oppositions such as *outside/inside*, *transcendental/empirical*, etc., depend on a point of differentiation, and the claim is that the moment of speech, where *signifier* and *signified* seem given together, and where inner and outer or physical and mental are for an instant perfectly fused, serves as the point of reference in relation to which all these distinctions are posited. Note that Derrida—like Saussure—himself creates a chain of related but non-identical terms and concepts, including *differance, supplement, trace, hymen, espacement, greffe, pharmakon, parergon*. However, he would also like to prevent any of his terms from becoming 'concepts' of a new science. In an interview on his positions in 'Semiologie et grammatologie' (1968), he identified his double science or double reading not with a mode of discourse that would lie outside or beyond semiotics but with a special practice within semiotics. One can then say that in every semiotic proposition or system of research, metaphysical presuppositions will cohabit with critical motifs by virtue of the fact that up to a certain point they inhabit the same language, or rather, the same system of language (Derrida 1972: 49–50).

Although Derrida's deconstruction reveals 'irrationalities' in our systems and theories, it is not a kind of 'new irrationalism', as is often suggested. It only reveals contradictions and paradoxes, which semiotics cannot escape. Generally, semiotics is not the self-consistent discourse of a science but is a discourse of a text. What deconstruction advises then is not a change of direction—but a shift from semiotics to a new discipline, namely, that of grammatology. Notice that in either case, there is no escape from textuality; one can only engage in it from a more critical viewpoint.

In 'Semiotics and Deconstruction', a lecture delivered at the International Conference on the Semiotics of Art, sponsored by the University of Michigan, Jonathan Culler (1978) observes that the importance of the present moment is that various traditional disciplines are now beginning to relate their own work to semiotics. At the same time, semiotics is facing an attack from traditional humanists, who are enraged about the fact that a discipline with scientific pretensions should claim to treat products of the human spirit. There is, however, a more radical critique which focuses on the same point about scienticism. Take J. Hillis Miller's (1976) argument that there is a clear distinction between what might be called to conflate two terminologies, Socratic (theoretical, or canny) critics on the one hand, and Apollonian/Dionysian (tragic, or uncanny) critics, on the other.

The promise of a rational ordering of literary study based on advancements in Linguistics would see the first group, i.e. the *canny critics,* try to create a language sciences under a collective enterprise such as 'the human sciences', penetrable by only one tool, namely, thought. It is not surprising if they literally follow what Nietzsche did in this respect.

The *uncanny critics*, on the other hand, do not believe in the possibility of general and systematic theories, because they have discovered that by careful working through individual texts, whether literary or philosophical, one is led to unmasterable paradoxes, which refer to the domain of signification. This is often cited as a post-structuralist or deconstructionist attitude. But one could still ask these question: are the proponents of semiotics 'lulled by the promise of rational ordering'? Do we really have 'unshakeable faith' in thought, rather than in the powerful interpretive account of linguistics and semiotics? Derrida's reading of Saussure in *Of Grammatology* is severely critical of the logocentrism of Western culture—the 'metaphysics of presence' that texts simultaneously affirm and undermine. Then there is the notion of meaning as something present in the consciousness of the speaker at the moment of utterance: what is it that the speaker 'has in mind' as he speaks. Derrida is interested in the way in which this logocentrism is 'deconstructed' in texts that affirm it. As a critique of logocentrism, Derrida argues that since Saussure defines language as a system of signs, the central question becomes that of the nature and identity of signs and their constituents, with a focus more precisely on their inter-relationship.

It may be mentioned here that the primacy of speech and thought over the written word had been realized by others, too. For instance, Nietzsche had an unshakeable faith that thought, using the thread of logic, can penetrate the deepest abysses of being.

SPOKEN VERSUS WRITTEN

The dichotomy of the spoken versus the written is not new. What is new is the claim that has been independently voiced by many that writing is an act of 'double articulation'. Speech implies an intricate process of selection of certain linguistic entities, appropriate to a given context or for an intended content, and their combination into linguistic units of a higher degree of complexity. The term 'double articulation' in the linguistics tradition suggests that 'speaking' (or 'organizing' one's speech) involves organizing ourselves twice—once to create lexis from the basic speech units, i.e. sounds, and then again to create sentences from these words. This two-step process completes the cycle of signification, beginning its journey from symbols as signifiers (sounds) and ending in a signified (meaning).

At the point of textual construction, this 'duality of patterning' is readily apparent: the author selects words and combines them into sentences according to the syntactic system of the language he is using; sentences in their turn are combined into utterances. But here there are interesting questions that remain hidden. First, are the *oral texts*—which is what folklore is—subject to this double articulation? In what way are they different from the written act of creativity? These are not easy questions and they do not have easy answers either. However, I would like to take the position that if we are to use the concept of double articulation from a text theoretic point of view (and not from a purely linguistic angle), folk-texts are instances of an interesting paradox. They are products of a single articulation that allows plurality to be reflected in the way the folk-texts are constructed and narrated, and also in the way they could be heard and understood or interpreted.

Second, here is where the pressure of the mass bound by a common code or convention puts pressure on the folk narrators, because they are by no means completely free agents in their choice of words. Their selection of names and certain limited words and expressions would of course respond to the need for localizing their texts (in a particular time and space), but their overall choice must be made from the lexical storehouse at the disposal of their culture with which they and their readers or addressees are familiar. Here, we have to assume that in the optimal exchange of information in a performance situation, whether it is a socio-cultural ritual or a bed-time story-telling event dominated by grandmas, the speaker and the listener have at their disposal more or less the same 'filing cabinet of prefabricated representation': the addressee of a verbal message selects one of these 'preconceived possibilities'. The addressee is supposed to make an identical choice from the same assembly of 'possibilities already foreseen and provided for'. Thus, the efficiency of a speech event in the case of a folk narration demands the use of a common code by its participants, which is inherently characterized by the feature of 'single articulation'. At least, this should be largely so. In comparison, the author of the written word is more free to practise a *grammatical and lexical violence*. That she can do it becomes a source of her cause for celebration. That keeps her going.

Third, in certain ways, writing relates the displaced speaker to the space she belongs to. I like the way Rajeev S. Patke (2001) describes this matter. Writing translates the diasporic into metaphor, Patke argues, where the figure of the cusp can serve as a geometrical emblem. As metaphor, suggests Patke, the diasporic refers to a state of being in two minds about itself. Likewise, translation may also be said to be a thought in two minds about itself. Both are figures for gain-in-loss. Just as selves translate across environments, likewise, texts live in a diasporic relationship between languages. Both diaspora and translation here may be viewed as metaphors for poetry: first, because in a poem, senses migrate from the world of experience to the world of expressions, and second, because pastness, loss, negation, absence, and desire all get translated, where ideas, events, feelings and convictions travel from the memory into a trace of being which recovers a part from evanescence. That is why all poets are, in a sense, engaged in acts of translation, and every translation is a kind of migration, a lamenting recuperation of love.

Lamentations apart, it is interesting to note that notwithstanding the theoretical points of debate as outlined above, there are now attempts to blur the dividing lines between the spoken and the written word, the text and its translation, or even the folk-knowledge and the documented history. I would like to end this monologue in the first person with an instance of this kind of an attempt, which can be seen in narratives like *Zindagiinaamaa: Zindaa Rukh*, a fiction in Hindi by Krishna Sobti, published in 1979 (winning her the Akademi Award in 1980, and also the Sahitya Shiromani Award in 1980). The novel was a surprise to the Hindi literary world because of the author's shift to the genre of 'historical' fiction. I must mention here that Krishna Sobti's reading of history does not deal with rebellions. It does not project any radical solutions, but it does create a world where caste and religion are peripheral and where the divisions of the male and female territories are blurred even while the conventional roles are supported.

Like in *Zindagiinaama*, I could present scores of other writings, such as Satinath Bhaduri's *DhoRaai carit maanas* or Amiyabhushan Majumdar's *Dukhiyaar kuTi*, both in Bangla (appearing in the 1950s and 1960s), where history is viewed not through cyclical patterns and archetypal characters but through folk traditions, rituals, ceremonies and marriage ties. In particular, in *Zindagiinaama*, feminine voices, maternal images, images of birth and nurturing and of continuity abound. The actual historical records are found to be irrelevant to the lives of the people by the author, and the historical processes stand reversed in their daily interaction with each other across barriers of castes and communities. The freedom that festivals and marriages provide for crossing these barriers is remarkable. Women voice their concern in different ways, prioritizing different issues: the oral takes over the written, and songs and ceremonies reflect this reality. They discuss war and peace, economic need, the British Raj, Victoria's reign, and the aggressiveness of the rulers. There is an earthiness about the narrative, a closeness to nature, a pride in the community.

Folk culture is seen here as a living tradition which knows no division, no difference of status. It is not a layered tradition which hierarchizes and distances one set of people from another. It rather has a levelling force which inculcates the feeling of solidarity. I would like to end my piece where Krishna Sobti began, with the following lines:

> History/what is not
> And history/what it is
> Not that
> which is secured in
> the royal archives with
> date and time in the
> chronicle
> But that
> which flows within the
> consciousness of the people's mind
> Flows, flourishes and spreads
> and lives in the
> ordinary people.
>
> (tr. in Jain 1996: 166–67)

Bibliography

Abrams, M. H. 1953. *The Mirror and the Lamp: Romantic Theory and the Critical Tradition*. New York: Oxford University Press.

Acharya, Phanibhusan. 1994. 'Mandirgaatrer prasaadhanrataar haater aaynaay', *Desh,* 111.

Adiga, Gopalakrishna. 1952. *NaDedu banda daari*. Mysore: Vishwa Sahitya Male.

Adorno, Theodor W. 1973a. *Negative Dialectics*. New York: Seabury.

———.1973b. *Philosophy of Modern Music*. New York: Seabury.

———. 1974a. *Minima Moralia: Reflections from Damaged Life*. London: New Left Books.

———. 1974b. 'The Stars Down to Earth: The *Los Angeles Times* Astrology Column I: A Study in Secondary Superstition', *Telos,* 19: 13–90.

Agger, Ben. 1979. 'Work and Authority in Marcuse and Habermas', *Human Studies*, 2: 191–208.

——. 1989a. *Fast Capitalism: A Critical Theory of Significance*. Urbana, IL: University of Illinois Press.

——. 1989b. 'Do Books Write Authors? A Study of Disciplinary Hegemony', *Teaching Sociology*, 17(3): 365–69.

———. 1990. *The Decline of Discourse: Reading, Writing and Resistance in Postmodern Capitalism*. London: Falmer Press.

——. 1992. *The Discourse of Domination: From the Frankfurt School to Postmodernism*. Evanston, IL: Northwestern University Press.

——. 2002. *Postponing the Postmodern: Sociological Practices, Selves, and Theories*. Lanham, MD: Rowman & Littlefield.

Agger, Ben. Forthcoming. *Self and Cybersociety*. New York: Blackwell.

Ahmad, Aijaz (ed.). 1971. *Ghazals of Ghalib*. New York: Columbia University Press.

Almqvist, Bo. 1991. *Viking Ale*. Aberystwyth, Wales: Boethius Press.

Althusser, Louis. 1970. *For Marx*. London: Allen Lane.

Annamalai, E. 1998. 'Nativity of Language', in Rajendra Singh (ed.), *The Native Speaker: Multilingual Perspectives*, Language and Development Series, Vol. 4. New Delhi: Sage, pp. 148–57.

Aronowitz, Stanley. 1981. *Crisis in Historical Materialism*. New York: Praeger Publishers (2nd edn, 1990, Minneapolis, MN: University of Minnesota Press).

Arrojo, Rosemary. 1996. 'Postmodernism and the Teaching of Translation', in Cay Dollerup and Vibeke Appel (eds), *Teaching Translation and Interpreting* 3. Amsterdam: John Benjamins, pp. 97–104.

Averbach, Margara. 2000. 'Translation and Resistance in Native North American Literature', *American Indian Quarterly*, 24(2): 165–81.

Babler, Otto Frantisek. 1970. 'Poe's "Raven" and the Translation of Poetry', in James S. Holmes (ed.), *The Nature of Translation: Essays on the Theory and Practice of Literary Translation*, Approaches to Translation Studies, l. The Hague and Paris: Mouton, pp. 192–200.

Bachelard, Gaston. 1958[1964]. *The Poetics of Space*, tr. by Maria Jolass. New York: Orion Press.

Balavant, Baba. 1941. *Mahaanaac*. Lahore: Singh Brothers.

———. 1951. *Bandargaah*. Lahore: Singh Brothers.

Bandyopadhyay, Rangalal. 1852. 'Bangla kabitaa biSayak prastaab' ('A Proposal on Bengali Poetry'), lecture at the Bethune Society, 13 May, Kolkata.

———. 1858. *Padminii Upaakhyaan* (A historical romance based on Todd's *Annals and Antiquities of Rajasthan*). Kolkata.

Barth, J. Robert. 1987. *Romanticism and Transcendence: Wordsworth, Coleridge, and the Religious Imagination*. Columbia, MO: University of Missouri Press.

Barthes, Roland. 1975. *Vers une esthétique sans entraves*. Paris: U.G.E.

———. 1978. 'The Image', paper given at a colloquium at Cerisy-la-Salle.

———. 1986. *The Rustle of Language*, tr. by Richard Howard. Oxford, UK: Basil Blackwell.

Bassnett-McGuire, Susan. 1980. *Translation Studies*. London: Methuen and Co. Ltd.

Bassnett-McGuire, Susan and André Lefèvre . 1993. 'General Editors' Preface', in Edwin Gentzler (ed.), *Contemporary Translation Theories*. London and New York: Routledge & Kegan Paul, pp. ix–x.

Basu, Buddhadev. 1930. *Bandir bandanaa*. Kolkata: D.M. Library.

———. 1937. *Kankaabatii*. Kolkata: Kabita Bhavan.

———. 1943. *Damayantii*. Kolkata: Kabita Bhavan.

———. 1948a. *Draupadiir SaaRii*. Kolkata: Kabita Bhavan.

———. 1948b. *An Acre of Green Grass—A Review of Modern Bengali Literature*. Delhi: Orient Longman.

Baudrillard, Jean. 1981. *For a Critique of the Political Economy of the Sign*. St. Louis, MO: Telos Press.

———. 1983. *Simulations*. New York: Semiotext(e).

Belitt, Ben. 1978. *Adam's Dream: A Preface to Translation*. New York: Grove Press.

Bell, Daniel. 1960. *The End of Ideology*. Glencoe, IL: The Free Press.

Berman, Marshall. 1982. *All That Is Solid Melts into Air*. New York: Simon & Schuster.

Bhabha, Homi K. 1994. *The Location of Culture*. New York: Routledge.

Bhaduri, Satinath. 1949–51. *DhoRhaai Carit Maanas*, Vols 1 and 2. Kolkata: Bengal Publishers.

Bhagat, Niranjan Narhari. 1949. *Chandolaya*. Ahmedabad: Indradhanu Book House.

Bhattacharya, Krishnachandra. 1928[1992]. 'Manane swaraaj'. Repr. in Anjan Sen, Birendra Bhattacharya and Udaya Narayana Singh (eds), 1992, *Eurokendrikata o Shilpa-Sanskriti*. Kolkata: Gangeo Patra, pp. 9–17. Tr. as 'Swaraj in Idea' (1952) by the author in *Visva-Bharati Quarterly*, 20(2).

Bhattacharya, Sukanta. 1948a. *ChaaRapatra*. Kolkata: International Publishing House.

———. 1948b. *Ghum nei*. Kolkata: Saraswati Library.

Bhowmick, Jayanta. 1995. 'Piggy-tail', *Desh*, 89.

Borges, Jorge Luis. 1940[1976]. 'Tlön, Uqbar, Orbis Tertius', inEmir Rodríguez Monegal and Alastair Reid (eds), *Borges, a Reader* (orig. pub. in *Sur*, 1940, Buenos Aires, tr. by Alastair Reid). New York: Dutton, pp. 111–22.

Bradbury, Malcolm. 1983. 'Modernism', in Roger Fowler (ed.), *A Dictionary of Modern Critical Terms*. London: Routledge & Kegan Paul.

Brossard, Nicole. 1984. *Journal intime: ou Voilà donc un manuscrit*, tr. by Bev Curran and Mitoko Hirabayashi as *Resubian Nikki*. Montreal: Les Herbes Rouges.

Brossard, Nicole. 1988. *La Lettre Aerienne*, tr. by Marlene Wildeman as *The Aerial Letter*. Montreal: Les editions du remue-menage, Toronto: The Women's Press.

———. 1992. 'Writing as a Trajectory of Desire and Consciousness', in Alice A. Parker and Elizabeth A. Messe (eds), *Feminist Critical Negotiations*. Amsterdam: John Benjamins, pp. 179–85.

Brown, C. P. 1842. *Sumati-Shatakam with English Rendering*, ed. and repr. in 1973 by C. R. Sarma. Hyderabad: Andhra Pradesh Sahitya Akademi.

Carlyle, Thomas (tr.). 1824. *Wilhelm Meister's Apprenticeship and Travels*, 2 vols (from *Wilhelm Meisters Lehrjahre*, 1795–1796, by Johann Wolfgang von Goethe). Edinburgh: Oliver and Boyd.

Catford, J. C. 1965. *A Linguistic Theory of Translation*. London: Oxford University Press.

Chakraborty, Bhaskar. 1994. 'Dhaaraabaahik samaacaar', *Desh*, 59.

Chattopadhyay, Shakti. 1976. 'Why I Hate the Literary Race', *Sunday*, 1 August, 4(19): 4.

Chaudhury, Pramatha. 'Kathaar kathaa'. *Bharati*, JyaiSTha, 1309b.

Chaudhuri, Sukanta (tr.). 1987. '"Ha-ja-ba-ra-la" of Sukumar Ray', *The Illustrated Weekly of India*, 14 June, pp. 36–39.

———. 1997. *The Select Nonsense of Sukumar Ray*. New Delhi: Oxford University Press.

Cheyfitz, Eric. 1997. *The Poetics of Imperialism: Translation and Colonization from the Tempest to Tarzan*, expanded edition. Philadelphia, PN: University of Pennsylvania Press.

Chomsky, Noam. 1957. *Syntactic Structures*. The Hague: Mouton.

Congrat-Butlar, Stefan. 1979. *Translation and Translator: An International Directory and Guide*. New York: R. R. Bowker Company.

Coseriu, Eugenio. 1988. *Schriften von Eugenio Coseriu (1965–1987)*, ed. by Jorn Albrecht. Tubingen: Narr.

Crystal, D. 1987. *The Cambridge Encyclopedia of Language*. Cambridge, UK: Cambridge University Press.

Culler, Jonathan. 1978. 'Semiotics and Deconstruction', lecture delivered at the International Conference on the Semiotics of Art, University of Michigan.

Curran, Bev and Mitoko Hirabayashi (trs). 2000. *Translation in Three Dimensions: Nicole Brossard in Japanese*. Tr. of Nicole Brossard's *Journal intime: ou Voilà donc un manuscrit* as *Resubian nikki*. Tokyo: Kokubunsha.

Das, Sisir Kumar. 1991. *A History of Indian Literature*, Vol. VIII. New Delhi: Sahitya Akademi.

Dash, Dinesh. 1942. *Kabitaa*. Kolkata: Purvasha.

Dasgupta, Alokeranjan. 1988. 'Translating: Practice Creates Theory', inaugural lecture at the Regional workshop on Literary Translation (Director: Alokeranjan Dasgupta & Jagannath Chakraborty), 5–25 January, Sahitya Akademi, Calcutta.

———. 1991. 'Translating: Practice Creates Theory', in Ayappa Paniker (ed.), *Making of Indian Literature: A Consolidated Report of Workshops on Literary Translation: 1986–88*. New Delhi: Sahitya Akademi, pp. 237–43.

Datta, Sudhindranath. 1930. *Tanvii*. Kolkata: Kabita Bhaban.

———. 1935. *ArkesTraa*. Kolkata: Bharati Bhavan.

De, Bishnu. 1933. *UrbaSii o AarTemis*. Kolkata: Buddha Basu.

De, Bishnu. 1941. *Puurbalekhaa*. Kolkata: Prajnan Raychaudhury.

———. 1947. *Sandviiper car*. Kolkata: Chinmohan Sehanabish.

de Beaugrande, Robert. 1978. *Factors in a Theory of Poetic Translating*. Amsterdam and Assen: Van Gorcum.

De Lima Costa, Claudia. 2000. 'Being Here and Writing There: Gender and the Politics of Translation in Brazilian Landscape', *Signs: Journal of Women in Culture and Society*, 25(3).

Derrida, Jacques. 1968. 'Semiologie et grammatologie', *Social Science Information*, 7(3) : 133–48.

———, 1972. *Positions*, tr. by Alan Bass. Paris: Minuit.

———.1976. *Of Grammatology*, tr. by Gayatri Spivak. Baltimore, MD: Johns Hopkins University Press.

———.1978. *Writing and Difference*. Chicago, IL: The University of Chicago Press.

———.1994. *Specters of Marx*. New York: Routledge. .

Dryden, John. 1711[1800]. 'The Life of Lucian', first printed in octavo in 1711. Repr. in 1800 in *The Critical and Miscellaneous Works of John Dryden* (London: T. Cadell, jr, and W. Davies).

Dundes, Alan (ed.). 1965. *The Study of Folklore*. Englewood Cliffs, NJ: Prentice-Hall.

Dutt, Hur Chunder and Kailash Chandra Basu. 1853. Lecture given at the Bethune Society, Kolkata.

Dutta, Michael Madhusudan. 1853. 'Letter to a Friend', as quoted in P. Guha-Thakurta, *The Bengali Drama: Trubner's Oriental Series*, 2001, New York: Routledge, p. 74.

Eliade, Mircea (ed.). 1987. *Encyclopedia of Religion*, in 15 volumes, 2nd edn 2005, ed. by Lindsay Jones. New York: Macmillan.

Eliot, T. S. 1932. *Selected Essays 1917–1932*. New York: Harcourt, Brace and Company.

Firth, Raymond (ed.). 1957. *Man and Culture: An Evaluation of the Work of Bronislaw Malinowski*. London: Routledge & Kegan Paul.

Fitzgerald, Edward 1851[1980]. 'Letter to the Rev. Cowell, dated 22 March, 1851', in Susan Bassnett-McGuire (ed.), *Translation Studies*, London & New York: Methuen, p. 3.

Fitzmaurice-Kelly, James. 1917. 'Translation', in *Encyclopedia Britanica*, Vol. 2, 11th edn. London: Enclyclopedia Britanica, pp. 183–88.

Foucault, Michel. 1972. *The Archaeology of Knowledge*. New York: Pantheon.

Foucault, 1977. *Discipline and Punish*. New York: Pantheon.

Frazer, Sir James. 1890. *The Golden Bough: A Study in Magic and Religion*, in two vols. New York London: Macmillan.

Freud, Sigmund. 1900. *The Interpretation of Dreams*, tr. from German *Die Traumdeutung* (1899). Leipzig und Wien: Franz Deuticke.

Gachechiladze, Givi R. 1967. 'Realism and Dialects in the Art of Translation', *Babel*, 13(2): 87–91.

Gangopadhyay, Sunil. 1971. Sahitya no. 1379b, *Desh*.

——— [Sanatan Pathak]. 1975. 'Bankimcandra', *Desh*, 26 April no. 991–92; 3 May, no. 65–66.

Gentzler, Edwin. 1993. *Contemporary Translation Theories*. London and New York: Routledge & Kegan Paul.

Godard, Barbara. 1990. 'Theorizing Feminist Discourse/Translation', in Susan Bassnett and André Lefèvre (eds), *Translation, History and Culture*. London: Cassell, pp. 87–96.

———.1995. 'The Translator's Diary', in Sherry Simon (ed.), *Culture in Transit: Translation and the Changing Identities of Quebec Literature*. Montreal: Vehicule Press.

Gorjan, Zlatko. 1970[1987]. 'On Translating Joyce's *Ulysses*', in S. Holmes, Frans de Haan and Anton Popovic (eds), *The Nature of Translation: Essays on the Theory and Practice of Literary Translation*. Bratislava: Publishing House of the Slovak Academy of Science, pp. 201–207.

Gramsci, Antonio. 1971. *Selections from the Prison Notebooks*. London: Lawrence and Wishart.

Guo Jian. 1999. 'The Politics of Othering and Postmodernization of the Cultural Revolution', *Postcolonial Studies*, 2(2): 213–29.

Gunn, D. M. 1971. 'Thematic Composition and Homeric Authorship', *Harvard Studies in Classical Philology*, 75: 1–31.

Gupta, Amitabha. 1989. *Uttar-aadhunik kabitaa, I*. Kolkata: Alochana Chakra.

Gupta, Ishwar. 1958. *Kabijiivanii*. Kolkata: Calcutta Book House.

Habermas, Jurgen. 1971. *Knowledge and Human Interests*. Boston, MA: Beacon.

———.1981. 'New Social Movements', *Telos*, 49: 33–37.

———. 1984. *The Theory of Communicative Action*, Vol. I. Boston, MA: Beacon.

———. 1987a. *The Philosophical Discourse of Modernity*. Cambridge, MA: MIT Press.

———. 1987b. *The Theory of Communicative Action*, Vol. 2. Boston, MA: Beacon.

Handoo, Jawaharlal. 2000. *Theoretical Essays in Indian Folklore*. Mysore: Zooni Publications.

Hartmann, R. R. K. 1990. 'The Not So Harmless Drudgery in Finding Translation Equivalents', *Language and Communication*, 10(1): 47–55.

Hartley, John. 1990. 'Culture and Popular Culture: The Politics of Photopoetry', in Malcolm Kelsall, Martin Coyle, Peter Garside and John Peck (eds),

Encyclopedia of Literature and Criticism. London: Routledge, p. 1098–1109.

Harvey, David. 1989. *The Condition of Postmodernity: An Enquiry into the Origins of Cultural Change*. Oxford, UK: Blackwell.

Hawes, Tara. 1995. 'Janet Frame: The Self as Other/Othering the Self'. *Deep South*, 1(1), paper originally given at the Identities, Ethnicities, Nationalities Conference, LaTrobe University, Australia.

Hegel, G. W. F. 1967. *The Phenomenology of Mind*. New York: Harper & Row.

Hirsch, E. D. 1967. *Validity in Interpretation*. New Haven: Yale University Press.

Horkheimer, Max. 1972. 'Traditional and Critical Theory', *Zeitschrift für Sozialforschung*, Frankfurt: Institute for Social Research (1937), tr. by Matthew J. O'Connell et al., in his *Critical Theory: Selected Essays*. New York: Herder and Herder. p. 188–243.

Horkheimer, Max and Theodor W. Adorno. 1972. *Dialectic of Enlightenment*. New York: Herder and Herder.

Huggan, Graham and Winfried Siemerling. 2000. 'U.S./Canadian Writers' Perspectives on the Multiculturalism Debate', *Canadian Literature*, 164: 82–111.

Huntington, Samuel P. 1976. 'The Change to Change: Modernization, Development and Politics', *Comparative Politics*, 3: 283–322.

Hussain, Yusuf (tr. and ed.). 1977. *Urdu Ghazals of Ghalib*. New Delhi: Ghalib Institute.

Husserl, Edmond. 1939[1973]. *Experience and Judgement*, tr. by J. S. Churchill and K. Ameriks. London: Routledge.

Ikôme, Otto M. 1994a. 'Tell Me Not: Comments on P. Dasgupta', *Meta*, 39(2): 397–400.

———. 1994b. 'A Bended Proximation: Comments on Tiffou ("Basic Distortions in a Translation")', *Meta*, 39(2): 338–41.

———. 2001. *Translating into English*. Université du Québec, Télé-université, Sainte-Foy, Québec (including audio recording).

———. 2004. 'If Only We Could Translate the (Under)mined Wisdom in Our Oral Traditions: Epasa Moto or the Enigma of Cameroonian Literacy', paper presented to the Roundtable Conference on African Studies, 'Globalization and the New World Order: Challenges and Opportunities for Africa and the African Diaspora', 25–27 March, at Kentucky State University.

Jacoby, Russell. 1976. 'A Falling Rate of Intelligence?' *Telos*, 27: 141–46.

———. 1987. *The Last Intellectuals: American Culture in an Age of Academe*. New York: Basic Books.

Jacoby, Russell. 1999. *The End of Utopia: Politics and Culture in an Age of Apathy*. New York: Basic Books.

Jain, Jasbir. 1996. 'Postcolonial Realities: Women Writing History', in Harish Trivedi and Meenakshi Mukherjee (eds), *Interrogating Post-Colonialism: Theory, Text and Context*. Indian Institute of Advanced Study, pp. 161–76.

Jakobson, Roman. 1959. 'On Linguistic Aspects of Translation', in R. A. Brower (ed.), *On Translation*. Cambridge, MA: Harvard University Press.

——. 1981. *Selected Writings III: Poetry of Grammar and Grammar of Poetry*, ed. by Stephen Rudy. The Hague: Mouton.

Jameson, Fredric. 1991. *Postmodernism, or the Cultural Logic of Late Capitalism*. Durham, NC: Duke University Press.

Jarvis, Charles (tr.). 1742. *Life and Exploits of Don Quixote de La Mancha,* tr. from the original Spanish of Miguel de Cervantes. London: S. A. and H. Oddy.

Jay, Martin. 1984. *Adorno*. Cambridge, MA: Harvard University Press.

Jennings, Humphrey (ed.). 1987. *Pandaemonium: The Coming of the Machine As Seen by Contemporary Observers, 1660–1885*. London: Picador.

Jermyn, S. 1989. 'Loaves of Bread and Jugs of Wine: Three Translation of Omar Khayyám', *Meta*, 34(2).

Joshi, Suresh. 1956. *Upajaati*. Vadodara.

Joyce, James. 1922. *Ulysses*. Paris: Sylvia Beach (serialized in *The Little Review*, 1918–1920).

Jung, C. G. 1977. *Collected Works of C. G. Jung*, ed. by C. G. Jung, G. Adler and R. F. C. Hull, Vol. 18, *The Symbolic Life: Miscellaneous Writings*. Princeton, NJ: Princeton University Press.

Kastovsky, Dieter. 1990. 'Word-formation and Translation', *Meta*, 35(1): 45–49.

Kay, P. and W. Kempton. 1984. 'What Is the Sapir-Whorf Hypothesis?' *American Anthropologist*, 86(1): 65–79.

Kellner, Douglas. 1997. 'Intellectuals, the New Public Spheres and Technopolitics', *New Political Science*, 41–42: 169–88.

Kenner, Hugh. 1954. *Introduction to Ezra Pound's Translations*. New York: New Directions.

Kipling, Rudyard. 1902. 'The Beginning of Armadillos', in his *The Just-So Stories for Little Children*. London: Macmillan.

———. n.d. *In Black and White*. New York: Washington Books, Inc.

Lal, Ananda. 1987. *Rabindranath Tagore: Three Plays*, tr. from Bengali and with an introduction, Classics of the East Series. Calcutta: M. P. Birla Foundation, reprinted in 2001, New Delhi: Oxford University Press.

Lal, P. 1975. Foreword to Jaikishandas Sadani's *Kamayani* by Jaishankar Prasad. Calcutta: Rupa & Co., pp vii–ix.

Lang, Berel. 1986. 'Post-modernism in Philosophy: Nostalgia for the Future, Waiting for the Past', *New Literary History*, 18(1): 209–23.

Layton, Robert. 1989. 'Introduction', in R. Layton (ed.), *Conflict in the Archaeology of Living Traditions*. London: Unwin & Hyman Ltd, pp. 1–21.

Lefèvre, André. 1970. 'The Translation of Literature: An Approach', *Babel*, 2: 75–79.

———. 1971. 'The Study of Literary Translation and the Study of Comparative Literature', *Babel*, 17(4): 13–15.

———. 1975. *Translating Poetry: Seven Strategies and a Blueprint*. Assen and Amsterdam: van Gorcum.

Lévi-Strauss, Claude. 1955. *Structural Anthropology*. Garden City, New York: Anchor Books.

Lilova, Anna. 1993. 'Categories for the Study of Translation', in Palma Zlateva (ed.), *Translation as Social Action: Russian and Bulgarian Perspectives*. London and New York: Routledge, pp. 5–10.

Lima Costa, Claudia de. 2000. 'Being Here and Writing There: Gender and Politics in Brazilian Landscapes', *Signs: Journal of Women in Culture and Society*, 25(3): 727–60.

Lukács, Georg. 1971. *History and Class Consciousness*. London: Merlin.

Lyotard, Jean-Francois. 1984. *The Postmodern Condition: A Report on Knowledge*. Minneapolis: University of Minnesota Press.

Maddern, Marian. 1977. *Bengali Poetry into English: An Impossible Dream?* Calcutta: S. Ghatack from Editions Indian.

Majumdar, Amiyabhushan. 1959. *Dukhiyaar KuTii*. Kolkata: Neo-Lit Publishers.

Marcuse, Herbert. 1955. *Eros and Civilization*. New York: Vintage.

———. 1964. *One-Dimensional Man*. Boston, MA: Beacon.

Mardhekar, Bal Sitaram. 1947. *KaaMhiiM Kavitaa*. Mumbai: Yugavani Prakashan.

Marx, Karl. 1967. *Capital Vol. 1: A Critique of Political Economy*. New York: International Publishers.

Marx, Karl and Friedrich Engels. 1848[1967]. *The Communist Manifesto*. New York: Pantheon.

Maslin, Matthew. 1996. *Waiting for Foucault*. Located at http://www.cyberartsweb.org/cpace/theory/maslin/Opening_Remarks_719.html.

Merleau-Ponty, Maurice. 1964a. *Sense and Non-Sense*. Evanston, IL: Northwestern University Press.

———.1964b. *Signs*. Evanston, IL: Northwestern University Press.

Merwin, W. S. and J. Moussaieff Masson. 1981. *The Peacock's Egg: Love Poems from Ancient India*. San Francisco: North Point Press.

Mileur, Jean-Pierre. 1985. *Literary Revisionism and the Burden of Modernity*. Berkeley, CA: University of California Press.

Miller, J. Hillis. 1976. 'Steven's Rock and Criticism as Cure', *Georgia Review* (Summer), 30(2): 330–48.

Mitra, Arun. 1986. *Khunjte Khunjte Eto Dur*. Kolkata: Dey's Publications.

———. 1990. *The Quest Goes On and Other Poems*, tr. by Surabhi Banerjee from Bengali. New Delhi: Sahitya Akademi.

Mitra, Premendra. 1932. *Prathamaa*. Kolkata: Indian Associated Publishing House.

———. 1948. *Pheraarii Phauj*. Kolkata: Signet Press.

Mufwene, Salikoko. 1998. 'Native Speaker, Proficient Speaker and Norms', in Rajendra Singh (ed.), *The Native Speaker: Multilingual Perspectives*, Language and Development Series, Vol. 4. Thousand Oaks, CA, New Delhi: Sage, pp. 111–23.

Mukhopadhyay, Subhash. 1946. *Padaatik*. Kolkata: Kabita Bhavan.

———. 1950. *CirkuT*. Kolkata: Prashanta Bhattacharya.

Muktibodh [Gajanan Madhav]. 1964. *Chand ka Muh Teda Hai*. Delhi: Bharatiya Jnanpith.

———. 1984. 'Brahma-raakshasa', in *Pratinidhi Kavitaayen*, ed. by Ashok Vajpeyi. Delhi: Rajkamal Prakashan.

Nama, Charles Atangana. 1990. 'A History of Translation and Interpretation in Cameroon from Precolonial Times to Present', *Meta*, 35(2): 256–369.

Narasimhaiah, C. D. and C. N. Srinath (eds). 1985. *Problems of Translation*. Mysore: Dhvanyaloka.

——— (eds). 1986. *Kipling's India*. Mysore: A Dhvanyaloka Publication.

Newmark, Peter. 1981. *Approaches to Translation*. Oxford, UK: Pergamon Press.

———.1988. *A Textbook of Translation*. New York: Prentice Hall.

Nida, E. A. 1964. *Towards a Science of Translating*. Leiden, UK: E. J. Brill.

———.1975. *Language, Structure and Translation: Essays by Eugene A. Nida*, selected and introduced by Anwar S. Dil. Stanford, CA: Stanford University Press.

Niranjana, Tejaswini. 1992. *Siting Translation: History, Poststructuralism and the Colonial Context*. Hyderabad: Longman.

O'Shaughnessy, Arthur. 1872. *Lays of France*. London.

Pal, Sanyam. 1995. 'Tomaake prakrita bhaalobaasi', *Desh*, 89, 1995.

Paniker, K. Ayyappa. 1994. 'The Anxiety of Authenticity: Reflections on Literary Translation, *Indian Literature*, 162: 128–38.

Parsons, Talcott. 1961. *The Social System*. Glencoe, IL: Free Press.

Patke, Rajeev S. 2001. *The Ambivalence of Poetic Self-exile: The Case of A. K. Ramanujan* (unpublished mss).

Paz, Octavio. 1971. *Traducción: Literatura y Literalidad*. Barcelona: Tusquets Editores. Tr. by Irene del Corral, 1992. 'Translation, Literature and

Letters' in Rainer Shulte & John, Biguenet (eds). *Theories of Translation: An Anthology of Essays from Dryden to Derrida*. Chicago, IL: The University of Chicago Press.

Pegacheva, Z. 1959. 'Nekotorye pshihologischeskye voprosy obucheniya ustnomu perevodu', *Bulletin'kolokviuma po eksperimental'noj fonetike i psihologii rechii (Bulletin of the Colloquium in Experimental Phonetics and Speech Psychology)*, 2: 130–48. Moscow: Izdatel'stvo Moskovskogo Gosudarstvennogo Pedagogischekogo Instituta Inostrannyh Yazykov (MGPIIJ).

Peeradina, Saleem, Jayant Parkh, Rasik Shah, and Ghulam Mohammed Sheikh (tr.). 1991. 'Magan's Insolence' (orig. by Sitanshu Yasaschandra in Gujarati), in Meenakshi Mukherjee and Nissim Ezekiel (eds), *Another India: An Anthology of Contemporary Indian Fiction and Poetry*. New Delhi: Penguin, pp. 221–24.

Popovič, Anton. 1976. *Dictionary for the Analysis of Literary Translation*. Edmonton: University of Alberta.

———. 1988. *Theory of Literary Translation*, tr. from *Teória umeleckého prekladu: aspekty textu a literárnej metakomunikácie*. 2. prepac. a rozš. vyd. Bratislava: Tatran, 1975.

Pound, Ezra. 1911–12. 'I Gather the Limbs of Osiris'. *The New Age*, 10 (November–February issue).

Prasad, G. J. V., 'The Untranslatable Other: The Language of Indian English Fiction', in R. S. Gupta (ed.), *Literary Translation*. Delhi: Creative Books, 1999.

Prasad, Jaishankar. 1936[2003]. *Kaamaayanii*. New Delhi: Prakashan Sansthan.

Raffel, Burton. 1971. *The Forked Tongue: A Study of Translation Process*. The Hague: Mouton.

Ray, Sukumar. 1921[1986]. *Sukumar Racanaabalii*, ed. Prafulla Kumar Patra. Calcutta: Patra's Publications.

Rege, P. S. 1950. *Dolaa*. Panjim: Dattaram Vaman Naik.

Richards, I. A. 1929. *Practical Criticism*. New York: Harcourt Brace.

Richards, Nelly. 1993. 'Cultural Peripheries: Latin America and Post-modernist De-centering', *Boundary*, 2(20): 3.

Rose, M. G. (ed.) 1981. 'Introduction: Time and Space in the Translation Process', in M. G. Rose (ed.), *Translation Spectrum: Essays in Theory and Practice*. Albany, NY: State University of New York Press, pp. 1–7.

Rosenblatt, L. 1984. *Literature as Explorations*. New York: Modern Language Association.

Rothenberg, Jerome. 2004a. *Writing Through: Translations and Variations*. Middletown, CT: Wesleyan Press.

Rothenberg, Jerome. 2004b. 'Translation as Composition/Composition as Translation', talk delivered on the occasion of receiving the ALFONS ET Sabio Translation Award from San Diego State University on 22 March 2004; also available at *Cipher Journal*: www.cipherjournal.com/html/rothernberg_traslation_ composi.html.

Rubin, David (tr.). 1976. *A Season on the Earth: Selected Poems of Nirala*. New York: Columbia University Press.

Sadani, Jaikishandas (tr.). 1975. *Kamayani* by Jaishankar Prasad (tr. from Hindi). Calcutta: Rupa & Co.

Samad, Abdus. 1995. 'Mahamayii Thyeng', *Desh*, 83.

Sapir, Edward. 1912. 'Language and Environment', *American Anthropologists*, 14: 226–42.

———. 1916. *Time Perspective in Aboriginal American Culture: Study in Method.* Ottawa: Government Printing Bureau.

———. 1924. 'The Grammarian and His Language', *American Mercury*, 1: 39–44.

———. 1929. 'The Status of Linguistics as a Science', *Language*, 5: 207–14.

———.1956. *Culture, Language and Personality*, ed. by David G. Mandelbaum. Berkeley and Los Angeles: University of California Press.

Sarma, Arobinda Nath (tr.) 1984. '"I Am There", in Eight Poems by Nirmal Prabha Bordoloi', *Indian Literature*, 27 (4): 19.

Sartre, Jean-Paul. 1956. *Being and Nothingness*. New York: Philosophical Library.

—— 1976. Critique of Dialectical Reason. London: NLB.

Satchidanandan, K. 1984. 'Translating Poetry', tr. by E.V. Ramakrishnan, *Chandrabhaaga II*, 11(Summer): 39–40.

Saussure, Ferdinand de. 1916. *Cours de Linguistique Generale* tr. as *Course in General Linguistics*, 1966 by W. Baskin. New York: McGraw-Hill.

Savory, T. 1957. *The Art of Translation*. London: Jonathan Cape.

Selver, Paul. 1966. *The Art of Translating Poetry.* London: Jon Baker.

Sen, Anjan. 1988. *Tin visshe din raatri*. Calcutta: Hardya.

———. 1993. 'Uttar-aadhunikataa: Kaal, aitihya, lokabritta', *DraSTabya*, 2(3): 50–66.

Sen, Anjan and Udaya Narayana Singh (eds). 1976. *Kabitaar bhaaShaa* (in Bengali). Calcutta: Gaangeya Patra.

Sen, Samar. 1937. *KayekTi Kabitaa*. Kolkata: Samar Sen.

———. 1939. *Grahan*. Kolkata: Samar Sen.

Shannon, C. E. and W. Weaver. 1948. 'The Mathematical Theory of Communication', *Bell System Technical Journal*, 27: 379–423 (July) and 623–56 (October). Reprinted in Weaver, W. and C. E. Shannon. 1949. *The Mathematical Theory of Communication*, Urbana, IL: University of Illinois Press.

Siemerling, Winfried. 1994. *Discoveries of the Other: Alterity in the Work of Leonard Cohen, Hubert Aquin, Michael Ondaatje, and Nicole Brossard*. Toronto: The University of Toronto Press.

Simon, Sherry. 1996. *Gender in Translation: Cultural Identity and the Politics of Transmission*. London and New York: Routledge.

Singh, Mohan ('Diwaanaa'). 1931. *Jagat tamaashaa*. Lahore: Lahore Book Shop.

———. 1945. *SuuphiyaaM de kalaam*. Lahore: Lahore Book Shop.

Singh, Namvar. 1970. In Ashok Vajpeyi (ed.), *Sidhi lekhak shivir ke dastaavez*, based on Writer's Workshop, 14–16 March. Bhopal: Purvagraha.

Singh, Rajendra (ed.). 1998. *The Native Speaker: Multilingual Perspectives*, Language and Development Series, Vol. 4. New Delhi: Sage.

Singh, Udaya Narayana. 1966. *Kavayo vadanti*. Calcutta: Mithila Darshan.

———. 1989a. 'Introduction', in P. R. Dadegaonkar and G. Umamaheswara Rao (eds), *CALTS Working Papers*, 1, Hyderabad: University of Hyderabad, pp. 5–22.

———. 1989b. 'Language of Literature and Fine Arts', in Udaya Narayana Singh and S. Padikkal (eds), *Suniti Kumar Chatterji: An End-Centenary Tribute*. New Delhi: Sahitya Akademi.

———. 1989c. 'Tin vishve din raatrir paaTh', *Saamprata*, 3(1): 74–84.

———. 1990. 'Dynamics of Textuality and Configuration of Space', *International Journal of Translation*, 2(2): 25–48.

———. 1992a. *Language Development and Planning: A Pluralistic Paradigm*. Shimla: IIAS and New Delhi: Munshiram Manoharlal.

———. 1992b. 'On Aesthetics of Neologism and Neotaxis, or When Do We Create When We Translate?' in Amiya Dev (ed.), *Papers in Comparative Literature*, Vol. 2. *The Aesthetics of Translation*. Calcutta: Jadavpur University, pp. 21–35.

———. 1993. 'Bankim as a Language Planner', in Bhabatosh Datta (ed.), *Bankimchandra: Essays in Perspective*. Calcutta: Sahitya Akademi, 351–58.

———. 1994a. 'Translation as a Way of Growing', *Meta* (Numero Speciale: La Traduction vue de l'Extererieur), 39(2): 401–403.

———. 1994b. 'Praying for the Pigeon', *Indian Literature*, 163(1): 84–96.

———. 1996. *'Kanchaniya' of Lalit* (tr. for Sahitya Akademi). Delhi: Sahitya Akademi [Unpub.]

———. 1997. *Raviindranaathak Baal-saahitya*. Tr. from Rabindranath Tagore's Bengali original into Maithili. New Delhi: Sahitya Akademi.

———. 1998. 'Speech as Chaos: Translation as Cacophony', keynote address delivered at the Central Institute of English and Foreign Languages, Hyderabad, 16–20 March.

Singh, Udaya Narayana. 2000a. '"The Village God" of Ramdeva Shukla', *Indian Literature*, 195 (January–February): 51–59.

Singh, Udaya Narayana. 2000b. '"The Dew Drops' of Ashtabhuja Shukla', *Indian Literature*, 195 (January–February): 83.

———. 2001. 'Another India: Voices from the Periphery', unpublished paper presented at the international conference on Peripheral Centres, Central Peripheries: Anglophone India and Its Diaspora(s), University of the Saarland, Saarbracken, August.

———. 2004. 'The Agency of Language', in Udaya Narayana Singh, N. H. Itagi and Shailendra Kumar Singh (eds), *Language, Society and Culture: ZICR: Visitations to 21st Century Reality.* Mysore: Central Institute of Indian Languages, pp. 6–21.

———. 2006a. 'Another India: Voices from the Periphery', in Martina Ghosh-Schellhorn with Vera Alexander (eds), *Peripheral Centres, Central Peripheries*, Transcultural Anglophone Studies, Vol. 1. Berlin: Lit Verlag, pp. 251–61.

———. 2006b. 'Nirupam, Nirupam!', tr. of Shakti Chattopadhyay's 'Jhaauyer Daake', *Indian Literature,* 201.

Singh, Udaya Narayana and Krishnanjan Bhattacharjee. 1999. 'Translating Abstractness', paper read at the ICOSALL Conference, Panjabi University, Patiala; 9–11 January.

Singh, Udaya Narayana and Mahendra K. C. Pandey. 1996. 'Conjectures on translation', in S. K. Verma and Dilip Singh (eds), *Perspectives on Language in Society: Papers in Memory of R. N. Srivastava.* Delhi: Kalinga.

Singh, Udaya Narayana and S. K. Pattanayak. 1990. 'Is Translation Amenable to Theorization?', in P. Dasgupta and N. Krupanandam (eds), *CALTS Working Papers,* 2. Hyderabad: University of Hyderabad, pp. 4–45.

Singh, Udaya Narayana, with Rizio Yohannan Raj. 2006. *Second Person Singular*, tr. from his *MadhyampuruS ekvacan* (Maithili). New Delhi: Katha.

Sharma, B. C. Ramachandra. 1952. *Hrudaya giita.* Bangalore: Sai National Mart.

———. 1953. *ELu suttina koTe.* Bangalore: Sai National Mart.

Smith, James and Horace Smith. 1841[2003]. 'An Address Without a Phoenix', in their *Rejected Addresses: or, the New Theatrum Poetarum.* London: Methuen & Co., pp. 15–16.

Snell-Hornby, Mary. 1988. *Translation Studies: An Integrated Approach.* Amsterdam: John Benjamins.

Sobti, Krishna. 1979. *Zindaginaamaa: Zindaa Rukh.* Delhi: Rajkamal.

Sri Aurobindo. 1972. *The Future Poetry* and *Letters on Poetry, Literature, and Art.* Pondicherry: Sri Aurobindo Ashram.

Srinath, C. N. and T. V. Subbarao (trs). 1987. *Sumati Satakam*, tr. from Telugu into English. Bangalore: Atmakala Publications.

Steiner, T. R. 1975. *English Translation Theory, 1650–1800*. Amsterdam and Assen: Van Gorcum.

Stoberski, Zygmunt. 1972. 'The Role of Translations in the Development of World Culture', *Babel*, 18(4): 21–28.

Tagore, Rabindranath. 1894. *Sonaar Tari*. Kolkata: Dwarakanath Lane, Kalidas Chakraborty.

———. 1927. 'Modern Poetry', essay available at http://www.cscs.umich.edu/~crshalizi/Poetry/Tagore/modern-poetry.html, accessed on 22 May 2009.

Talgeri, Pramod. 1988a. 'Intercultural Hermeneutics and Literary Translation'. Unpublished Ms. based on his (1981) 'Die Darstellung fremder Kultur in der Literatur–Die Suche nach einer erweiterten identität der eigenen Kultur', in Ralph Kloepfer and Gisela Janetzke-Dissner (eds), *Erzählung und Erzählforschung im 20, Jahrhundert. Tagungsbeiträge*, Eines symposions der Alexander von Humboldt-Stiftung Bonn-Bad Godesberg veranstaltet, 9(14): 123–28.

———. 1988b. 'The Role of Culture in Successful Translation', in Pramod Talgeri and S. B. Varma (eds), *Literature in Translation: From Cultural Transference to Metonymic Displacement*. Bombay: Popular Prakashan, pp. 22–26.

Tandon, Purushottamdas (ed.). 1913. *BrajabhaaSaa-SurakoSa*. Allahabad: Hindi Sahitya Sammelan.

Tirumalesh, K. V. 1990. 'Translation as Literature Three', *International Journal of Translation*, 1(2): 1–11.

Toporov, V. N. 1992. 'Translation: Sub specie of Culture', *Meta*, 37(1): 29–49.

Toury, Gideon 1998. 'Hebrew [Translation] Tradition', in Mona Baker, assisted by Kirsten Malmkjaer (ed.), *Routledge Encyclopedia of Translation Studies*, London and New York: Routledge, pp. 439–48.

Trivedi, Harish. 1992. 'Omar Khayyam in India: An Evolution Through Persian, English and Hindi', in Amiya Dev (ed.), *Papers in Comparative Literature, 2: The Aesthetics of Translation*. Calcutta: Jadavpur University, pp. 35–62.

Trivers, R. 1985. *Social Evolution*. Mento Park, CA: Cummins.

Vatsyayana, Sacchidananda Hirananda (ed.). 1943. 'Ajneya', *Taar Saptak*. Delhi: Pratik Prakashan.

Venuti, Lawrence. 1992. 'Introduction', in L. Venuti (ed.), *Rethinking Translation: Discourse, Subjectivity, Ideology*. London: Routledge, pp. 1–17.

Verma, Sriram. 1970. In Ashok Vajpeyi (ed.), *Sidhi lekhak shivir ke dastaavez*, based on Writer's Workshop, 14–16 March. Bhopal: Purvagraha.

Weissbrod, Rachel. 1998. 'Translation Research in the Framework of the Tel Aviv School of Poetics and Semiotics', *Meta*, 21(3): 1–13.

Whorf, B. L. 1938. 'Some Verbal Categories of Hopi', *Language*, 14: 275–86.

Whorf, B. L. 1940. 'Science and Linguistics', *Technological Review*, 42: 229–31, 247–48.

Whorf, B. L. 1950. 'An American Indian Model of the Universe', *IJAL*, 16: 57–72.

——. 1956. *Language, Thought and Reality: Selected Writings of Benjamin Lee Whorf*, ed. by John B. Carroll. New York: Wiley.

Will, Frederic. 1993. *Literature as Sheltering the Human*. Lewiston, ME: Edwin Mellen Press.

Wilss, Wolfram. 1982. *The Science of Translation: Problems and Methods*. Tubingen: Gunter Narr, tr. from *Übersetzungswissenschaft. Probleme und Methoden*. Stuttgart: Ernst Klett Verlag.

Wittgenstein, L. 1959. *Philosophical Investigations*, tr. by G. E. M. Anscombe. Oxford, UK: Blackwell.

———. 1976. *Philosophical Investigations*. Oxford, UK: Blackwell.

———. 1986. *The Blue and Brown Notebooks*. New York: HarperCollins.

Zimnyaya, Irina. 1993. 'A Psychological Analysis of Translation as a Type of Speech Activity', in Palma Zlateva (ed.), *Translation as Social Action: Russian and Bulgarian Perspectives*. London: Routledge & Kegan Paul, pp. 87–100.

Credits

Every effort has been made to obtain permission from all copyright holders, but in some cases this has not proved possible. The publishers, therefore, wish to thank all authors and copyright holders who are included without acknowledgement. Dorling Kindersley (India) Pvt. Ltd, licensees of Pearson Education in India, apologize for any errors and omissions in this list and would be grateful to be notified of corrections that should be incorporated in the next edition.

Chapter 1

36 Guo Jian, 'The Politics of Othering and Postmodernization of the Cultural Revolution' (© 1999 by Taylor & Francis), used with the permission of Taylor & Francis, licence number 1819391456401, dated 30 October 2007, and of the author.

38 Jerome Rothenberg, *Writing Through: Translations and Variations* (© 2004, Jerome Rothenberg), used with the permission of Rothenberg.

40–42 Matthew Maslin, *Waiting for Foucault*, written as an undergraduate paper under George P. Landow, Professor of English and the History of Art, Brown University, used with the permission of Landow.

Chapter 2

54–55 Original Bhojpuri text and its translation in Udaya Narayana Singh, *"The Village God' of Ramdeva Shukla* (© 2000 by Sahitya Akademi), used with the permission of the Akademi.

55–56 Original Maithili text and translation in English in Udaya Narayana Singh, *'Kanchaniya' of Lalit* (© 1996 by Sahitya Akademi), used with the permission of the Akademi.

60–63 Sitanshu Yasaschandra's Gujarati poem (translated by Saleem Peeradina, Jayant Parkh, Rasik Shah, and Ghulam Mohammed Sheikh as 'Magan's Insolence'), published in Meenakshi Mukherjee and Nissim Ezekiel (eds), *Another India: An Anthology of Contemporary Indian Fiction and Poetry*. Used with the permission of Yasaschandra (© original Gujarati poem), Mukherjee (© 1991 by Meenakshi Mukherjee and Nissim Ezekiel for the translation), and Peeradina et al.

Chapter 4

94 Arun Mitra, 'Ornament' (© by Arun Mitra's estate), used with the permission of his daughter, Mrs Uma Bose. Surabhi Banerjee's translation of this poem (© 1990 by Sahitya Akademi) used with the permission of the Akademi and Banerjee.

Chapter 5

98–99 K. Satchidanandan, 'Translating Poetry' (© 1984 by K. Satchinanandan for the original poem; © 1984 by E.V. Ramakrishnan for the translation), used with the permission of Satchidanandan and Ramakrishnan.

112–13 Translated song of Tagore (C. F. Andrews' translation) from his play *Aruup ratan* in Ananda Lal's *Rabindranath Tagore: Three Plays* (© 1987 by Ananda Lal), reproduced with Lal's permission.

113 Translated song of Tagore from his play *Aruup ratan*, in Ananda Lal's *Rabindranath Tagore: Three Plays* (© 1987 by Ananda Lal), reproduced with Lal's permission.

Chapter 6

130 Bhaskar Chakraborty's poem in *Dhaaraabaahik samaacaar* (©1994 by Bhaskar Chakraborty), reproduced with his permission.

130 Sanyam Pal, *Tomaake prakrita bhaalobaasi* (©1995 by Sanyam Pal), reproduced with his permission.

130–31 Jayanta Bhowmick's poem (© 1995 by *Desh*), reproduced with his permission.

131 Phanibhusan Acharya, *Mandirgaatrer prasaadhanrataar haater aaynaay* (© 1994 by *Desh*), reproduced with his permission.

Chapter 7

159 Anjan Sen, 'Kathaa' (© 1988 by Anjan Sen), reproduced with his permission.

160 Anjan Sen, 'AakaraN' (© 1988 by Anjan Sen), reproduced with his permission.

Chapter 8

166 Arun Mitra, 'Come Rain, Come!' (© by Arun Mitra's estate), used with the permission of his daughter, Mrs Uma Bose. Surabhi Banerjee's translation of this poem (© 1990 by Sahitya Akademi) used with the permission of Sahitya Akademi and Surabhi Banerjee.

Chapter 10

p. 197 Excerpt from Jasbir Jain's 'Post-Colonial Realities: Women Writing History' (© by Jasbir Jain), published in Harish Trivedi and Meenakshi Mukherjee (eds), *Post-Colonialism: Theory, Text and Context*. Used with Jain's permission.

Index

About the Author

Udaya Narayana Singh is Tagore Professor, Rabindra Bhavana, Visva-Bharati and Director, Indira Gandhi Centre for National Integration (IGCNI). He has been the Director of the Central Institute of Indian Languages (CIIL), Mysore from December 2000 to early June 2009. He is a renowned linguist as well as a reputed poet, playwright and essayist in Maithili and Bengali. He set up the Centre for Applied Linguistics and Translation Studies (CALTS), the Centre for Distance Education and the Study India Program (SIP) at the University of Hyderabad, and has taught at the Universities of Delhi, Baroda and Surat. As a creative writer, he has published four collections of poems and twelve plays in Maithili (he writes under the pen-name 'Nachiketa'), and six books of literary essays and two volumes of poetry in Bengali, besides translating several books. His recent authored volumes include an anthology of poems in Maithili—*Madhyampurush Ekvachan* (2005), which has been translated and published in English (with Rizio Yohannan Raj, 2006), Tamil (2008) and German (2009); a play in Maithili—*No Entry: Maa Pravisha* (2008); a collection of one-acts—*Priyamvadaa aa anya ekaankii* (2008) in Maithili; a collection of nonsense rhymes—*Khaam-kheyaali* (2003) in Bengali; and *India Writes: A Story of Linguistic and Literary Plurality* (2006). Presently, he is the Chief Editor of the state-of-the-art Maithili bi-monthly, *Mithila Darshan*.

Professor Singh has also edited/co-edited many volumes, and contributed numerous chapters to edited volumes and articles to journals. His most recent edited volumes include *Culturation: Essays in Honour of Jawaharlal Handoo* (2001); *Linguistic Landscaping in India* (jointly with N. H. Itagi 2002); and *Language, Society and Culture* (jointly with N. H. Itagi and S. K. Singh, 2004). He has been the chief editor of the journal, *Indian Linguistics*, and general editor of the 'Language and Development' series (LAD) from Sage, and of the Longman–CIIL series of bilingual dictionaries from Pearson (forthcoming). He has also been the mentor or chair of several interesting academic projects, including the *Linguistic Data Consortium for Indian Languages* (LDC-IL), *National*

Testing Service (NTS), *National Translation Mission* (NTM), and CIIL's *Bhasha Mandakini* series of documentation. Under the last project, Professor Singh has designed and created 545 short films in English on teaching of Bangla, Tamil, Kannada and Marathi.

A poet-invitee at the Frankfurt Book Fair (2006)—India Guest of Honour presentation—and the leader of the Cultural Delegation of Writers to China (2007), Professor Singh has visited and lectured in Bangladesh, the Caribbean, China, Germany, Iceland, Italy, Mauritius, Nepal, Pakistan, Russia, Singapore, Sri Lanka, Sweden, Thailand, the UK and the USA, and has received several grants and honours.